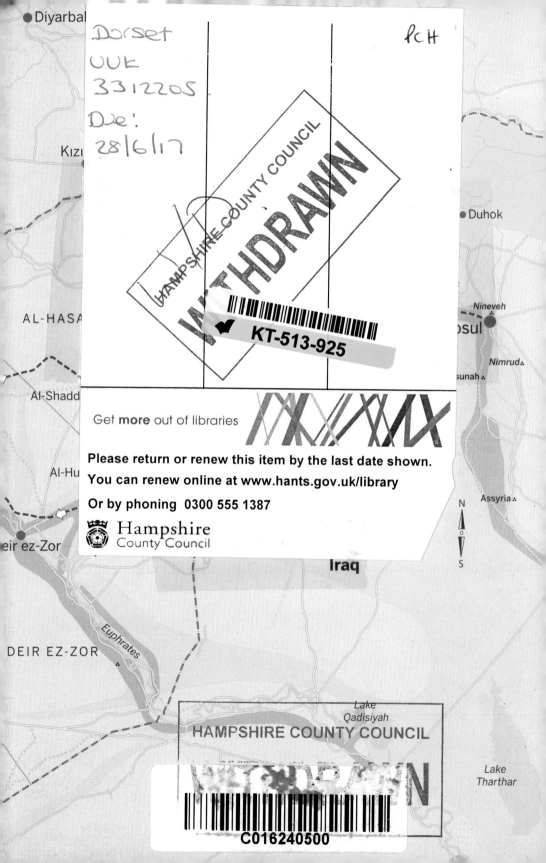

My Journey into the Heart of Terror

Ten Days in
the Islamic
State

MY JOURNEY INTO THE HEART OF TERROR

Jürgen Todenhöfer

Translated by A.O. May

GREYSTONE BOOKS
Vancouver/Berkeley

Copyright © 2016 by Jürgen Todenhöfer
Translation copyright © 2016 by A.O. May
All photographs copyright © 2016 by Frederic Todenhöfer,
except photographs 17 and 47, which are taken from IS videos
Maps copyright © 2016 by Peter Palm, Berlin
Originally published in Germany as *Inside IS* by C. Bertelsmann
Verlag in 2015

16 17 18 19 20   5 4 3 2 1

Greystone Books Ltd.
www.greystonebooks.com

Cataloguing data available from Library and Archives Canada
ISBN 978-1-77164-224-8 (cloth)
ISBN 978-1-77164-225-5 (epub)

Editing by A.O. May
Copyediting by Shirarose Wilensky
Jacket design by Peter Cocking
Jacket photo collage by Frederic Todenhöfer
Text design by Nayeli Jimenez
Printed and bound in Canada by Friesens
Distributed in the U.S. by Publishers Group West

We gratefully acknowledge the financial support of the Canada Council
for the Arts, the British Columbia Arts Council, the Province of British
Columbia through the Book Publishing Tax Credit, and the Government
of Canada through the Canada Book Fund for our publishing activities.

Greystone Books is committed to reducing the consumption of old-
growth forests in the books it publishes. This book is one step toward
that goal.

For Frederic, who made a huge contribution to the journey and to the development of this book. Without him this book would not exist.

TABLE OF CONTENTS

Introduction

I N THE MANY court cases I have been involved in, first as a junior lawyer and later in my short time as a judge, I often found myself on an emotional roller coaster. After the prosecutor's arguments, I usually thought the accused was a scheming scoundrel. But as soon as the defense made its case, everything looked completely different. I was all for leniency. Assessing who was right and to what extent were the most difficult decisions of my life. One side is hardly ever completely without fault, and there are almost always arguments in favor of the other side. Rarely did I feel that the final decision was absolutely correct.

The lesson I took from this was that if you want to find the truth, you must speak to both sides. Even when the world has already pronounced its judgment. An important principle of Roman law is *audiatur et altera pars* ("listen to the other side"). So in the eighties, I spent time with different groups of mujahideen in what was then Soviet-occupied Afghanistan. Then I spoke twice with Marshal Sergei Achromejew, the head of the Soviet military in Moscow, even though the Soviet government had publicly declared that if they caught me, they would have me flogged and then shot. For hours we discussed whether it would not be smarter for the Soviet Union to withdraw from Afghanistan. Achromejew was a very open man and he knew how to listen.

It was Easter 1975 when I met with the Chilean dictator Augusto Pinochet in Punta Arenas to negotiate the release of 4,500 political prisoners, most of whom were Marxists. But I was also there to understand the situation in Chile after the fall of Salvador Allende. After meeting with Pinochet, I flew to the capital, Santiago, to speak with the leaders of the opposition, the Christian Democrats Eduardo Frei Montalva and Patricio Aylwin. Back in Germany, I was subjected to a torrent of abuse for my attempt to build an objective picture of the situation. I was labeled "a supporter of dictatorships." Even though many thousands of prisoners were later set free, this did not change the fact that for many years I was drowned out at large events by the chants of furious crowds waving banners depicting Pinochet.

Despite this, in my search for the truth I stuck with my strategy of speaking with both sides whenever possible. Mostly this strategy garnered indignant protests from those who pass judgment on the world from the comfort of their armchairs and are convinced that they alone are in possession of the truth. I spoke on numerous occasions with Hamid Karzai, the president of Afghanistan, but I also spoke with leaders of the Afghan Taliban. For countless deskbound strategists, such as the former chief of staff of the German armed forces Harald Kujat, I was from then on the "mouthpiece of the Taliban." For others I was quite simply a "terrorist sympathizer."

I temporarily lost the label "terrorist sympathizer" when I met Bashar al-Assad many times in Damascus in 2012. I met with him not only to conduct an interview for the ARD (German public broadcasting consortium) program *Weltspiegel* but first and foremost to establish direct contact between Assad and the U.S. administration. I was firmly convinced that the USA could reach a peaceful settlement in Syria with the help of their allies Saudi Arabia and Qatar, who were supplying the insurgents with weapons. Assad was open to far-reaching concessions, and I passed this information along to the American government. But the U.S. government absolutely refused to speak with him.

Another wave of outrage washed over me. "Ethical" Germany turned up its nose. Politicians and journalists foamed at the mouth as they asked how I could speak to a man who had so much blood on his hands. And all the while they would have given their eyeteeth for a meeting with George W. Bush, who had infinitely more blood on his hands. *Die Welt* wrote: "The interview is faintly reminiscent of earlier conversations of other idealistic journalists and misguided thinkers who met the nice, heroic Joe Stalin during the war or who extolled the virtues of the amazingly knowledgeable leader from Berghof before the war, who was after all only striving for the things all of us strive for, such as the right to self-determination for all people, including the Germans."

Stalin and Hitler! You can't get any lower than that. No one was interested in the fact that no Western journalist before me had ever had such a hard-hitting conversation with the Syrian president. There was also little interest in the fact that at the same time as I was speaking with Assad, I was having countless conversations with his opponents, the fighters of al-Qaeda, the Free Syrian Army (FSA), and other rebel groups. Even former West German chancellor Willy Brandt developed his *Ostpolitik,* or "new Eastern policy," only after sitting down with the ruthless Leonid Brezhnev. But for my critics, this proven past success was no justification for my actions.

THE WEST DIVIDES the world into good and bad, and as former U.S. president Jimmy Carter has said, since the time of George W. Bush, it has harbored a deep-seated aversion to having conversations with its enemies. Carter made that statement in 2005, after George W. Bush forbade him from making a previously arranged visit to Damascus. The "axis of good" doesn't speak with the "axis of evil." If you go ahead and do it anyway, you have to deal with social sanctions.

This is what Ines Pohl, then editor in chief of the German daily newspaper *taz,* wrote to me in June 2014, comfortably convinced that she was occupying the moral high ground: "Dear Mr. Todenhöfer, *taz* will not publish the piece you offered us. A large majority of the editors have spoken against publishing reports from you in *taz.*

It is not about your innately radical pacifist arguments but about you as a writer, in other words, about the position you have taken for the past three years on Assad and the subject of genocide. I respect my editors' judgment. With best wishes, Ines Pohl, editor in chief, *taz*."

Should I even reply to such a sanctimonious letter? I did reply, because I will not give up hope that one day the morally superior mainstream in Germany who oppose negotiations will indeed change their thinking. I hope that they will recognize that even when dealing with dictators, it is always better to negotiate than go to war. That our enemies are precisely the ones we must talk to. That they will understand that if we don't do this, our world will be destroyed in the chaos of endless conflict. So I wrote:

Dear Ms. Pohl,

I am amazed. I write as someone who has traveled halfway around the world many times to speak with many governments as well as many opposition movements in order to help find a peaceful solution to the crisis in Syria. Who has spent a gazillion euros to pay for prosthetics for fifty tiny victims of the war in Syria. Who every month looks after the living expenses of a family in Homs who has lost its wage earners because of Assad's security forces. Who because of this has been labeled an enemy of the state by the Syrian government's intelligence service and who therefore can no longer get a visa to visit the country. Such a level of self-righteousness on the part of "a large majority" of your editorial team leaves me flabbergasted. It must feel good to write such a disparaging letter from your air-conditioned office. Congratulations! I am always pleased to meet real heroes. Now I know where to find them.

Amazed in Munich,

Yours, JT

BEING SNUBBED BY some media outlets and by the German upper class has never bothered me. And neither have the death threats that continue to pile up. One day, at the most intense point of the discussions about Syria, during which the late Peter Scholl-Latour,

Germany's best-known expert on the Middle East, kept up a cease-less crusade of systematic rabble rousing, I found an expertly tied hangman's noose with its gaping mouth at the entrance to my office. A supporter of the Syrian rebels wrote on my Facebook page: "Jür-gen Hodenköter (Jürgen Dogballs) is paid by Mossad!!! Death to Höfer!!!" One soldier wrote: "Such an asshole. Colonel Klein wiped out 100 assholes and saved German soldiers. Hopefully a suicide bomber will blow Todenhöfer to bits!!!" Next to the Israeli flag was the Facebook comment: "God take Todenhöfer to his side. As soon as possible." A radical Muslim raged: "You bastard. You enjoy the highest level of trust in our countries and then you sell us out to the Amis (the Americans) ... You will not die a natural death." Another: "You shouldn't be allowed to live!" The next: "Off with your head, Mr. Doofenhöfer (Idiot-höfer)!!!" And an aggrieved radical leftist wrote: "I will stab you to death, you filthy bastard."

All I know is that I cannot let myself be swayed by these peo-ple. My desire to discover the truth runs too deep. And it is more important.

Birth of the "Islamic State"

T HE "ISLAMIC STATE," or IS, seems to have emerged only recently from the shadows of history, immediately occupying a central position on the world political stage. But IS has existed for some time. It is the child of the 2003 Iraq War.

In August 2007, I first met one of its fighters in Ramadi, the hotly disputed capital of Anbar Province in Iraq. Rami was a twenty-seven-year-old history student who had joined the terrorist group after American GIs shot his mother during a home search. Right in front of him. "What would you have done?" he asks me bitterly, when he sees that although I understand his pain, I cannot begin to understand his decision. It's easy, he tells me, to express noble sentiments about resistance and terrorism when you're living in peace and comfort. Had I ever considered what must go through a suicide bomber's mind just before he blows himself up? When I remain silent, he continues: "Stop attacking us and humiliating us. Clear off back to your own countries. Then al-Qaeda will disappear on its own."

THE RISE OF al-Qaeda as a factor in the chaotic struggle for power in Iraq began four years earlier. In 2003. Abu Musab al-Zarqawi, a thirty-seven-year-old Sunni Muslim from Jordan, was its public face. Originally, Zarqawi had planned to overthrow the Jordanian monarchy with his Party of Monotheism and Jihad. But the U.S. invasion of Iraq suddenly offered him completely different options. Finally, he could fight the Americans and wage jihad against Shia Muslims, whom he regarded as "apostates" (Muslims considered to be "betrayers of Islam" for apparently having abandoned Islam or questioned any of its fundamental creeds). After the fall of Saddam Hussein, the Shias assumed absolute power in Iraq. Sunnis had previously been highly influential in the government, but the Shias brutally banished them from political life.

Soon after the U.S. invasion, Zarqawi began to build up a fighting force in Iraq. The force included a small number of Arab fighters that he smuggled into Iraq from Syria with the help of al-Qaeda. In total, Zarqawi gathered about two thousand highly effective fighters. One thousand of these were in Anbar Province. The remainder fought mostly in Diyala Province northeast of Baghdad and in some Sunni neighborhoods in Baghdad. Zarqawi profited from the resentment of the now marginalized Sunni population. His preferred targets were Iraqi soldiers, police officers, and, most especially, Shias. According to U.S. reports, in August 2003, his fighters blew up the Imam Ali Mosque in Najaf, the third-holiest Islamic site for Shias. Waves of bloody attacks followed one after the other.

The U.S. occupation forces liberally attributed almost every attack in Iraq to Zarqawi. And so it was that Zarqawi's reputation began to outstrip his operations. The fact that in addition to al-Qaeda there was a far more powerful "citizen resistance" against the U.S. occupation, with a considerably larger number of fighters, was systematically kept quiet. That would have been difficult to explain on the American home front. After the fall of Saddam Hussein, the U.S. government needed an impressively diabolical image of the enemy to justify to voters the endless war with Iraq. Zarqawi seemed a good fit for the role of omnipresent terrorist.

Zarqawi became known around the world thanks to cynical video productions of the beheadings of Western hostages. In 2004, a video surfaced with the title "Abu Musab al-Zarqawi slaughters an American." In it, the American Nicholas Berg has his head cut off—ostensibly in revenge for the "shameful actions" of the USA in the notorious Abu Ghraib jail outside Baghdad. Berg and later victims were dressed in the orange overalls worn by the inmates at Abu Ghraib. The videos differ from the current beheadings under IS leader Abu Bakr al-Baghdadi in that the bloody executions were shown in their entirety. Other than that, al-Baghdadi's publicly staged brutality is similar in many respects to that of Zarqawi.

IN THE FALL of 2004, Zarqawi officially joined al-Qaeda. Publicly his terror group went by the name al-Qaeda in Iraq (AQI). At that time, al-Baghdadi was sitting in an American prison in Baqubah, north of Baghdad. In the meantime, Zarqawi continued his murderous rampage. He was so brutal that finally Osama bin Laden's representative Ayman al-Zawahiri complained in writing to Zarqawi that too many civilians were being killed in his suicide bombings. And more Shias were being killed than Americans. Unlike Zarqawi, bin Laden and Zawahiri were striving for reconciliation between Sunnis and Shias.

But Zarqawi was not to be stopped. Not on any front. Everywhere he appeared, there was controversy about the brutality of his actions and the severity of his AQI interpretation of sharia (Islamic law), even though he could enforce sharia in only a few places. In those places, rigid, puritanical rules were imposed. Smoking, drinking alcohol, and music were forbidden.

Zarqawi's ruthless methods were similar in many respects to those of the early Wahhabis on the Arabian Peninsula more than 200 years ago. And these, in turn, were reminiscent of the Kharijites, who murdered Ali, the Prophet Muhammad's son-in-law, more than 1,300 years ago. Anyone who deviated even an inch from their strict beliefs was mercilessly and bloodily persecuted. It didn't matter if that person was a woman, a child, or an old man. Twenty-first-century extremists are often called modern-day Kharijites.

In June 2006, U.S. forces succeeded in eliminating Zarqawi at Baqubah by means of a targeted air strike. With two five-hundred-pound bombs. The USA desperately needed a success-ful mission in Iraq.

Al-Qaeda in Iraq, however, continued to fight. In October 2006, al-Qaeda in Iraq changed its name to the Islamic State in Iraq (ISI), after collecting into its fold many smaller resistance groups. Its new leader was the Egyptian Abu Ayyub al-Masri. The group's leading spiritual emir was the Iraqi Abu Abdullah al-Rashid al-Baghdadi—not to be confused with the current "caliph," Abu Bakr al-Baghdadi. Whether or not this spiritual emir existed and just what his signifi-cance was are matters that are still in dispute. ISI fighters numbered about two thousand as before. For political reasons, however, the USA continued to attribute almost all attacks, even those of other resistance groups, to ISI/al-Qaeda.

IN THE MEANTIME, the U.S. government was suffering significantly both politically and militarily as a result of growing resistance in Iraq. And it was getting war weary. Despite an extensive search, the weap-ons of mass destruction that were the alleged reason the U.S. had been drawn into this war were nowhere to be found. Instead, the number of fallen GIs was climbing relentlessly. So the USA changed its strategy. In Iraq, as in other places, you get a lot further with a sackful of money than you do with an army of tanks. Thanks to fan-tastically large payments in the millions of dollars to the chronically weakened Sunni tribes, the USA finally got them to agree to a military ceasefire. Awakening Councils were formed. These councils in turn created powerful Sunni militias. To distinguish them from ISI, which included some foreign fighters, they were called the Sons of Iraq.

Motivated by the promise that they would later be included in the power structures and prosperity of Iraq, Sunni tribes drove the increasingly unpopular ISI out of their strongholds. Small ISI cells managed to survive, especially in Baghdad, in Diyala Province, and in the large cities of Anbar, Fallujah, and Ramadi. ISI found itself in crisis and its very existence threatened. Yet the "civilian resistance" forced the Sunni tribes to be cautious when they attacked. After all, unlike the ISI fighters, their members now had the promise of civilian jobs to which they could return.

In return for the ceasefire, the American forces withdrew to their base camps, where they dug themselves in like moles. GIs were rarely seen on the streets of Iraq. The American account that the Iraqis had been brought to their knees by Bush's reinforcements, the so-called surge, is a public-relations myth. At that time, I was with the moderate resistance fighters in Anbar Province. And sometime later, I was in Baghdad. The USA had lost the war in Iraq, plain and simple. But thanks to their monetary gift, they could at least save face, and when they withdrew in 2011, they could act as though they had eked out a victory after all.

Anyway, neither the American nor the Iraqi governments kept their grand promises to the Sunnis. In fact, the Sunnis, and above all members of the one-time ruling Baath Party, continued to be largely excluded from political life in Iraq. And after the routing of ISI, they received no more money either. Many young Sunnis were again without work. Instead of being rewarded, the Sunnis were oppressed and hunted down by death squads. As revenge for the difficult years under Saddam, Iraq's Shia prime minister Nouri al-Maliki set up an anti-Sunni regime of terror. The West knew what was happening. But it wasn't interested.

AFTER THE ISI leader al-Masri and the first al-Baghdadi were killed in U.S. air strikes in April 2010, thirty-eight-year-old, PhD-educated Abu Bakr al-Baghdadi took over leadership of the overextended ISI cells in May 2010. They were still under the jurisdiction of al-Qaeda.

In 2011, during the so-called Arab Spring, impoverished former members of Saddam's command joined ISI. They had been shut out of the Iraqi forces in 2003 and had never been given another chance to join up. And so ISI grew once again into a small, powerful fighting force. Al-Baghdadi resumed Zarqawi's campaign against the Shias and Maliki's government. With the same brutality and the same rigid AQI interpretation of sharia Zarqawi had employed.

At the same time, armed resistance against Assad in Syria was gaining momentum, and at the end of 2011, al-Baghdadi founded the terrorist organization Jabhat al-Nusra under the leadership of the Syrian Abu Mohammad al-Julani. In the following months, al-Nusra fought the Syrian regime with increasing success. At first, the ties to ISI and al-Qaeda were kept quiet. And for good reason: al-Qaeda and the Iraqi ISI were not well loved by the Syrian people.

The "Alawi heretic" Assad was a perfect bogeyman for the rebels. He was secular, Alawi (Alawis practice a secretive form of Shia Islam), one of the leaders most closely connected with Shia Iran, and supposedly secretly pro-West, or even pro-Israel. And he was a dictator. Most of the rebels I met in Syria thought Assad was Israel's ally, even though Israel often bombed his positions. In Syria, like everywhere else in the world, the bogeyman defies logic.

FROM THE BEGINNING, many Middle Eastern and Western governments were involved in the insurgencies in Syria, and all of them were hugely interested in a coup in the country. Saudi Arabia, Qatar, the USA, France, Great Britain, and others tried to strengthen resistance to Assad. With money and weapons. As well as by means of media campaigns—primarily on al-Jazeera and al-Arabiya—that were reminiscent of the disinformation campaign in the 2003 Iraq War. While I was in Syria, I spent my evenings reading Western news reports on the Internet, and I often thought the Western media was writing about a completely different country from the one I was experiencing so intensely every day.

The weapons that helped turn what had been initially peaceful demonstrations in Syria into ruthless civil war were delivered to Turkey with the USA's kind permission, either by ship in gigantic cargo containers or by air. From there, the weapons were transported to Syria and handed over to the rebels. Smaller smuggling routes led through Lebanon and later through Iraq.

The deliveries were approved by CIA officers. From undisclosed locations, they decided who got which weapons. In this way, the Americans could supposedly ensure that weapons did not go directly to Jabhat al-Nusra or other extremist groups—though they had no control once the weapons passed into Syrian territory. They were aware that the weapons would eventually end up with terrorist groups—as was anyone with even a passing knowledge of the military situation in Syria. The most militant rebel groups could always find the best weapons on the other side of the border. Often the groups considered to be more moderate simply sold the foreign weapons on to organizations with ties to al-Qaeda. A bloody and lucrative arms trade arose in Syria.

Private donors and organizations from Saudi Arabia and Kuwait also contributed money, weapons, and fighters on a vast scale. Most of the money and weapons went to radical Islamic groups. This was forbidden under the laws of these countries, but that did little to deter them.

By 2013, Jabhat al-Nusra had grown to be the strongest rebel group in Syria. It was so powerful that al-Baghdadi felt compelled to declare publicly that Jabhat al-Nusra was none other than ISI in Syria. When he had done that, he asked al-Julani to swear allegiance to him. Al-Julani, however, refused, preferring to swear allegiance to the leader of al-Qaeda, Ayman al-Zawahiri. Al-Julani wanted to be a subsidiary that reported directly to head office, not a subsidiary of a subsidiary.

So, al-Zawahiri asked al-Baghdadi to let al-Nusra and ISI operate as separate entities "as before" so that both organizations could concentrate on their respective territories. Al-Baghdadi categorically refused and explained that from now on, al-Nusra was part of ISI. When Zawahiri and al-Julani didn't agree, al-Baghdadi officially split from al-Qaeda and declared that al-Julani was an apostate. As a result, more than half the al-Nusra fighters defected to al-Baghdadi and pledged their allegiance to him.

Raqqa and northeastern Syria now came under al-Baghdadi's control. He changed the name of his organization from ISI to ISIS, also referred to as ISIL (the Islamic State in Iraq and al-Sham—the Levant). Later, he called ISIS simply IS, the "Islamic State." The name no longer acknowledged any geographic boundaries. The aspirations of IS are, after all, global. When Abu Bakr al-Baghdadi declared the caliphate of the "Islamic State," there were already more than 6 million people living in territory he controlled.

II

How Close Can We Get?

VERY EARLY ON, I suggested that arms shipments from Saudi Arabia and Qatar had led to a radicalization of the situation in Syria. Peaceful demonstrators striving for democracy in Tunisia and Egypt had earned my complete sympathy. But the dream of peaceful demonstrations in Syria was over as soon as one segment of the population received and began to use weapons. From this point on, another kind of human being took over leadership of the rebellion. The peaceful demonstrators were pushed aside, and they retreated.

The armed rebel units radicalized with breathtaking speed. The French philosopher André Glucksmann once said in the German magazine *Der Spiegel:* "Terrorist methods have poisoned the goals of almost every modern freedom movement, from Algeria to Vietnam. When the methods are dreadful, they destroy even the noblest goals." Terrorist organizations are stepping forward more and more aggressively. First, Jabhat al-Nusra with its close ties to al-Qaeda, then ISI, which originally started in Iraq and changed its name numerous times, to ISIS, ISIL, and, now, IS.

My repeated warning about the inexorable empowerment of terrorist organizations was rejected in Germany as a conspiracy theory.

People thought I wanted to discredit the moderate rebels. But even leaders of the Free Syrian Army, which the West regarded as moderate, told me their fighters were defecting to the extremists in droves. They went because Jabhat al-Nusra and ISIS paid better and fought more ruthlessly. The West refused to acknowledge this development. In May 2013, when I told the American government of Assad's interest in a mutual exchange of information about terrorist organizations in Syria, the USA refused. "We won't speak with that rogue," was their childish reply, even though it would not have been necessary to speak directly with the government. A dramatic mistake for which Christians, Shias, Yazidis (a Kurdish religious sect), and the whole world have had to pay a high and bloody price. The USA hadn't wanted to be informed about terrorism in Syria, and it was probably surprised by the momentum and power of IS's victories. Or had the USA knowingly taken IS's march to victory into account, as ex-DIA (Defense Intelligence Agency) head Lieutenant General Michael Flynn stated bitterly in an interview with al-Jazeera in 2015?

IN JUNE 2014, when fewer than four hundred IS fighters drove twenty thousand Shia-Iraqi soldiers and thousands of police officers from the predominantly Sunni town of Mosul, I decided I had to visit Mosul. I knew the town, which had once had a population of 2 million, from earlier travels, and I could not figure out how IS fighters had been so successful against an Iraqi army equipped with the latest in modern weaponry. I called Sunni friends in Mosul and asked if they could smuggle me into the town IS had conquered. "Not a chance," came the answer. They had just fled Mosul and did not dare return.

I called members of the moderate Sunni resistance that had fought successfully first against Bush's troops and then doggedly against the Shia-Iraqi Maliki government. But they also refused to get me into Mosul. Their fear of IS was too great, even though the civilian Sunni resistance claimed to have twenty thousand armed fighters in and around Mosul. Apparently, their Kalashnikovs were no match for the modern weapons IS had captured from Iraqi divisions as they fled. Everything was a bit murky.

To shine some light on the situation, I flew with my son, Frederic, to Erbil, the capital of the autonomous Kurdistan Region in Iraq. The town lies fifty-five miles east of Mosul. In Erbil we met with high-ranking Kurds, townspeople who had fled Mosul, and members of the Sunni resistance. But even here, no one was willing to guide us to the new IS stronghold. So we decided instead to visit two refugee camps and then drive to Gwer, where the front lines between the Kurdish Peshmerga (military forces) and IS were located. Gwer lies thirty-seven miles southwest of Erbil. The date was August 20, 2014. The outside temperature was 109 degrees Fahrenheit. The air was comfortably dry.

IN THE FIRST camp we visit, about three thousand people are sheltered in tents set up by the UNHCR (United Nations Refugee Agency). Sunnis, Shias, Yazidis. Everything is in short supply. But no one complains, even though they only get to eat once a day. We see sanitation ditches they dug themselves, women washing clothes, children playing. Everyone is trying to make the most of the situation. Everyone has something to do. Life goes on, no matter how hard it is. They have left everything behind, given everything up. Some of them have experienced awful things. Who knows when they will return home— if ever? Most of them fled from Mosul, which is now occupied by IS. As long as nothing changes, they will remain here.

When we are ready to leave, I see children playing soccer with an empty plastic bottle. Street soccer at the end of the world, I think. Seconds later, I am in the thick of things, trying to get possession of the bottle so that I can kick it a few yards forward. Or dribble it. More and more children join in. Finally, a grown-up is playing with them. And a foreigner at that!

Frederic is telling a couple of curious boys who approached him that we are from Germany. "Oh! Almanya! World champion!" Frederic and the boys exchange high fives. Then Frederic sees a boy wearing an Italian soccer jersey. Well, Frederic laughs, he really should be wearing a German jersey now. He certainly can't be seen wearing an Italian jersey any longer. But Frederic knows that the children here have completely different things to worry about.

After a quarter of an hour, I'm dripping with sweat. Despite that, fifteen minutes playing soccer have done me good. We hit the road. As we discuss street soccer in the car, I notice that I have left my rucksack containing my money and my passport back at the camp. We turn around immediately.

Suddenly a severe sandstorm kicks up. It gets thicker and thicker, until we can't see anything at all. All kinds of things are flying up around the car—stones, clumps of dirt, cans, branches, sand, garbage! For minutes on end there is banging and rattling. We hunker down in our seats and put our arms up to protect our faces. Objects are banging against the windshield so hard that we are afraid it's going to shatter. It begins to hail, but with all the other noise we can hardly hear it. We are just hoping another car won't come down the road in the opposite direction and crash into us!

Suddenly, it's all over. We can see again. All that is left is the rain still pelting down as hard as before. The windshield is cracked. We drive back to the camp very carefully. In the pouring rain, Frederic gets out and runs into the camp. The bag is still lying there where I left it. Next to the soccer pitch. Everything is still inside. I've been lucky. And I got to play soccer with well-mannered and well-behaved children. Frederic is soaked to the skin. I give him my jacket.

THE SECOND REFUGEE camp is in an old school opposite a church. Three hundred and fifty Christians are sheltered here. Seventy-two families in all. The church organizes food and drink. The people are happy that they are at least getting some help. Most of them have fled here from Mosul as well. Just like the Shias, Sunnis, and Yazidis we saw in the first camp. After conversations that leave a deep impression on us, we set out for Gwer and the front lines.

In the fields next to the country road, we see earthen berms, primitive defenses against IS. At one of the many Kurdish military checkpoints, we are advised to travel no farther. IS is still in the area. There are many snipers, especially to the right of the road. Gwer was retaken by Peshmerga troops only a few days earlier after a massive U.S. bombardment. IS moved just one village farther away. The strategic situation really hasn't changed much.

At the next checkpoint, we are warned about IS once again. But all I can see on the road are passenger cars and trucks, and I ask our driver to keep driving. Then, all of a sudden, the roads are empty. Once in a long while we see a truck. Our driver is getting more and more nervous, and in desperation he asks a soldier standing by the roadside a barrage of questions: "Are we really allowed to continue driving? Isn't it too dangerous? Why aren't we seeing cars anymore? Why do the villages look uninhabited? Where are the snipers?" I can imagine what is going through his head. He keeps taking deep breaths to calm his nerves.

I decide to pay strict attention to what the soldiers at the checkpoints are saying. To our amazement, they say: "Come on through." But after a while, there are no longer any vehicles to be seen on the road. As far as the eye can see, no one but us. Now even I am becoming uneasy. Have we already driven past Gwer and on to the other side of the front lines? The road yawns empty in front of us. Here and there are a few abandoned houses.

To our right, no more than a mile away, is where the new IS camp should be. They must have seen us. Perhaps they'll think we're here to sell them something. Hopefully! Our driver keeps saying that he's never been here before and he's afraid. He says he doesn't want to make a wrong turn. Frederic tries to take his mind off things by telling him little jokes. Somewhere around here there must be another Peshmerga checkpoint. Otherwise, the last checkpoint would not have waved us through. But, then again, you can rarely rely on logic in war-torn areas. When will we find the next checkpoint? It must be coming up, dammit. I really don't want to fall into a deadly trap like I did in Libya in the heated atmosphere of the so-called Arab Spring. Frederic keeps giving me questioning looks.

Thank goodness, two Peshmerga appear about a hundred yards

in front of us. We drive up to them. They point their Kalashnikovs directly at us at close range. I step out of the car to defuse the situation and show them we are unarmed. Now somewhat friendlier, the Peshmerga tell us that they drove IS from this place a few days ago. IS is now on the other side of the Zab River. About half a mile away. There is a bridge over the river.

A car screams up, stuffed with more Peshmerga soldiers. At the wheel sits a cool-looking young fighter, a keffiyeh, or scarf, on his head and gold sunglasses standing proudly on the bridge of his nose. I tell him, in a friendly fashion, that we would very much like to see his base camp. And then I simply get into the car with them. That always works. Even here. It is crowded and uncomfortable in the car. I'm sitting on some sort of handgun, and I try to move as little as possible. With a screech of tires, we're off. Our driver from Erbil and Frederic follow in the taxi.

We drive up a hill and get out. From this vantage point, we have a good view over the village, the bridge, the river, and the neighboring village. The one IS has moved to. All the fighting troops in the camp quickly gather around us. They are happy when we introduce ourselves. Thrilled, they shake our hands. These are civilized young men. They are well nourished and very clean and neat. Do these likeable young men stand the slightest chance against the Spartan troops of IS?

A few of the Peshmerga set themselves up behind a concrete wall with their Kalashnikovs and pose with their weapons directed at the IS positions. Wearing warlike expressions, they gaze out in the direction of the enemy. They wait patiently while Frederic photographs them. I tell them about my Kurdish friend Hussein, whom I play soccer with every Saturday in Munich. I ask them why 100,000 proud, world-renowned Peshmerga are asking the Americans and Europeans for help instead of confronting IS directly on their own. After all, they have quite the reputation as guerilla fighters. They laugh self-consciously. "What are we to do? We have nothing but these Kalashnikovs and small weapons! IS has modern weapons. And that is a huge problem for us."

Apologetically, they continue: "Anyway, we haven't received any orders to drive IS out. If our president gave us the order to drive IS out of Mosul, then we wouldn't hesitate for even a second. We would engage in battle proudly and fearlessly. And we would win!" But even the legendary Peshmerga seem to be afraid of IS. Like the whole Iraqi army. The IS strategy of spreading fear and terror by means of brutal medieval-style beheadings seems to be working.

The leader of the Peshmerga points to the village on the other side of the river, where IS has dug in. For the moment, IS is quiet. Apparently, to avoid provoking more American air strikes. But precision air strikes that spare civilians are difficult when the enemy takes cover among the inhabitants of a village. In the future, that will be the main problem with U.S. bombings. Especially in a large town like Mosul.

After an hour, we make our farewells. On the other side of the river, the black flag of IS is flying.

BACK IN ERBIL, I meet with leaders close to the president of the Kurdistan Region. They are proud to inform me that the Kurds seized one-third of the mostly ultramodern weapons of war left behind when the Iraqi army fled from IS. Weapons with a value of approximately US$4 billion. When I ask whether their flourishing country couldn't buy more weapons on the international black market, my question is met with an amused smile. Of course they could. "But why would we buy weapons when we are getting them from the Europeans for free? It might sound odd, but for us, IS is a gift from heaven. We Kurds have never been closer to our political goals than we are today." How can you blame the Kurds for making the most of the situation?

III

Conversation with a Jihadist

INCREASINGLY, IS WAS dominating world media reports. And my thinking. For weeks, I had been poring over a book about the conflicts in Iraq and Syria. But I couldn't find any sufficiently authentic information about IS. Who were these bloodthirsty terrorists who routed entire armies? Who celebrated their deliberate killing of civilians with sadistic glee?

In June 2014, before I left for Erbil, I had tried to establish Internet contact with these declared enemies of Western civilization. It was the German jihadists who interested me most of all.

I asked my son to help with my research. I have to say, it took me a while to convince him. We had to assume that all our online activity would be monitored by Western intelligence services. And Frederic had no desire to be pulled out of bed at five o'clock in the morning by officers of the state. Although everything we did was legitimate. It was even in the public interest to find out more about the German jihadists. Apart from that, both Frederic and I were journalists. And Freddy was my most valued colleague in this work.

To put my cards on the table, I informed the office of the federal chancellor and an influential member of the cabinet, as well as the editor in chief of ARD—my friend Thomas Baumann—about my research mission. However, I didn't go into my plans in detail. I was already regarded as a friend of Assad, and I had no desire to be defamed as a supporter of IS as well.

On our very first evening of research, June 9, we found more than eighty German jihadists on the Internet. Each of them received a letter from Frederic that I had drafted the night before. It was Frederic's job to edit and sign it.

Hello...

My name is Frederic Todenhöfer, and I am writing to you on behalf of my father, Jürgen Todenhöfer. We found you here on Facebook. From the posts we've read and the pictures we've seen, we conclude that you are in Syria. I don't know if you are familiar with my father and his work, but in recent years he has made an effort to present a fair picture of Islam. He has been to Syria many times, both before and during the war. He thinks this war is terrible, as are all wars. But he doesn't assign blame to just one side. He believes that no wars are ethical. He has learned this many times in many wars. Beginning with the Algerian War of Independence in the sixties.

In Syria, he talked with members of all the main rebel groups. Even with groups who had ties to al-Qaeda. And with the government.as well. He always speaks with both sides in every conflict. For this reason, he would very much like to speak with you or with your friends. He would like to know why you are doing what you do.

Best,

Frederic

FIFTEEN OF THE people we contacted replied. Most of the chats or Skype conversations that resulted were short. Connections were constantly disrupted. The people at the other end of the line were suspicious. Despite this, we kept up communication with two people for a period of many months. It was clear to them that I disapproved of their political stance and their brutal behavior. Despite that, they seemed to have a keen interest in sharing their side of the story. The

Skype conversations were tedious from a technical point of view because the Internet connections were, for the most part, very bad. I came away from many of our hours-long Skype conversations with a hellish headache. Not only because of the technical difficulties but also because of the content of our conversations.

SALIM, HIS BATTLE name, is a straightforward, one could almost say good-natured, thirty-year-old jihadist from Frankfurt. When our contact with him broke off at the end of July, he was a fighter for the jihadist group Jund al-Aqsa, which was mostly made up of foreigners. Before that, he had been a fighter with Jabhat al-Nusra and IS. In our interviews, he clearly distanced himself from IS. He is a young man full of contradictions. He told us that he had, in his words, messed up big time in Germany. He wanted to make up for this in Syria by "defending Muslims against Assad." Frederic and I often talked about whether we could persuade him to stop and make a normal life for himself somewhere else. But when contact ceased completely at the end of July and he was never online after that, we had to assume that either he was dead or he had been captured. Here is an extract from a conversation on June 19.

Salim: I came here because I am a true believer. I know that one day I will die. There is no one who can deny that one day he will have to answer to God. I am convinced that what I am doing here is the right thing. Because of my religion. Regardless of whether it is the right religion or not. Everyone claims his religion is the right one. The Christian says that Christianity is the true religion. The Jew claims Judaism is the true religion. The Muslim says the same of his own religion. If he didn't say that, he wouldn't be a Muslim. I am a fundamentalist because I base everything on the Quran. I try, as best I can, to serve God by following the Quran.

If you try to bring the truth of this war out into the open, you won't have a very successful career as a journalist. Politics is based on lies. Democracy itself is a swindle. Democracy is based on lies. Everyone tries to lie for his own benefit. If you try to write the truth about us, you'll find you have tough times ahead of you. Everyone knows the Syrian regime is a criminal regime. The Americans know it, too. The Germans are prepared to go into Afghanistan, into Kunduz and places like that. But no one is prepared to come here to help. Every fighter who comes here is immediately a Salafi [Salafism is an ultra-conservative movement within Sunni Islam] in your eyes. Everyone who comes to fight in order to defend his brothers and to defend Islam and its values. We say in Islam: "All Muslims are brothers." I would even die for you if you were a Muslim. It doesn't make any difference to me whether I know you or not. But the moment a Muslim leaves his comfortable home and fights for Allah, you immediately see him as a terrorist. As soon as an American or a German in the German army does the same thing, he's hailed as a hero. Saying that publicly won't do much for your career.

JT: For me it's not a question of advancing my career. I'm trying to discover the truth.

Salim: I really wanted to go to Afghanistan. I landed here by accident. I'd been to the Pakistani consulate to get a visa. Unfortunately, that didn't work. If I had the opportunity to go to Afghanistan today, I'd leave right away. That's what I dream of. I have a few friends there. I think the people in Afghanistan are more organized and friendlier than the people in Syria. They don't like foreigners like me here.

 To tell the truth, I've asked myself, hmm, why is he writing to me now? Why does he want an interview? I was there. I know how it goes. I was in Frankfurt then, and I know all those people. Pierre Vogel [a German Salafi preacher well known for being a convert and former boxer] and others who gave speeches. Whenever a television team or a newspaper came, they gave interviews. But the media distorted everything. They twist your words around. Then it's shown on television with some scary music playing in the background. And all so people get a bad impression of Islam. Pierre Vogel, the former boxer, is a Salafi now! He's never said anything awful. But the media is interested in making Islam look bad. And that's exactly what I'm worried about. That you will interview me and then edit our conversation so it reads: Salim is engaged in jihad and killing people and so on. That's the way it always goes.

JT: **It's not my intention to distort what you say.**

Salim: What do you think of this persecution of Muslims? Everything is always the Muslims' fault. Are Salafis bad people?

JT: **Have you seen my video** *Feindbild Islam* **[Islam as the Enemy]?**

Salim: I couldn't open it. It's not as though we have a truly free Internet here. You can buy fifty megabytes for about three or four euros. And with a video, of course, that's quickly used up.

JT: **Okay. So I'll just ask you a few questions instead. Why is there no jihad in Saudi Arabia?**

Salim: Because there is no such thing as Saudi Arabia. There's just Saudi America. Apart from that, we engage in jihad only when Muslims are being attacked. And that's not the case in Saudi Arabia. Mind you, there's no true sharia there. If sharia was in place there, there would be no brothels and no alcohol.

JT: **So sharia in Saudi Arabia is only for the man on the street?**

Salim: Exactly. That shows that the king of Saudi Arabia doesn't actually have anything to do with Islam. Despite that, the Muslims who live there are satisfied with what's happening. Many don't know Islam at all even though they live in Mecca or Medina. But they are not being oppressed. No one's being arrested and beaten on account of his beard or thrown into prison because he says: *"La ilaha illallah"* ["There is no god but God"]. That happens here in Syria because the majority are Alawis and Shias. Sunnis are being oppressed by Bashar al-Assad because he's an Alawi. There were demonstrations in Daraa.

And how did Assad and the government respond? They used force immediately. That's how it all began. First of all, there was the FSA, the Free Syrian Army. They were the first to engage in jihad here. They fought with shotguns and other simple weapons. It didn't take long for al-Qaeda to arrive and the jihad began. Al-Qaeda brought weapons and Jabhat al-Nusra came into being. Ahrar al-Sham and all those other groups arose. And so the jihad got underway.

I came here because I'm trying to practice true Islam. Because I'm convinced that when I die, God will call me to account. He will ask me: Have you lied? Did you drink alcohol? Did you cheat or do anything else you shouldn't have done? So now I'm just trying to be a better person. When Muslims are attacked, jihad is the duty of every Muslim.

JT: How come Jabhat al-Nusra and ISIS arose so suddenly?

Salim: I'm not really smart. The heads of our organization have many goals. Some pursue the goal of money and sell weapons. For them, war is a good thing. They make good money from it. Some want to found a state they can rule later. I'm not interested in those things. All I think about is how I can protect my brother in Islam, my sister in Islam, and their children, and how I can be a better person.

JT: Do you believe al-Qaeda has anything to do with the Assad government behind the scenes? Is there contact between them as some people claim?

Salim: Assad could never under any circumstances have founded al-Qaeda because al-Qaeda is so old. Just as the governing body of al-Qaeda and the people in it . . .

JT: And ISIS?

Salim: There are people who say IS is working with the government. The leader of IS, al-Baghdadi, is always fighting Muslims, receives all those assets seized in war, and is super good at promotion. They have an unbelievable amount of money, but all they do is stir up trouble. They don't understand jihad. They don't understand Muslim culture. They don't know that you have to give people time. So people have been smoking for forty years and along comes IS fighting everyone who smokes and cutting off their hands and I don't know what else. That's not acceptable! That is not Islam. The Germans who come here are completely wound up. They are happy and they think IS, that is Islam. But they don't understand anything at all about Islam. They don't know that Islam is also love and wisdom. I can't just suddenly take cigarettes away from someone who smokes. Say he's been smoking for forty years. I must get him to the point where he begins to hate these cigarettes so he can begin to leave them alone. Not because he is afraid of me, but because he is afraid of Allah, his master and his creator.

JT: Why do most Germans and most international jihadists join IS?

Salim: Because IS has such a strong presence in the media with its propaganda and calls to join up. They are simply unbeatable in this area. Also, people are naïve and dazzled by their black flag and *"La ilaha illallah."* They all wear beards and advocate absolute sharia. But they've got it all wrong. First, you must fight the enemy. You can't fight your own people until you have conquered the enemy. A caliphate has duties. That's what these people don't realize. All they see is beard, beard, beard, beard. And all they think is "Wow! Sharia, sharia. We're on absolutely the right track with our flag." But they're mistaken. Before you can punish a man, you must have given him something. I can't just go and punish a child if I'm not the person who looks after this child, who gives him his food. If I'm a father and my son makes a mistake, I can punish him. Because I'm the one who is bringing him up. I'm the one who gives him his clothes, his food, everything. The one who offers him protection. But if your child is failing in school, I can't just go up to him and hit him. I'm not his father, after all. I don't feed him or protect him. Nothing. IS doesn't give their people anything! They oppress their citizens more than they oppress their enemies. When I started out with them, I told them all this.

JT: And what did the people from IS say to that?

Salim: They are blind. They don't understand at all. All they see is sharia, sharia, sharia. They are always right and everyone who is not with them and with al-Baghdadi is wrong. That's how they think.

JT: At that time, al-Baghdadi was sitting in an American jail in Iraq.

Salim: Right. After the 2003 war, IS wasn't actually achieving anything in Iraq. They were kicked out of Iraq because of their lack of success. They came here to Syria and messed up jihad. They broke us up instead of bringing us together. Jabhat al-Nusra had been such a success here. They were so successful. They liberated many areas from government control. So we could move freely, eat, all those things. That's what Jabhat al-Nusra, and Jaish al-Hor, and Ahrar al-Sham, and the other groups achieved.

JT: You are really bitter about IS.

Salim: I don't have much of a brain, but I try to use what little brain I have. I try to examine things very carefully. I don't just look at the surface. When I work with someone, I try to understand him. What are his goals? Why is he doing this? Is he doing this because he wants money or to seize assets in war or because he wants to sell weapons? Does he want to trade oil or gas? What are his goals? I am here to free people from the oppressive Assad regime. That is jihad. And whoever dies during jihad is a martyr. But most people who die with IS, die fighting Jabhat al-Nusra. That's just insane. Just ask completely normal young people, normal Arabs, who have nothing to do with this revolution, who are just refugees. None of them think IS is a good thing.

JT: What does IS want?

Salim: IS wants power. They want to found a state. Al-Baghdadi has his own agenda. He's just been making a mess of things. Therefore it's of utmost importance that you as a journalist come here to report on the situation. You'd give people a rude awakening and shake them up a bit. I think your report would really make an impression. Of course, only if German television broadcasts it. If you came here and got to know the real mujahideen [those who perform jihad] then you'd stop calling these people terrorists. The only goal of true mujahideen is to protect people and give them what is rightfully theirs.

JT: Yes, but through war. Surely, you must have had to kill a lot of people as well.

Salim: Yes, of course. As you just said, we're in a war.

JT: What does war mean to you?

Salim: Killing is... In battle you don't think much. You only think about staying alive and functioning. You get tunnel vision. When you go out on an operation and the government is right there in front of you, and they're firing at you from helicopters, airplanes, tanks, and everything—and you're trying to fight with your ridiculous Kalashnikov. Right then, you aren't thinking at all. You are so busy with your life, your death, and the noise. You are afraid. My fear is not that I am going to die. Because, *alhamdulillah* [praise God], *inshallah* [God willing], if my intention is pure, then I will be dying for Allah. When you do something, you must be doing it for Allah and not so people will say how strong and courageous you are. If that's the case, the thing isn't worth anything at all. People who aren't really acting for Allah go to hell. The mujahid fights for God and not for himself.

Anyway, first of all you're busy with yourself and with the bombs. You are afraid. My fear is not that I will die. My fear is that I might be wounded and then get treated badly or that I might lose an arm or something. Then I wouldn't be able to fight anymore. That is my fear.

Then you fire your gun and perhaps you kill someone. Some people kill. Others don't. It's not always easy to kill someone in war. After all, the other person is fighting as well. Let's assume we want to storm a checkpoint. Before we storm this checkpoint, we fire on it heavily. From a distance of about five hundred meters [yards]. We bombard this checkpoint with everything we have. Then we advance on the checkpoint, one step at a time. By the time we arrive at the checkpoint, we've bombarded it so heavily that the house is completely destroyed. We've wiped out so many people that no one really knows who killed who. Everyone fired on the house. You only know for sure that you've killed someone when you take part in a special operation. For example, when you storm houses or sneak into checkpoints to set explosive charges and then sneak out again, or things like that. In normal warfare, no one can say if he's killed someone or not because mostly you're shooting from a distance. No one can say for sure how many people he's killed unless he's in a special group or part of a special operation.

Mostly we just sit there shooting, five or six hundred meters [yards] apart. Everyone shoots. Eventually, a couple of us are killed and a couple of them are killed. But nobody knows who killed who. Later, when we take the square, so many dead are lying there. No one can say, I killed that one, unless he is a sniper or was very close to the enemy. Do you know what I mean?

JT: So, roughly, how many people have you killed?

Salim: Like I told you, I'm nothing special. I'm not an amazing mujahid. You really are very curious, aren't you?

JT: Yes, I am.

Salim: Numbers aren't important. If I've killed someone it's only because he fought Muslims and wanted to kill me or my brothers.

Of course, this person also has a family. He also has a mother, who is now crying for him. Perhaps he also has children and a wife who is now a widow. But it is war, after all. In this case, you've got no choice but to think mostly of yourself. Of course, the best thing would be if we could all live in peace together. That would be the best thing.

I hate war, and I hate these things. I tell you truthfully, they make me feel sick. Really. I feel nauseous after a fight, after war. Your shoes are full of blood. You're slopping around in blood. You take this checkpoint and take the weapons from the dead. You take their magazines, you put on their flak jackets. That is disgusting. For example, I might have one shoe full of blood. That's revolting. It's stuck under your fingernails, down in between your fingers, all over your hands. I like to keep myself clean and tidy. I hate that. I hate disorder, and I hate dirt and nasty smells, and all those things. That's not my thing at all. What can I say? I don't have a passion for killing.

It was like that with boxing. I used to box and wrestle. I never liked to wrestle much. I really didn't want to have the other person's sweat all over me. Other people's sweat disgusts me. That's why I always tried to keep my opponent at arm's length and knock him out as quickly as possible. I didn't want him to sweat and slobber all over me. The best thing would be if we could live here without war. In a war you kill people fairly often.

JT: Sometimes you don't sound at all like a cold-blooded murderer.

Salim: Because I'm not. I'm someone who sometimes cries himself to sleep.

JT: How many people have you killed? Ten, twenty, fifty?

Salim: I've never killed fifty people. I'd have to be Rambo to do that. I'm not a sniper, either. I have a colleague who kills all the time. All the time, all the time. I wouldn't be able to handle that. He just makes himself comfortable, singles someone out, pulls the trigger and—wham!—he's taken that person's life. You know what I mean?

I'm a normal fighter. I fight with RPGs [rocket-propelled grenade launchers], so with a bazooka, or with an AK-47, a standard Kalashnikov. This Kalashnikov can fire up to seven to eight hundred meters [yards]. But at that distance, it isn't deadly. A sniper or a tank gunner, he kills a lot of people. When a tank gunner takes aim, the whole house falls down.

JT: Do you often see innocent people die?

Salim: No. Because we don't shoot civilians. We only fight people we meet in war, in battle. We never just go into the home of someone who is, say, an Alawi or a Shia and kill him.

Nevertheless, everyone who participates in war is guilty. I, too, am guilty. When I kill, I am guilty. Because I can choose to go along or not to go along. I can choose to fight or not to fight. I can choose to go to Turkey or some other country and get a new passport made and start a new life. But I have never killed an innocent person. I have never said: "Hey, I think I'll storm a house now and kill a kid or a woman or something." Only checkpoints, enemy barracks, just war.

JT: But the soldiers are not all contract killers. There are young men like you. Their families said: "You should join up." And there are mothers on both sides.

Salim: Yes, you're right. That's why I say killing is not anything beautiful. Because the person you killed also has a mother who will cry for him, a wife and children he'll leave behind. But, as I said, it's war after all. The best thing would be if no mother cried, if no one cried. If no woman had to be alone because of all this.

JT: So let's say tomorrow there was the possibility of a peaceful solution. Would you and the people you know be prepared to say: "We accept the solution if it can be an honorable and fair peace"? Would you accept that? When will the war end? You know there are parts

of Syria where Assad has a lot of support. What if everyone came together and united?

Salim: The war would just start all over again. Because everyone has a different point of view. Some people really want peace. They have no idea about Islam. They are not interested in whether democracy or sharia or whatever rules here. They simply want to live in peace. And I can understand that. It's a human instinct. People want to live and survive. People do whatever they can to survive. But if, as you suggest, we were to unite now, and if there was peace, perhaps I'd be okay with that. But! The Islamists might not agree because this peace would be based on the interests of people who don't hold the same beliefs they do. And a Muslim, of course, wants sharia and wants to live in a caliphate. So what are the Americans, NATO, and the EU afraid of? Sharia. Because just and fair sharia is strict.

JT: But in Syria not all people are Sunnis, right? There are other groups there as well, including secular groups. Would it really be fair to say: "Sharia for all"? Or are you saying that everyone must live under sharia? If that's your view, then there should be sharia in Germany as well, because there are Muslims who want sharia here, too.

Salim: Muslims want to live according to sharia. Why? Sharia, when correctly understood, protects people's rights. It is fair to everyone. It protects every Muslim. When the Jews were persecuted in Andalusia, where did they flee to? To Morocco, where they still live today and where they have founded a large community. Sharia protects all people. It doesn't matter whether they're Jews, Muslims, or Christians. Allah says in the Quran: "No one is forced to convert. You have your religion; we have ours." Everyone can believe in what he wants to believe in. Islam means we honor this. We give money to everyone who is hungry. We protect everyone who is oppressed. Do you understand? That is true sharia. Sharia is not mutilating women or circumcision, cutting off hands and war and slaughtering everyone who is not a Muslim. No. That is not our mission. What IS is doing has nothing to do with Islam. They haven't understood Islam.

Someone who has really understood Islam doesn't just rip a sentence from the Quran out of its context. Take, for example, the sentence: "Kill them wherever you find them!" What you need to know is why this verse was revealed, when, and what comes before and after it. Instead of just yelling the verse: "Kill them wherever you find them!" Should I kill everyone now? Should I kill my mother now? No. There are people who simply take it out of the context of the war that was being fought at the time. Christians and Jews do it, too. These people have no clue.

The best way to show what is going on here in Syria would be to somehow drum up a camera team and make a really honest documentary. That shows everything from a different perspective. That tries to be honest. Then you'd see how people live here. How they think. We're not radical. We aren't Salafis. We wouldn't—I would never—just kill a Christian or a Jew or a Buddhist or someone. We are Muslims. All we want is peace, and we want other people to live in peace as well.

JT: When an Alawi walks down the street where you are, what happens to him?

Salim: He has his religion. I have mine. He doesn't attack me. I don't attack him. So he's free to walk down the street.

With IS he would be dead right away. But we're not like that. We have packets of cigarettes here. I don't smoke myself, but some people do. There are people here who don't wear beards. People who listen to music as well. Everyone can do what he likes as long as he doesn't harm anyone else. Everyone must answer to Allah on his own. Whatever you do is between you and God. You will stand before him alone. Your reckoning will be with him alone. So you can do what you like here, as long as you don't harm other people around you. That is the true Islam. I want people to know the true Islam, even if they are Christians. What I would like is if you were to come here and make a documentary to show how we do things. To show the kinds of values we have and the morals that guide our lives in Islam. According to our moral code, all Muslims and Christians can live in peace and live together.

People need to understand sharia. A child abuser is killed. But if someone steals, his hand is not cut off right away. Sharia would not be sharia if a poor man who has nothing to eat at home gets his hand cut off. That is not sharia. And the kind of sharia where the king stuffs himself and my neighbor starves is not the kind of sharia I want either. That is not sharia. Sharia means everyone can eat, everyone has a right to protection, to peace, and everyone has the right to live safely and not be robbed. The thief has his hand cut off only if he has everything and still steals a woman. That is sharia.

JT: Did you ever steal anything in Germany?

Salim: I got into a lot of trouble in Germany. (Laughs.) I dealt stuff, I beat people up, I lied. Everything that you can do, I did, other than killing people and stuff.

JT: And what if they'd cut your hands off?

Salim: I would have said: "No, I don't believe in that." I would have been against that. Because I did not understand Islam. I wasn't poor and I didn't have any reason to steal. But now I understand Islam. Sharia is mercy and wisdom. It pays attention to the life circumstances of individuals. Before people are punished, they are given one more chance. "Come to us if you have nothing to eat. Come to us if you need something, but you must not take what does not belong to you."

JT: There appear to be about three hundred Germans who have gone to Syria. Why do some of them return to Germany and some don't?

Salim: Some of them would like to go back, but they're afraid they'll be arrested right away if they return to Germany. But if they haven't done anything, they have nothing to be afraid of. But let's say if I were to go back to Germany, then there's no doubt I would go to jail. I'm not stupid. I know for sure that the police, the authorities, and the BKA [German federal criminal police], the secret service, and the intelligence service are listening in on my conversation with you right now. They read my Facebook posts and hack my Facebook account. But if they're doing that, they'll see that I'm just a normal person who sometimes writes to women and things like that. No one can make me feel ashamed. The only person who could make me feel ashamed is God. But if I were to return to Germany, I know I'd have all kinds of problems because I've been here for so long. Eighteen months or so. They make things difficult for anyone who's simply been in contact with someone in Syria. They throw him in jail. Right away, he's a Salafi and extremely dangerous. It doesn't matter if he's committed a crime or not. The system in Germany isn't fair. Not for Muslims.

Many of my friends don't write to me anymore because they're worried that being in touch with me will get them into trouble. They don't call me anymore or don't answer when I call them because it's no secret that the authorities listen to everything.

JT: But why do some people return? Are they going to Syria, taking part in jihad for a couple of months, and then going back to school? Are they going home to their towns and saying to girls they meet: "Hey, I just waged jihad"?

Salim: I don't know. Perhaps they didn't find what they were looking for. Perhaps they weren't treated right. Perhaps some of them came here just to see what was going on. Perhaps some of them just wanted to say: "Hey, I waged jihad," and then they come back and say they killed fifty people. They tell that to their friends to gain their respect.

JT: So what did you do before when you were still in Germany?

Salim: I trained in the sports and fitness business. Before that, I grew up in a group home. In a residential home and all that. So, of course, Germans could say: "Whoa. A migrant, a difficult past. That's the reason he joined jihad." No. It's true I was in a home and I wasn't good in school and got into trouble all the time. That I was a dealer and all that. But that's not the reason I came here. Just before I came here, everything was just fine. I was making a lot of money. I had girlfriends and all the fringe benefits. I looked pretty good. I had money and I had a good body. Actually I still have a pretty good body. But I knew beyond a doubt that I was going to die someday, and as I said, I didn't want to go to hell. I'm afraid of going to hell. And then I said, I've just got to start serving my Creator. I've got to be a better Muslim. I've got to stop lying and dealing. I've got to stop putting women down, getting mixed up in bad things, hurting people. I've got to change my life. I've got to change and do something good. That's the most important thing for me.

JT: But, Salim, if you wanted to do something good, couldn't you have chosen something other than going to war?

Salim: I could have done anything. But the genuine Muslim chooses according to Islam. And, according to Islam, the best thing to do, *la ilaha illallah,* is to engage in jihad. So that you don't turn your back on your Creator. A Muslim is not just anyone. He is someone who devotes himself to God. Before, I had a different girlfriend every week, and I got into fights and drugs. But a real Muslim devotes himself to God. It is Allah who gives you your mother. Your merciful and kindhearted mother. Who feeds you and lets you see, who allows your heart to beat, and who, without having to give a reason, could simply take your life away. For death doesn't need a reason. Allah gave me strength so I can work. Allah could take away my strength. Allah gives me health and sickness. Allah controls everything. Whoever doesn't give him thanks is the worst person. The best deed, according to Islam, is jihad. It is proof you love Allah. A Muslim loves

Allah more than he loves himself. He loves Allah more than sleep. He loves Allah more than food. During Ramadan, he fasts for more than fourteen or fifteen hours. It is hot. He does it just for Allah. That is why a Muslim offers his blood, all of it, without holding back. I don't hold back my blood. I don't hold back my strength. I have desires, too. I would love to live in a villa and have many women, be rich, do whatever I want. But I am a human being. Human beings are weak. Human beings love parties, women, alcohol, just having fun. A Muslim is allowed to have fun as well but only in moderation. For the person who enjoys himself too much loses his sense of compassion for others.

Jihad is the best deed. Fair, justified jihad. You've got to be fair and just. Take September 11, for example. Airplanes crash into the World Trade Center and thousands of innocent people die. That is not jihad. Jihad is when you protect poor people and help them, not when you kill innocent people.

JT: So why are so many young people joining IS, which you say is insane? Or Jabhat al-Nusra?

Salim: You've said it. You're telling the truth about these crazy people. You said it really well. What about human rights? What about protecting a person and standing up for his rights? All IS does is kill people. They are murderers. And when they say they are Muslims and judging people according to Allah's law, where are the courts? They kill—wham. Someone smokes—wham—they take his hand right off.

JT: But al-Qaeda is just as awful.

Salim: I don't know.

JT: Yes, but you just said that 9/11 had nothing to do with a just jihad. It wasn't honorable. You don't go to paradise for something like that. You go straight to hell.

Salim: But I don't believe that al-Qaeda had anything to do with 9/11. I just have to say that.

JT: But bin Laden himself said he had inspired people and appealed to them to do that. That makes him guilty. To massacre innocent people is to massacre innocent people. It doesn't make any difference to me if the perpetrator is wearing a uniform or a mask or whether it's all done by computer. For me, it's always murder. It is just not okay to murder innocent people.

Salim: You are right. On every point.

JT: You believe that, too?

Salim: Yes, absolutely. Whoever it was behind the September 11 killings. But I'm afraid. Of God. Later, when Allah says: "I am the one who gave this person life and you are the one who has taken his life from him. Who are you then, who has taken his life?"

JT: Exactly. And that is why I say that IS is just as awful as al-Qaeda.

Salim: I would never do these things. If I was with al-Qaeda and if my boss said: "You know what? You're going to Frankfurt now. And your task today is to go back and fly into the Commerzbank." Why should I do something like that? Perhaps my mama is going to be in the bank today with my little brother. Perhaps someone else's mother is going to be there that day, and perhaps she's a Christian. She goes high up in the tower with her little children and simply wants a chance to see the view and show it to her little children. Why should I come and...? No, I wouldn't do that. I have no special knowledge of Islam. I'm telling you the truth. All I have is a humble desire to please my Creator.

JT: In your opinion, do people who go to Syria and then return to Germany pose a threat?

Salim: Nope.

JT: Do you believe that a group in Syria might say it's time to go and get something going in Germany?

Salim: I don't know. No idea. Whatever happens, they shouldn't kill any innocent people. No innocent people, no innocent people.

I am a Muslim, and I must defend the honor of my Prophet. What I'm about to tell you could undermine everything I've said to you so far. But I don't want to lie to you. If someone were to insult the Prophet, I would react very strongly. According to Islam, the punishment for this person is death.

JT: But surely you know that people who insult the Prophet want to provoke you. They want Muslims to run through the streets crying: "Blood, blood, we want blood!" So that the next day some newspapers have the photographs they want and can say: "Just look at these insane Muslims. You insult them and they freak out and kill people." That's their goal.

Salim: I'll come clean. If I were in Germany and someone insulted my Prophet, I would probably knock his teeth out. But first, I would check. Is this guy in his right mind? If he's some poor person who doesn't know what he's doing, then I would let him go. But there are people who are very clever, who bait you because they hate Islam. I would kill them. Perhaps I've just destroyed my credibility as far as you're concerned. That's all the same to me, because I'm not saying all this so I look good to you...

JT: If I were you, I wouldn't listen to such provocation and I would leave. There are so many idiots, and you shouldn't let idiots get to you.

Salim: I would do the same thing if someone were to insult Jesus. I think I love Jesus more than many Christians. Jesus, Abraham,

Moses, Noah, David, and all the prophets, they are all part of the same religion. Every one of these prophets said: "Pray to the one true God! And don't pray to anyone else." Jesus didn't say: "Pray to me." All of them were monotheists. Jesus, too. But what did Christians do to this belief in one true God? They made three gods: Father, Son, and Holy Spirit. But Jesus said quite clearly in the Bible: "I am only the shepherd sent to the House of Israel."

JT: You forgot the Virgin Mary.

Salim: (Laughs.) Right, I forgot the Virgin Mary. But, as I said, they were all part of a monotheistic religion, even Mary. I love Jesus. I wish I'd lived in his time, and then I would have followed him. I would love to have been one of his followers. If someone were to insult Jesus or David or Abraham or any of the other prophets, I hope, *inshallah,* that I would find a path between not listening and knocking their teeth out. But it would hurt me deeply.

JT: I think Allah would prefer that. No reaction would be the best reaction. There's no rule that says: "Kill all the ignorant people and those who provoke you." Better just to not let yourself be provoked in the first place! In the end, you Muslims are hurting yourselves most of all. And that's the bad thing about it. If you look at the media reports, everyone's saying: "Now the Muslims are cutting each other's heads off." Sunnis against Shias and Alawis. Everyone against everyone else. And the West fans the flames, saying: "Just look at those crazy people! Someone's just got to draw a cartoon of Muhammad and they go completely mad."

Let's change the subject. What do your parents think about what you're doing?

Salim: Home. Come home. Come home.

JT: Do you still speak to them sometimes?

Salim: Only with my mom. I don't know my father. He abandoned me a long, long time ago. I have a little brother as well. I've never, never made my mother sad, thank God. And I always listened to her. My family is very poor. My mom has just a temporary residence permit. She doesn't have a passport. She only gets two hundred euros and she's not allowed to work. She is really poor. I love my mom more than anything.

JT: But she must be sad now.

Salim: She's sad, but she understands. She knows I'm a better person than I was, that I have a moral code and values I live by. She knows that if I'd stayed in Germany, so many things could have gone wrong. Because of my friends and their bad influence, and perhaps I might have started to deal drugs again. Perhaps I would have landed in jail again. She knows I'm really helping here, and, I hope, I'm a different Muslim now. As I said, I'd really like it if you made a video, a report, but probably I'm just dreaming about that. That'll never happen, but it really doesn't matter.

JT: Where do you come from originally?

Salim: My mom is Moroccan. My father is Turkish.

JT: What's your favorite soccer team?

Salim: Real Madrid overall, but Schalke was my favorite German team.

JT: Schalke?

Salim: What's wrong with Schalke? You must support Dortmund.

JT: No, Bayern. That's where I live, after all.

Salim: Bayern? Oh. Okay, I must admit FC Bayern has really improved their game. Lots of short passes! The kind of soccer they are playing now is very, very good.

JT: Let's get back to your life for a moment. For example, what do you have to do tomorrow?

Salim: First of all, I'm going to stay awake until morning prayers. That'll be in about an hour and a half. At 4:00 AM. Then I'll pray and lie down for a while. I'll sleep until nine or ten and then I'll get up. I'll do a few push-ups, a few sit-ups. Then I'll go out and ask the guys what's up for the day. Have we been attacked? Right now it's quite quiet. A few days ago, we were on a mission. Yesterday and today, there's nothing going on except MiG airplanes flew over and bombed us. When there's nothing to do, I stay at home and eat and sit around with my brothers. Or I train.

My house is right next to the border with the enemy. They're about sixty or seventy meters [yards] away. If I go to my front door, I'm right in the middle of the fighting. My house is right on the border with the neighboring town. The fights take place between my town and the town down the road. Bullets are always flying, bombs are falling, there are snipers. But I love it.

AT THIS POINT, our conversation was interrupted for several minutes. Salim apologizes. It was a false alarm.

Salim: We're always ready. If something were to happen now, I'd be ready right away. I always have my AK-47 with me. I have my handgun with me at all times, as well. So we're always ready if something happens. Other than that, we live a completely normal life. You can lead a completely normal life here. You can get married. You can even live here with kids. It's just that planes are flying over all the time and bombing us. But other than that, we live a completely normal life. I could show you all that if you were here. I could show you how we go off to fight. I have four good bulletproof vests, thank God.

One of them is from a friend who became a martyr. I got it from him. I got everything of his, weapons, bulletproof vests. If you came here, for a week or so, we would, of course, give you all these things so you'd be safe.

JT: So I could become a martyr as well? What is your task right now?

Salim: Our most important task is to hold this village.

JT: Who are you holding it for?

Salim: For the villagers. So that the Assad government doesn't come and slaughter people.

JT: Who is coordinating all this? Who's in charge of the town?

Salim: I have to say, it's all badly organized, very badly organized. But it's getting better. Thank God we now hold many towns. And in these towns there is no IS, just Jabhat al-Nusra, Ahrar al-Sham, Jaish al-Hor, and other groups. Jund al-Aqsa, that's the best group because the brothers are really great brothers. That's my group. Our task is to stop Assad's soldiers from taking the town. And to make sure that everyone can live in relative freedom. Of course, there's no fornication here, and you can't just, how do you say it, have sexual relations with a woman outside marriage. Naturally, that's not okay. And there's no alcohol, either. But people smoke, some of them listen to music. Everyone does his own thing. No one is forced to pray.

And that's partly because IS is not here. If IS was here, there'd be heavy fighting between IS and Jabhat al-Nusra and Ahrar al-Sham. Those would be really ugly fights. IS is always trying to come here. But they can't. For IS we are—I am a *murtad,* an apostate.

AT THIS POINT, we lost our connection. Permanently. We never heard from Salim again. Freddy and I had hoped to convince him to end his jihad and make a new life somewhere else.

IV

Things Get Serious

FOR A WHILE in the early summer of 2014, we were in contact with a number of Germans fighting for IS. Then, from one day to the next, our communications stopped. One of the young men made an official announcement: "I have spoken with one of the people in charge. He would like your Skype address. He said you shouldn't contact anyone else here. From now on, he will look after everything for you." A few days later, Abu Qatadah got in touch.

Abu Qatadah is over thirty. He is physically imposing. He is about five foot nine and must weigh at least three hundred pounds. He's like a youthful Bud Spencer as jihadist. Of all the people we talk with, he is the most accomplished intellectually and the most skilled in matters of ideology. He has a comprehensive knowledge of history. His answers are ruthless and incisive. He obviously has an official function in IS's media department, but he doesn't spell out what it is. He used to be a Protestant. He's German to the core. His parents are German. His grandparents were German. He comes from the Ruhr region near the Rhine. From Solingen.

The conversations with him included here have been edited for length. The first one took place on September 9, 2014.

Abu Qatadah: Hello? The sound quality is really bad.

JT: I can hear you.

Abu Qatadah: Good. Let's give this a try then.

JT: How hot is it with you?

Abu Qatadah: I don't know. During the day it's about thirty or forty [eighty or a hundred] degrees.

JT: That's normal, not so bad.

Abu Qatadah: It's bearable.

JT: Is it difficult to get a Skype connection out of Raqqa?

Abu Qatadah: If we want to use the Internet, we have to go to an Internet café. For security reasons. We can't make any telephone calls. That's why it's difficult to contact you.

JT: I wanted to restate what it is I'm interested in. I would like to understand what you really want, what your organization wants, and what most Germans there want.

Abu Qatadah: Okay.

JT: I would very much like to visit you in your conflict zones. But that isn't so easy to do.

Abu Qatadah: Why not?

JT: We should speak frankly about that. Naturally, there are problems about safety. You know that as well as I do. You could perhaps

guarantee my safety, but what does that get me if someone else then cuts my throat?

Abu Qatadah: I have spoken with my superiors. Your safety would absolutely not be a problem. We would guarantee it. We want you to give the world an accurate image of IS. So it's better if you come here. A Skype interview is all well and good, but we want to show the world what we're really doing. We want to show them how the state we have built here functions and what life is like for the Europeans and the Germans. So it's better if you come to us in person. Until now, the media has tried to fight us. I don't know if you've been following the situation, but they have shut down our social media accounts, and we have scarcely any access to the outside world.

JT: I'm listening.

Abu Qatadah: Before you come, we'll discuss what you'd like to see, all the places you can visit. We'll put people at your disposal and, of course, provide accommodation, a house, and all that. Everything you need and is in our power to give you. We could also organize interviews with many of the Germans if you'd like.

JT: I'm not an overly fearful person and I've been in many war zones. Despite that there is still an element of risk. When I visit a war zone— I've just been in the Gaza Strip—then of course I look around to make sure I'm not about to be blown to bits. But how can you guarantee my safety? After all, there are other rebel groups in your area.

Abu Qatadah: No, in our region there are no other groups.

JT: How can I get to you?

Abu Qatadah: Via Turkey. We control two border crossings. At one of the crossings there's Gaziantep on the Turkish side—roughly where the German Patriot missiles are installed—and Jarabulus on the Syrian side. At the second crossing, there's Urfa on the Turkish side and Tel Abyad on the Syrian side, if I'm not mistaken.

JT: How far away from you is that?

Abu Qatadah: I'm not sure, 130, 150 kilometers [80, 90 miles] or so. I'm in Raqqa right now. That's in the northern part of Syria.

JT: Who would pick us up?

Abu Qatadah: I think I'll be there because I speak German, and a few others from our group will be there as well. We'll pick you up personally.

JT: But where are the security checks? So I get there and perhaps I find you—and you find me—and then someone says: "But that's an enemy. He has always publicly attacked IS." How can you guarantee that won't happen?

Abu Qatadah: I don't know how many Muslims you've met and whether you know Islamic law. The Christians who live here in Raqqa, they pay this—I don't know what it's called in German—protection tax or whatever. In Arabic it's called jizya. Based on the current price of gold, that's about US$630 a year. That's the price for rich people. Poor people pay about half that. And for this they get protection. No Muslim is allowed to attack them. Anyone who attacks them despite this is brought before the Islamic courts and sentenced to death.

The shura council—I don't know if that means anything to you—anyway, the council that reports directly to the caliph gives its word that it guarantees your safety. And if something were to happen (laughs)—that's bad news for you. But the person would be punished that's one hundred percent certain.

JT: But that doesn't do me any good.

Abu Qatadah: For our part, I can guarantee there won't be any attacks or anything like that. Of course, in the end it's up to you whether you believe me or not. All I can do is make the offer.

JT: I would probably come with a journalist who would also require some sort of guarantee, so, for example, a letter from your emir or caliph that would have to say something like: "I herewith invite you and offer you hospitality and safety." Then the caliph's credibility is on the line. It doesn't have to be more than a couple of sentences.

Abu Qatadah: Okay.

JT: If he writes that, then he is giving his word that he takes responsibility for our safety. I would put my trust in a promise like that. Because if things go badly for me then, despite his assurance, that's not good for him either. Then no one would ever believe him again.

Abu Qatadah: Yes, of course. I think one way you can ensure your safety is to make this public in Germany or in the media or however you like. That way you put us at risk if something did happen to you—a rocket, a plane, or whatever—we would look bad. We're not interested in what any of the media say, but unfortunately for us, from then on many Muslims, and they are our main concern, would be against us. And, of course, we want to avoid that.

JT: If you were to give me a guarantee from the emir that says: "This man is our guest for one week and I guarantee his safety"—that would be enough for me.

Abu Qatadah: That shouldn't be a problem. We could prepare the letter. We could have it signed and stamped. So the way it works here is that each province has its own stamp and signature. That can be arranged.

JT: When I say the emir, I mean al-Baghdadi.

Abu Qatadah: I don't think it will go that far. My superior has complete freedom to act in his jurisdiction because the emir doesn't want to be personally bothered with such matters.

JT: Then we have a problem. I still have some living to do. Give some thought as to how I might get a guarantee from your emir. And now I would very much like to ask you a few questions and discuss them with you. Do you have time?

Abu Qatadah: Yes, I have time.

JT: We'll see how far we get. How old are you?

Abu Qatadah: Thirty-one.

JT: What motivated you personally to go to Syria?

Abu Qatadah: My personal path to Syria was a long one. I didn't travel to Syria directly from Germany. I spent time in a few other Arab countries first. Only then did I travel to Syria.

JT: How long have you been in Syria?

Abu Qatadah: Hmm. What year is it? 2014?

JT: Yes, about that.

Abu Qatadah: Then I came to Syria in early 2013.

JT: Did you enter from Turkey?

Abu Qatadah: I was mostly in the area of Halab [Aleppo] and Idlib, so right close to the Turkish border.

JT: With which organization?

Abu Qatadah: With Jabhat al-Nusra. At that time IS didn't exist in Syria.

JT: What motivated you to come? Did you want to overthrow Assad? Did you want to help establish a caliphate? Did you have religious motives?

Abu Qatadah: It's not easy to explain. Syria has advantages over other countries. There are many prophesies about the Levant, Syria, Palestine, parts of Iraq, parts of Turkey, Jordan, Saudi Arabia. When war broke out, we sort of took the opportunity to settle in here. Because the region is of particular significance for Muslims, both because of its history and because of the prophesies.

JT: But what is it all about for you? Is it about living a particularly pure form of Islam or ending a dictatorship? What is the main driver for you?

Abu Qatadah: The main reason for me, at least today, is to found an Islamic state. Of course, at the beginning, when we got here the idea of an Islamic state was more theoretical than practical. At first, it was all about helping Muslims and freeing them from the dictatorship of Bashar al-Assad. Apart from that, it's much easier to travel to Syria than it is to travel to other countries. Today, if you want to go to Afghanistan to fight against the Americans, you might not even manage to get out of Germany. But in Syria, there are many emigrants from European or Western countries. Thousands of them. Because it's much easier than going to Afghanistan. Life here is also much more similar to life in Europe than life in Afghanistan is—and therefore it's much easier. It's difficult to go to Afghanistan.

JT: So whereabouts in Germany are you from?

Abu Qatadah: I'm from the Ruhr valley. I was self-employed for a while. In 2008, I gave up my business. Since then I've been mostly traveling.

JT: Self-employed in what area?

Abu Qatadah: Computer software and hardware.

JT: Which governments in the Arab or Islamic world are good governments in your opinion?

Abu Qatadah: None of them. (Laughs.)

JT: None of them?

Abu Qatadah: No, absolutely not.

JT: Not even Saudi Arabia?

Abu Qatadah: No, definitely not.

JT: But IS was funded by Arab countries, or am I mistaken there?

Abu Qatadah: That is propaganda to weaken the power of *al-Dawla al-Islamiya* [the Arab expression for IS]. At no time has IS received financial help from foreign countries. Perhaps there was the occasional private donor who could maybe raise US$10,000 or US$100,000. But as you well know, you can't wage war on US$10,000, or even on US$1 million. Essential income comes for the most part from assets seized in the war.

JT: I've visited Syria six times since the war began. I've met with rebel groups, with people from the FSA, from Jabhat al-Nusra, a group you were once a part of as well. People in the FSA told me that they got money from the Americans and from the Emirates.

Abu Qatadah: Yes, that's common knowledge. What few people in the West know is that Jabhat al-Nusra was sent into Syria by IS in

Iraq. Their leader, Abu Mohammad al-Julani, was ordered to Syria to represent the Islamic State in Syria. But he began to accept outside money and betrayed the common goal. At some point, Jabhat al-Nusra separated completely from the Islamic State, and for a while it joined up with the Free Syrian Army. To fight against the Islamic State. Because their financial backers from foreign countries—whether they were Arab countries, America, or European countries—demanded they do so.

JT: Who is financing Jabhat al-Nusra? Saudi Arabia or America?

Abu Qatadah: Officially neither. Unofficially both. In the end, it's all the same. Saudi Arabia can only finance a group if America approves of them financing the group, the so-called Islamic Front, for example.

JT: Is the American influence on Saudi Arabia that strong?

Abu Qatadah: Definitely. That's no secret.

JT: How many people does the "Islamic State" have in Syria and how many in Iraq? Just so I can get a rough idea.

Abu Qatadah: It's difficult to say. I asked some people higher up. Even they can only give an estimate.

JT: Their estimate?

Abu Qatadah: My superior, who is often in Iraq, told me a few days ago that in the past weeks and months alone, the number of our fighters in Iraq has increased tenfold. Off the top of my head, I'd guess between fifteen thousand and twenty thousand fighters.

JT: In Iraq.

Abu Qatadah: No, Syria and Iraq together. And on the administrative side—judges, managers, police officers, sharia police, and so on—I'd estimate about the same number.

JT: How important is the role of the Sunni tribes, the Baathists, and the other groups said to be connected to IS in Iraq? Those groups apparently fighting side by side with IS? Are they as important as IS? The Sunnis are claiming that there are many more of them. They're saying they have about twenty thousand fighters and you're saying they have far less.

Abu Qatadah: This talk about fighting side by side is not true. Since January 2014, so since the beginning of this year, there haven't been any coalitions with any other groups. The Islamic State no longer has ties to any other group. It could be that groups merge completely with IS and put their people and their weapons at our disposal and come under our command. Apart from that, coalitions are no longer tolerated.

JT: It's exactly the same in Syria?

Abu Qatadah: It's exactly the same in Syria.

JT: In your estimation, how many Germans are fighting with IS? And how many Germans are there in total fighting in Syria? Off the top of your head. In Germany, they say it's about three hundred.

Abu Qatadah: I can't confirm whether it really is three hundred. I also couldn't say if it's five hundred or a thousand. But in any case, I think about ninety percent of them are with IS. The rest are divided between Jabhat al-Nusra, the Islamic Front, and Ahrar al-Sham.

JT: But the overall number is not completely off base?

Abu Qatadah: I think the German government can make more accurate statements than we can.

JT: Do you want to come back to Germany someday?

Abu Qatadah: Definitely not. (Laughs.)

JT: And what do you think about the other members of the "Islamic State"? Do some of them want to return to Germany, or do they all want to stay?

Abu Qatadah: From the point of view of Islam, I think none will go back. But a person might get wounded or suffer from so-called homesickness. He might want to go back to his wife or to his children. Those are the other factors. So it could be that one or two go back. In January, when the fighting broke out, a few went back to their own countries—Germans, Belgians, but some Arabs, as well.

JT: In Germany, public prosecutors are standing by because you are not allowed to be active in foreign terrorist groups. That is an offense. And the penalties are severe. That is not exactly inviting, is it?

Abu Qatadah: Not really, no. But think of all those people who came back from Afghanistan anyway. You probably know about that. Their circumstances were all very different. Many of them expected to be put away for a long time. In the end, they got three, four, or five years, perhaps more. So, whatever reasons people have for coming back, that's all part of the calculation.

JT: The main concern here in Germany is that returning German jihadists will carry out serious attacks. I've spoken with many people who are fighting right now in Muslim countries. They told me: "But we're not fighting Germany. We're fighting in Syria against the regime there and not against the German government." What's your opinion? Should Germany be afraid of those who return?

Abu Qatadah: That's difficult to answer. From the Islamic point of view, Germany is considered to be an enemy of Islam, a country that fights Islam.

JT: By you, perhaps, but not by the majority of the Islamic world.

Abu Qatadah: German foreign policy concerning Israel is well known. Its foreign policy concerning Afghanistan is well known. The killing of Muslims in Afghanistan and in other countries is well known, weapons shipments around the world—weapons that are deployed against Muslims. Earlier we talked of Saudi Arabia. For example, we all know that troops in Saudi Arabia and the Saudi Arabian intelligence services were trained by Germany, that there are arms deliveries.

There's also the fact that—you must have seen this—that Kurt Westergaard was personally singled out and praised by Angela Merkel for his cartoons against the Prophet. [The Danish cartoonist Kurt Westergaard, whose controversial caricatures of Muhammad were published by the Danish newspaper *Jyllands-Posten* in 2005, was awarded a press freedom award by German chancellor Angela Merkel in 2010.] According to sharia, a person like that incurs the death penalty. By acting in this way, your government is demonstrating that it is an enemy of Islam.

JT: But not the German people.

Abu Qatadah: There's no difference—especially when you consider that Germany is a democracy. The people elect the government, and therefore, it follows that the people are happy with the government's actions. Or at least somewhat happy. You see that in surveys, as well. When you visit Internet forums or look at news sites, you see people largely in agreement about the fight against Islam. The so-called War on Terror. That's how Germany makes itself both a target and an enemy.

JT: It's one thing to criticize the German government's policies. I sometimes do that myself. But you see Germany as an enemy. What does that mean? Does that mean that those who come back will carry out attacks in Germany and carry on the fight here? Does Germany need to be worried if IS fighters return to Germany? Does Germany need to worry that there will be attacks?

Abu Qatadah: Right now that is definitely not our policy. Right now our policy is: if people leave us in peace, then we will leave them in peace. Having said that, if one day the borders of our state reach Germany, then we will fight people there as well. But there are no attacks or anything like that planned right now. At least not at the moment...

JT: So you don't believe that those who come back will carry out attacks?

Abu Qatadah: Maybe you saw what happened in France. The Belgian—or perhaps it was the other way around, the Frenchman who carried out an attack in Belgium, or the Belgian in France? I don't know exactly which it was, I've forgotten—the man who went into the Jewish museum and killed a couple of people with his Kalashnikov. [The attack happened at the Jewish Museum in Brussels. The attacker was French.] The fact is he wasn't acting on orders but on his own. It could well be that something like that could happen again. I'd be lying if I said it would never happen.

JT: What does the caliph have to say about that kind of attack?

Abu Qatadah: As I said, right now that's not the policy of the Islamic State. What should I say? These things happen.

JT: What do you think about the extent of the "Islamic State"? How large will it be one day?

Abu Qatadah: We know from the sayings of the Prophet Muhammad that at some point Islam will rule the whole world. That will happen. That is part of what we believe. And therefore I can say: "The Islamic State will rule the whole world."

JT: But the Quran states that there should be no coercion in matters of faith, and that Christians and Jews can keep their religions. Even under Muhammad, they could keep their religions.

Abu Qatadah: What you are saying is correct, of course. Perhaps you are aware that in Raqqa there is for all intents and purposes a peace treaty with Christians. We have spoken about this, that the Christians in Raqqa pay jizya, this protection tax. Christians have their rights. They can hold mass and pray in safety and so on. In Mosul, the Christians did not accept that arrangement. So they were given three weeks to meet with people from the Islamic State to negotiate the situation. But that meeting never happened. After that, the Christians were given three days to either pay the jizya or leave the country or be killed.

JT: And you think that's good?

Abu Qatadah: Definitely. I mean, otherwise I wouldn't be here and I wouldn't be with the Islamic State. That's legitimate and one of the laws of Islam. After all, Germany dictates to Muslims what they can and cannot do. We do exactly the same thing with Christians.

JT: But that is completely untrue. Muslims in Germany—I play soccer every Saturday with a few of them—vote for the party they want. They are for or against the government. For example, most people are against the war in Afghanistan. Muslims are not forced to follow any government.

Abu Qatadah: That is not quite correct. For proof, look no further than the closure of several mosques the German authorities found troublesome. That's clear proof that the so-called religious freedom of Muslims in Germany is pure German baloney.

JT: In Munich, which is where I live, they've just built a new mosque...

Abu Qatadah: You call it a mosque. In Islam, we wouldn't call it a mosque. If you open the Quran to surah 9, you'll read about mosques where people come to knowingly harm Islam. That's the case with most mosques in Germany. What they preach is not Islam. It's something else. The principles of their personal belief systems mixed with the principles of democracy, of other religions such as Christianity, or of some other ideologies. Then they mislead people by passing that off as Islam.

JT: I don't think I understand the position you're taking there. Would you characterize yourself as Salafi or Wahhabi?

Abu Qatadah: The problem with all these labels—Salafi or Wahhabi—is that they have nothing to do with religion. But if you're asking whether I follow Muhammad and his teachings, the ones he lived by in his day, yes, I am Salafi. Then, yes, that's definitely true.

JT: Earlier, you said that you don't think any country is good. Not even Saudi Arabia. But Saudi Arabia does the best it can to support Salafism and Wahhabism.

Abu Qatadah: That is another superficial observation. In Saudi Arabia, you find exactly the same moral decay you find in other countries. Sharia applies only to people unrelated to the royal family and who do not hold influential positions. So, the common people.

JT: Is there a country that comes somewhat closer to your idea of an Islamic state? Isn't there any Islamic country where you could say: "What they're doing here isn't too bad"?

Abu Qatadah: Definitely not. There is no Islamic country that comes even close to implementing sharia and adhering to it.

JT: In your push to conquer the world, sooner or later you will have to attack all these Muslim countries.

Abu Qatadah: That will definitely happen.

JT: If you believe that the "Islamic State" will one day achieve world domination, then for purely practical geographic reasons, the first countries you will have to conquer will be Islamic countries.

Abu Qatadah: The next country we'll seize will most likely be Saudi Arabia or Jordan, and we'll go on from there.

JT: Saudi Arabia will be happy to hear that.

Abu Qatadah: I don't think they will.

JT: If you declare these positions publicly, you're going to make a lot of enemies. The world is not just going to stand by and watch. Why isn't the Syrian government attacking you more aggressively? After all, they have airplanes that could strike your positions in Raqqa even more heavily.

Abu Qatadah: No doubt you're following what's been happening: we're beginning to hit Assad's positions hard. Since we've been able to push back other groups such as the Islamic Front, we've got a bit of breathing room. We attacked the military base in Raqqa. We managed to take it in less than two days. Of course, the counterattacks are stronger now. The fact is Assad is now sending in more rockets and more airplanes. In the past two days alone, Assad fired four Scud missiles at us, but they didn't hit anything important.

JT: But he could send even more planes.

Abu Qatadah: Planes come every day. That's nothing new. Every day, planes come and bomb something. But these planes and their bombs are not very accurate. There's also always the matter of the great expense of sending in one or more planes. That's a problem shared by many governments. Their expenditures are way too high. War is expensive. You're probably aware of that with America. The wars in Afghanistan and Iraq have almost bankrupted the country. Anyway, they've landed the country in financial difficulties because they can barely look after their own country, and now they have a huge national debt.

JT: Last week, I spent four days in Gaza. For the most part, Israeli planes hit very specific targets there. Mostly civilians, mind you.

Abu Qatadah: But the Israelis have money. The civil war in Syria has been dragging on for more than three years now. It's cost the Syrian government billions. You can't carry on that kind of war for long.

JT: Unlike you? You have a lot of money. I've read that IS raked in a lot of money in Iraq. More than US$1 billion. Is that true?

Abu Qatadah: Yes.

JT: I'm going to come back to Germany just quickly. What does Germany mean to you personally? When Germany plays soccer, are you at all interested?

Abu Qatadah: Absolutely not. I wasn't interested before either.

JT: When you lived in Germany, weren't there some things you particularly liked, things you enjoyed that you can experience only in Germany and nowhere else?

Abu Qatadah: That's a difficult question to answer. Of course, there's the landscape. I like Germany much better than some of the

Arab countries with their deserts and heat. But there are other things that are much more important for a Muslim.

JT: Which party did you vote for?

Abu Qatadah: I have never voted. Not even when I wasn't a Muslim. I never voted.

JT: What do you think of Ms. Merkel?

Abu Qatadah: The Prophet said that when a woman takes over the leadership of a country, the country will be ruined. Those who know Ms. Merkel and her political career know there's nothing behind her policies but self-interest. She wants above all to win and stay in power.

JT: I must disagree with you there. I find Ms. Merkel to be unusually competent. But let's change the subject. What's your most cherished memory of growing up in Germany?

Abu Qatadah: I don't know how to answer a question like that. Of course, there are things you enjoy doing when you're young that you can also do according to Islam. But we also have experiences here that are beautiful and that you wouldn't want to miss. Even if that's difficult for some people to believe.

JT: Are Muslims in Germany treated well or badly? Are they discriminated against or not?

Abu Qatadah: Definitely discriminated against. I converted to Islam in 2003. Shortly after that, I began to train as an office administrator in a large company. There were many Islamic duties, like Friday prayer, that I could not fulfill there. That is discrimination, of course. As a Muslim, you have duties, but you cannot fulfill them. Even when you try to work out a compromise with the boss. I'm not the only one this happened to.

JT: I have a Muslim coworker who prays five times a day. No one would ever stop him doing that. And he wouldn't allow anyone to stop him.

Abu Qatadah: But we're talking about the majority of people in Germany, and they forbid such things. Germany tells everyone about democracy and freedom. Everyone can do what he wants and the worth of every individual is sacrosanct. There are laws about religious freedom and the like. But then, despite these laws, there are female teachers who want to wear simple headscarves—which isn't even sufficient according to the rules of Islam—and they are not allowed to do so. So, ask yourself whether there's discrimination or not.

JT: What were you before you were a Muslim?

Abu Qatadah: I was a Christian, Protestant. But just like most Germans, I never really had anything to do with my religion.

JT: Where are your parents from? Did they come from Islamic countries or are they German?

Abu Qatadah: My parents are both German. My grandparents were German, too, and my great-grandparents.

JT: Why did you convert to Islam? What experience caused you to convert to Islam?

Abu Qatadah: It was a process over a number of years that finally led me to becoming Muslim. Because I had been involved with Islam.

JT: What do you think is better in Islam than in Christianity?

Abu Qatadah: It's a long list.

JT: But the religions are similar.

Abu Qatadah: Yes.

JT: Isn't Allah the same God as the one the Christians believe in? There's just one God, after all.

Abu Qatadah: Yes and no. The idea the Christians have of God as the Trinity, three-in-one, contradicts monotheism. For me, that was what made me realize that Islam is purer than Christianity.

JT: Most Jews also believe in only one God.

Abu Qatadah: We could discuss this for hours. The differences and what is wrong in other religions. But for me, the most important proof of the correctness of Islam is that the Jewish Torah no longer exists in its original form. Whereas the Quran exists exactly as it was revealed. If a person wants to know what God asks of him, first of all, you need instructions that lay out what God wants of people. And if these instructions have been falsified or are no longer authentic, then that is bad.

JT: I have read the Quran many times. With great interest and with great benefit to me. It says, roughly: "Whoever kills a man, it is as though he has killed all humanity. And if he saves a man, it is as though he has saved all humanity." I've seen a video from the "Islamic State" and it contains nothing but killing. You know the video I'm talking about? It was released about a month ago. There's a car driving along the highway, and whenever another car overtakes it, the window is wound down, the submachine guns come out, and there's shooting until all the people in the other car are dead. Do you believe that's Islamic?

Abu Qatadah: Those people in the other cars, the ones who were shot, were all members of the military in Maliki's regime in Iraq. That

means these are not completely innocent people. They are not innocent of having killed Muslims, they are not innocent of having fought
against the Islamic State, they are not innocent of having betrayed
their religion as a whole, and they are not innocent of having committed serious crimes against the Sunnis in Iraq. In light of this they
received, as the saying goes, the just punishment they deserved. The
Islamic State doesn't simply show up somewhere to shoot innocent
people in the bright light of day who have never fought against IS and
never had anything against Islam.

**JT: But did the shooters know beforehand exactly who was in the
cars?**

Abu Qatadah: Of course they did. These were planned attacks.

**JT: Extremely gruesome attacks. I've read a lot about Muhammad.
Muhammad and the God of the Quran were never as gruesome as IS.
Never as brutal. I've always considered Islam to be a very humane
religion. I've traveled the world for more than fifty years. I have never
experienced more benevolence and brotherly love than I experienced
in the Muslim world.**

Abu Qatadah: It is not as though IS doesn't give people a choice. Perhaps you were following events when the other groups began to fight
against us in Syria back in January. At the time, al-Baghdadi released
an audio message for our opponents. He said: "Lay down your weapons. We will accept your repentance, you can come over to us, we
will leave you in peace, we will not fight against you, and so on. But
if you continue with your attacks, we will be forced to pull our troops
from our other front lines and fight against you. And, with Allah's
permission, we will annihilate you." They continued to fight against
us. After that, we went after them hard. We drove them completely
out of the regions we control and we stripped them of all their weapons. We made millions from the assets we seized: weapons, money,
and the oil and gas fields that were under their control. Hundreds, if

not thousands, of people lost their lives. But it wasn't as though they had no choice.

JT: In your opinion, is it okay to kill civilians? Does IS kill civilians as well?

Abu Qatadah: No, definitely not. Anyone who says that is lying.

JT: I'll come back to that later. Just in general terms here: Where have the Western media got it wrong? What are the main lies from your point of view?

Abu Qatadah: Here's an example from a news report a couple of days ago. It stated that IS forced women to undergo female circumcision.

JT: But that was quickly retracted as incorrect information. Some human rights worker had mistranslated something or heard a rumor. Now she's being roundly criticized.

Abu Qatadah: But shortly before that almost exactly the same thing happened. It was reported that the women in Mosul were being forced to marry IS soldiers. That was all rubbish. Other media outlets stated we would kill or expel from Islam every person who had sinned or made some other kind of mistake. It's like that every day. You can come to Raqqa and see for yourself that none of this is true. If this was our model, we'd have to kill the complete population of Syria. Every one of them smokes, every one of them does plenty of un-Islamic things, and despite that, we've not killed any of them on that account. Unless there's an explicit Islamic judgment that calls for the death penalty.

JT: What is your opinion of Shias?

Abu Qatadah: The Islamic opinion is that Shias are apostates. Their apostasy is their death sentence.

JT: What does that mean in practical terms?

Abu Qatadah: The Shias have two choices. Either they repent and return of their own free will to the true Islam or they will be killed.

JT: That means if 80 million Iranian, Iraqi, and Syrian Shias don't repent and convert to Sunnism of their own free will, they will be killed?

Abu Qatadah: Right. Definitely, yes.

JT: Eighty million?

Abu Qatadah: If it has to be that way. (Laughs.) I mean that sounds, how can I put it, rather extreme...

JT: That sounds really extreme.

Abu Qatadah: IS tried to pursue a different policy with the Shias. In 2006, when IS first controlled regions in Iraq in Anbar and Fallujah. At the time, we tried to expel the Shias from the towns. We said to them: "Find somewhere else, you can go and live there." To put it politely, we drove them out. Unfortunately, this strategy didn't work out well. Because people who have been driven out always use force and try to fight their way back in. And that's just what happened.

What many people either did not see or kept quiet about was that the Shias in Iraq and in Iran committed many terrible crimes against the Sunnis. You saw this in Syria as well with Assad: people, babies, children were beheaded and skinned alive, and women were raped. So the way we mostly deal with Shias and Alawis is very simple: we capture them and we shoot them. (Laughs.)

JT: Do you think everything that is being said about the government of Iran, the government of Syria, and the government of Iraq is true? Isn't much of it fabrications or lies?

Abu Qatadah: I can't comment about Iran's nuclear projects and such. But statements about crimes against Muslims and against Sunnis are definitely not fabricated. Unfortunately, there are thousands, millions, of witnesses that these statements are true.

JT: What do you think of Hezbollah and Nasrallah?

Abu Qatadah: Nothing at all. (Laughs.) He's Shia, after all.

JT: What do you think of Hamas?

Abu Qatadah: Even less. Hamas is no different from Hezbollah, a democratic party disguised as Islam. If you go back twenty or thirty years, perhaps Hamas was different then. But these days, you can't expect anything of them. To make a long story short: brothers in the Gaza Strip have told us that Hamas is a worse enemy for us than the Israelis.

JT: You said that at the moment there are about fifteen to twenty thousand fighters in IS, correct?

Abu Qatadah: About that, yes.

JT: And basically, with the exception of the Christians and the Jews, who you can just about tolerate, you are declaring war on everyone who doesn't follow your interpretation of Islam. You want to conquer the world. The whole world knows that you are very brutal with those who oppose you. Don't you think that because of this, all the other Arab countries will unite very soon and say: "We can no longer tolerate these twenty thousand men who want to kill us all?"

Abu Qatadah: We think that's going to happen. There's no question that's going to happen. We're not afraid. Sometimes it's difficult to explain these things. If you had asked anyone three months ago: "Can IS win the victories they just won in Iraq and in Syria this past month?" one hundred percent of them would have said: "No, they'll never manage that." But we put our trust in Allah, and we know that everything comes from him and through him. And so we are absolutely sure that we can prevail in these matters. Even if the whole world joins forces against us. And we know that from history as well. The Prophet was also attacked by troops with superior numbers and weapons. Despite that, he was victorious. History repeats itself.

JT: But Muhammad was a prophet of compassion. He was merciful to his opponents. You, however, show no mercy to those who oppose you.

Abu Qatadah: That is not true. To give you a good example: after we took Mosul, we captured 4,500 soldiers from Malaki's army. We executed 1,700 of them. The other...

JT: Why did you execute 1,700 Shias? Because they were Shias?

Abu Qatadah: No. Wait. Here's the thing. Normally, we would have executed all the rest as well. The Islamic judgment about these people was clear. They fought for the government against Islam. That means apostasy. But because they were Sunnis and swore they would never do it again—never form an alliance against IS—we let mercy prevail. Even though it would have been very easy to kill them all. So you see, the mercy of the Prophet is being continued.

JT: You call that mercy?

Abu Qatadah: Yes, I call that mercy.

JT: Are you still in contact with your parents? You could communicate with them using Skype.

Abu Qatadah: From time to time, yes.

JT: And what do they say now that you have become such a ruthless fighter?

Abu Qatadah: My parents know I'm not the kind of person who would kill people without reason or with no sense of what is right or wrong.

JT: Have you killed people?

Abu Qatadah: I can't answer that. (Laughs.) That's quite possible. (Laughs.)

JT: Would you have any objection if I were to talk with your parents sometime, if I were to visit them? I disagree with you on many things. But I would very much like to speak with your parents.

Abu Qatadah: That's possible.

JT: Would it also be possible to interview the caliph?

Abu Qatadah: No. Definitely not.

JT: But he must give an interview sometime.

Abu Qatadah: I have spoken with my superiors and right now he will definitely not give an interview. And I don't think that's going to change in the next few years. Perhaps it will get to the point where he will appear in public in a video or something like that.

JT: He made an appearance in a mosque. Was that really him? [The notoriously secretive al-Baghdadi made an appearance at the Great Mosque in Mosul in July 2014.]

Abu Qatadah: Yes, he was there. You're only the second reporter or journalist we've spoken to. The first one was from Vice News. You're the first one from the West. The man from Vice News was Muslim.

LESS THAN TWO weeks later, on September 21, 2014, the conversation continued.

JT: No one in the world understands why IS cuts the heads off innocent people. That's just twisted. What's the reason for making these beheadings into such a spectacle? Why are these people being executed in public? These beheadings are unbelievably ruthless and gruesome. Even more gruesome than al-Qaeda. What are your reasons? There's no point in not addressing this directly.

Abu Qatadah: Are you talking now about the Americans or about the British? Or about Assad's soldiers?

JT: Actually, I'm talking about all of them. But first I'll ask about the two Americans.

Abu Qatadah: You've probably seen the videos. Ultimately, this was not our decision. The politicians from the countries these people came from had the chance, on more than one occasion, to protect their people and get them out. They deliberately turned a blind eye to these opportunities.

JT: You say you're guided by the Quran. I've told you many times that I'm of the opinion that the Quran is merciful. Where does it say in the Quran that you may kill innocent people? Innocent people. For example, James Foley was a journalist. He hadn't done anything. Neither of the journalists was your adversary, your enemy.

Abu Qatadah: You know as well as I do that the media, or rather journalists, are usually more dangerous enemies than soldiers on the ground.

JT: Public executions and the public decapitation of innocent people are the main reasons the majority of people around the world now accept American bombing raids. I know that many innocent people are killed in war. But they are not deliberately killed. You, on the other hand, deliberately kill demonstrably innocent people on purpose. That has completely changed the public mood. No one condones that.

Abu Qatadah: That may be true. But we are not afraid of an American attack. It's only a question of time. If you don't come to us, we will come to you, and then you'll see the confrontation firsthand. If you look at things carefully, you'll see that the Americans and their allies don't really have a plan, or a strategy, or a good idea how to fight IS.

What is happening now is basically the result of what happened during the war the USA waged in 2003 against Iraq. The USA did not win the war. It is clear that they lost the war in Iraq. The Shia government they left behind was not stable. The country is shattered. Whether the beheadings you're criticizing were necessary or if shooting these people with a pistol would have been sufficient is debatable. The fact is this provocation was deliberate. We wanted to send a message to the Americans.

JT: The whole world is asking why you are cutting the heads off innocent people. The Quran doesn't allow this. And what is it with the children? Children are also being killed.

Abu Qatadah: First of all you've got to prove we are also killing children.

JT: I've seen pictures of a girl whose head was cut off.

Abu Qatadah: These photographs come from the Yazidis and the Kurds. They do an excellent job of propaganda. Those are fakes. IS would never publish photographs like that of children.

JT: Now I'm going to get back to the journalists again. I knew James Foley personally because I spent time with him in Libya. We spent many days together in the same hotel during the uprisings. Why is IS of the opinion that they can just slaughter journalists?

Abu Qatadah: You have to look at the big picture. These weren't just any journalists, but journalists who had already written articles criticizing the Islamic State in Iraq. The second one, Steven Sotloff, had also served in the armed forces, as had the third one. They were not simply journalists without blood on their hands.

JT: So they'd criticized IS. That's good to know. I, too, have criticized IS. And weren't there some members of NGOs who were also killed? So now, just quickly. I'm not here to judge you, even though I am appalled. I'm telling you this because it has completely changed public opinion.

Abu Qatadah: Public opinion is always focusing on something. Basically, it's all the same to us. The Americans—and you probably know this better than many people—killed over a million children in Iraq alone. Innocent children. Through their infamous sanctions and the war. No one was interested in that. Now everyone's worked up because of a pair of Yazidis and three reporters whose government turned down the opportunity to buy their freedom.

After all, we held other journalists. The French bought the freedom of their people. I don't know if you knew that. We also had a German. His family bought his freedom because the German government didn't care about him. The German family paid a million euros for his freedom. These foreigners were being held with the three prisoners who were beheaded. Obama said he ordered the first air strike to protect American personnel in Erbil. We gave him the chance to protect his imprisoned citizens. But he wasn't the least bit interested. Because of some principle along the lines of "we don't deal with terrorists" or something like that.

JT: Why were the beheadings filmed?

Abu Qatadah: So we could show them to the world. So what did these people say before they were beheaded? What did the Briton— I've forgotten his name now—David, what did he say? "I am holding you personally responsible for this, David Cameron," he said. "You are responsible for my death." Why? Because the prime minister had had the chance to buy his freedom. It would have been easy for the British state to negotiate with another state. We told the Americans we wanted Aafia Siddiqui [a Pakistani terror suspect sentenced to eighty-five years in prison in the USA]. A woman in exchange for a male prisoner. They did not want to have the conversation.

JT: Were the people who were publicly executed anesthetized? Did they get any drugs?

Abu Qatadah: Of course not.

JT: How come they didn't react at all when they were killed?

Abu Qatadah: Because they had come to terms with their deaths. Every person knows in the last moments of his life that he will return to Allah.

JT: In Erbil, I heard from Kurd leaders that they had prisoners who had fought for IS. I asked if they would be willing to trade them. You have Kurdish and Yazidi men and women as prisoners. If you're interested, let me know. I would gladly help facilitate a prisoner exchange.
When I asked you recently whether there might be attacks in

Germany, you said no. Now Germany has delivered weapons to the Kurds. Has that changed IS's strategy?

Abu Qatadah: I can't answer that. Other people are responsible for such things.

JT: Could you try to find out?

Abu Qatadah: If a country like Germany takes an active role in this conflict, not just passively like before but by sending weapons, equipment, and instructors to Iraq or by bringing Kurds to Germany to train them, then it shouldn't be a surprise if our policies were to change as well.

JT: Germany was under severe pressure. You know that.

Abu Qatadah: You just need to have the courage to say no. Just say no. After all, Germany has enough problems of its own its politicians should be looking after instead of getting involved in things that have nothing to do with them. And if Germans think their politicians should play at being allies anyway, then later, if they've made their bed, they must lie in it, as the saying goes...

JT: Well, Germany refused to take part in the air strikes.

Abu Qatadah: Steinmeier [German minister of foreign affairs] made a good move there.

JT: That was Ms. Merkel's policy as well.

Abu Qatadah: In things to do with IS, people would do better to listen to Steinmeier. Even if I don't think much of him or any of Germany's policies.

JT: What did he get right about IS?

Abu Qatadah: That we cannot be stopped. You asked me: "Does IS want to take on the world?" I said yes. In 2003, the Americans went into Iraq, and in 2011, they had to retreat with the back of their military machine broken, billions in losses, and thousands of fallen soldiers. Just to save themselves from total humiliation. Back then, the Islamic State consisted of about five thousand men, who were engaged in what was effectively a guerilla war and they had no tanks or heavy artillery. According to the latest CIA reports, we now have more than thirty-five thousand men and over one hundred tanks, as well as airplanes and heavy artillery. Do the Americans really think they can win against us?

JT: Are the numbers mentioned by the CIA correct?

Abu Qatadah: It's hard to say if the numbers are correct. But I can give you some numbers. About fifty people a day join us from Russian-speaking regions. I've heard that in the last month, over six thousand new fighters have joined us. After we took Mosul, the number of our fighters in Iraq increased tenfold. Every army in the West dreams of numbers like these.

One of the commanders of the PKK [Partiya Karkerên Kurdistanê, or the Kurdistan Workers' Party] said that very thing just today. We're fighting them right now on the Turkish border. He said he has twenty years' experience in war. He's fought against the Turkish army, against helicopters, against airplanes, against everything you can think of. But he has never fought against fighters like the fighters who fight for IS. Whenever they shot up a car, ten more advanced. The simple reason is that our people don't mind dying. For the Islamic State. History always repeats itself. You can't stop an army that is ready to die and sacrifice everything.

JT: Are there soldiers among the German jihadists, people who used to be in the German army?

Abu Qatadah: Of course! I assume many of them were in the German army. Especially the converts. Robert B., for example, who was in the German army and then joined IS.

JT: Some newspapers are reporting that those who were not in the army and who don't have any other combat experience are used mostly for suicide attacks, as cannon fodder. Because they haven't learned how to fight.

Abu Qatadah: That is simply not true. Our people choose for themselves if they want to take part in missions that will end in martyrdom. No superior, no emir comes and decrees whether or not a person must carry out a particular mission. This is another example of Western media propaganda. They write that to stop young people from joining IS.

JT: Last time, you said that what the cartoonist Westergaard did was blasphemy. He was honored by the German chancellor for his work. Apparently, this warranted the death penalty. Did you mean the death penalty for Westergaard or for Merkel?

Abu Qatadah: Both.

JT: Earlier, we spoke of cruelty. I said that the demonstrated cruelty of IS, some of which has even been filmed, has completely turned around public opinion in Germany. I write regularly for the newspapers and I argue that air strikes are wrong. Even though I'm against IS, as you know. But the films and your brutality make it hard to advance that argument. Children are being shot for blasphemy. Heads are being cut off. You ostentatiously show the most gruesome scenes. You can't just say it's all Western media propaganda when you're making your own propaganda videos.

Abu Qatadah: What do you mean?

JT: That you're talking as though you are not really cruel at all. As though much of this cruelty has nothing to do with you.

Abu Qatadah: Cruelty is always relative. The videos of the beheadings were edited because we wanted to spare viewers, if you can call them that, the most gruesome parts. And as far as the other videos are concerned, the drive-by video, for example, where people are shooting at other cars, that video involved the military and not innocent people.

JT: But there are children who've been killed for blasphemy. There are photos where you can see girls with their heads cut off. I must ask you again: How do you reconcile this with the Quran?

Abu Qatadah: I sincerely doubt that these photos are authentic or that these terrible acts were carried out by us. There's an amazing function in Google Images. I don't know if you're familiar with it. You can upload a photo and, using data embedded in the picture, Google scans the photo. If it matches other photos in the Google databank, Google shows the original source for the photo. So you can see when it was first uploaded. Many people have done that and discovered these photos originally came from the war in Gaza or from the first war in Iraq or from the war against Assad, or something like that. In short, these are old pictures that are now being falsely attributed to us.

There was a photo being circulated by some Kurds. This photo gave the impression IS fighters were going to rape Kurdish women. But then it was discovered the photo was taken from an Indian Bollywood film and was being falsely attributed to us. That's the usual propaganda, and naturally you'd expect nothing else from people known for their lies. I'm surprised you of all people would fall for these propaganda lies.

JT: But the photos of decapitated heads in Raqqa. Those are real, aren't they?

Abu Qatadah: Definitely. Those I don't deny. In dealing with soldiers or any other enemy groups such as the Islamic Front, it's entirely possible we would do something like that. And we certainly wouldn't dispute that.

JT: But why cut off heads and then put them on show? If your enemy is dead, there's no need to humiliate and dishonor him as well by putting his mutilated remains on show.

Abu Qatadah: In many cases, the enemy is simply killed. And he doesn't deserve anything else. I can give you an example. About three months ago, a car bomb exploded in front of a hotel here in Raqqa. It was parked in front of a hotel full of Muslim women. Three or four women were severely injured, along with a few children. Four or five people died. We captured the five people responsible. In order to make an example of people like this, we cut their heads off or crucify them.

JT: I'll ask again. Are people also killed for blasphemy? Are children and young people also killed for blasphemy?

Abu Qatadah: If they've reached the Islamic age of adulthood, if they're considered to be in possession of their faculties, and if they then commit blasphemy, then definitely. No one is spared, just because he is sixteen or seventeen or perhaps even only fifteen years old. But I personally don't know of a single case in which any children or young people have been killed for blasphemy.

JT: At the same time as we're having these conversations, I'm reading the Quran for the third time. I've told you many times that the Quran is far more merciful than you are with the things you're doing. As you well know, 113 of the 114 surahs begin with the words: "In the name of Allah, the Beneficent, the Merciful!" The whole spirit of the Quran is different, gentler than the way you pursue your policies. That's why the reaction against you is getting more negative every day. More negative even than it used to be against the Taliban.

Abu Qatadah: The West's opinion of Islam is always negative. You saw that in Bosnia, you saw that in Chechnya, you saw that in Afghanistan, you saw that in Iran in 2003. And you see that today, and that's the way it will always be.

JT: Even Jabhat al-Nusra is beginning to look moderate in comparison with IS.

Abu Qatadah: (Laughs.) I really don't want to talk about that, because I don't want our conversation to become too political. But when you look at the policies of Jabhat al-Nusra or some of the other groups that call themselves Islamic, such as the Islamic Front here in Syria for example, then you will quickly understand that they're not really Islamic at all. That goes for Jabhat al-Nusra as well. Even when they declare allegiance to al-Qaeda, they're not far from the ideology of democracy and secularism.

JT: What is the difference between IS and al-Qaeda?

Abu Qatadah: Jabhat al-Nusra was sent to Syria by IS to support Muslims in their fight against Assad. But very quickly they turned and showed their true colors. They betrayed IS and came to arrangements with al-Qaeda in Afghanistan behind our backs. And they formed other odd coalitions. For example, in Deir ez-Zor Province with the FSA and with a few other groups in the Syrian National Council. They fought with them against IS, and that is apostasy.

JT: When you compare Osama bin Laden's ideology with the ideology of your caliph, what, in your opinion, are the crucial differences?

Abu Qatadah: Al-Qaeda at the time of Osama bin Laden is closer to us than the al-Qaeda of today. But one shouldn't forget that Osama bin Laden never had the political or military power Abu Bakr al-Baghdadi now has. So you can't make a direct comparison.

JT: But the ideologies are similar.

Abu Qatadah: The ideologies are similar. It should be noted, however, that Osama bin Laden was heavily influenced by the Muslim Brotherhood at that time. Which was usual back then, especially in the eighties and nineties.

JT: If you had to, how would you describe your Islam in two sentences?

Abu Qatadah: Our Islam is the true Islam, free from any contamination by other ideologies, whether it's democracy, secularism, Buddhism, Christianity, or anything else.

JT: So comparable to Wahhabi doctrine?

Abu Qatadah: You can't call it Wahhabi doctrine, because this doctrine existed before Wahhab existed. He lived in the seventeenth or rather eighteenth century. At that time, there were people who were living the true form of Islam. There were just very few of them.

JT: Is it IS's opinion that you must interpret the Quran literally, or must you separate the fundamental ideas in the Quran from their historical context?

Abu Qatadah: There are things in the Quran that you can understand only in their historical context. But of course you must take the answers literally without interpretation. This literal reading of the Quran is an important component of Islam. The people today who have strayed and got lost in other ideologies are mostly people who do not interpret the Quran literally. Instead, they begin to philosophize. Like the ancient Greeks.

JT: At the moment, who is your greatest enemy in military terms?

Abu Qatadah: Countries that have an air force. Assad or the Americans. But when it comes to foot soldiers, that's a very different question. The Americans don't want to send troops, the Germans don't want to send troops, the French don't want to send any, nor do the Australians, and neither do any members of the coalition. Why not? Because they know they don't stand a chance. And without troops on the ground, you can't win a war. Definitely not.

TWO DAYS LATER, on September 23, 2014, the conversation continued.

Abu Qatadah: Hello? Can you hear me?

JT: I can hear you, but I can't see you.

Abu Qatadah: We're having problems with the power supply.

JT: I've just received an email that a journalist from *Die Welt*, Alfred Hackensberger, has spoken with IS. Did you know that?

Abu Qatadah: Yes, I'm aware of that. The people who spoke with him are now being punished unfortunately (laughs), because they were in contact with the Western media without permission and, unfortunately, they said some rather stupid things.

JT: I hope they are not being punished too harshly!

Abu Qatadah: No, not too harshly. Perhaps a couple of months in jail or something like that.

JT: I wanted to talk about how we could organize the journey to Raqqa. But before we do that, I have two important questions because I'm quarreling with my friends about them at the moment. What is the main reason for your war? Does the fact that the Americans marched into Afghanistan have something to do with it? Or the fact that the

Americans invaded Iraq? Or does it have something to do with Palestine? Or the relatively aggressive policies of Western powers in the Middle East in the last two hundred years?

Abu Qatadah: Definitely that's part of the motivation, part of the reason people are fighting here. Simply because for centuries they've experienced Western aggression toward Muslims or Islam. To a certain extent, they grew up with it and, unfortunately, they're still seeing the consequences. Of course that has something to do with it. But it's not the only reason.

JT: If the Americans had not marched into Afghanistan or Iraq, and if all the past history with the French and the English had not happened, would you still be acting exactly the same way you're acting now?

Abu Qatadah: The establishment of an Islamic state has been the dream, the duty, of Muslims since they lost Andalusia. Since the time the Spanish in Andalusia fought the Muslims and began to occupy Islamic land. It is our duty to defend or reclaim Muslim land. And this would have happened somehow, if not with Afghanistan, then probably somewhere else. There's still Chechnya, Somalia, and other countries like that, where the war against the West is being actively fought.

JT: Have I understood you correctly? That the two things are connected? The war against aggressive American policies, against Russia's policies in Chechnya, and the dream of the "Islamic State."

Abu Qatadah: Yes, of course. The establishment of an Islamic state is the priority. The fact that Western powers or Russia have attacked or are attacking Muslims has naturally intensified the situation.

JT: During some of our conversations, we've spoken about the relationship between IS and the Alawis and Shias. If I remember correctly, you said: "Shias are not true Muslims. We will invite Shias to

convert to the real Islam. If they don't accept, then they will be killed."
I checked and there are 200 million Shias in the world. You cannot
seriously mean you want to eliminate them all if they don't convert
to Sunnism, to your true Islam.

Abu Qatadah: What can I say? In the end, those are numbers and
they are unimaginable for all of us. But as you know, it's easy to kill 6
million or x million, depending on how it's done.

You keep asking: "Why do you kill people in such a gruesome
way?" The fact is American air strikes took place before we killed
the first American. At the end of the day, it's the people who started it
who are the aggressors. And not just in Iraq today. It's been going on
for hundreds of years. You know that yourself. We can begin in Andalusia. After that, the occupation of Morocco and Algeria by France.
Then the French and the English in Egypt, the Italians in Libya and,
to some extent, in Tunisia, and so on. At some point, if you're constantly oppressing people and pushing them around, they're going
to say: "Enough."

**JT: Getting back to the 200 million Shias. If they say: "No, we don't
want to convert. We want to be Shias." What happens then?**

Abu Qatadah: You probably haven't yet read yesterday's announcement by al-Adnani, the spokesperson for IS. It will soon be translated
into English. He addressed Obama and the Western powers directly.
He said: "You are all welcome to come. We will be ready. Our deaths
will be martyrdom and your deaths will lead to hell. We know we will
be victorious. And if we are not, then our children will be the victors,
or our grandchildren, or our great-grandchildren."

We spoke about this the day before yesterday. The Americans
lost in Iraq and in Afghanistan. In Iraq, they tried to install the pup-
pet Nouri al-Maliki. He too was conquered. His security forces
essentially vanished into thin air. We seized all the armaments the
Americans had handed over to these Shias, so now we can fight the
rest of them.

JT: What will happen to the Shias?

Abu Qatadah: I don't know if you've seen the latest videos we released. With fewer than one hundred soldiers, we attacked the Seventeenth Division in Raqqa. There were eight hundred of them. In the end, they all gave up and fled. The process was repeated at the airport at Tabka. I don't know if you've been following that.

JT: I saw that.

Abu Qatadah: There were a few hundred of us and thousands of them. They had airplanes, tanks, and heavy artillery and I don't know what else. In the end, they took off like startled chickens, and exactly the same thing will happen with the Iranians.

JT: But what will you do with the Shias in Iraq and Iran who want to stay Shia?

Abu Qatadah: Well, they will all be executed.

JT: Are you quite sure you know what you are saying? I don't need to tell you that I'm not okay with that.

Abu Qatadah: That could well be. (Laughs.) The Shias aren't okay with that either.

JT: As we said before, Freddy and I would very much like to meet your mother and your father. Not to question them but just to get to know them.

Abu Qatadah: When I agreed to that, I assumed your conversation with my parents or with my mother would take place after you'd visited us. You must surely be aware that given the fact I'm having telephone conversations with you and you want to make contact with my mother, the intelligence services will, once again, turn up on my mother's doorstep and, to put it politely, be a real pain in the neck.

JT: I don't know if the intelligence services are listening in on our conversations. But I don't think they'll make trouble for your parents if I interview them. If a German citizen finds himself in trouble after an interview with me, then the intelligence services would soon find themselves in a tight spot as well.

Abu Qatadah: I don't have any objection if that's what you really want. You're welcome to make contact with my parents or old acquaintances or other family members. We'll see where that leads.

JT: May I have the telephone number, the address?

Abu Qatadah: I can give you the email address.

JT: Do you have a friend who you'd say understands you and who I should perhaps talk to?

Abu Qatadah: I've never had a wide circle of friends. Most of them came here with me or followed later, so there aren't very many you could talk to. Anyway, I've just sent you my parents' email address.

JT: Earlier, you said how badly Muslims are treated in the Middle East, in Arabia. But you are German, right? You weren't really treated badly, were you?

Abu Qatadah: In Germany?

JT: Yes.

Abu Qatadah: You don't have a clue, do you? You have no idea what it's like when someone from the intelligence services turns up on your doorstep at five o'clock in the morning and suddenly confiscates half your belongings, your computer, cell phone, money, and stuff like that. They confiscated money people had donated. The police still have that money. So I wonder what you mean when you say I've never really been subjected to violence or unlawful treatment. ·

JT: In Arab countries, people are killed, raped, bombed. In comparison, the distress of being woken up at five in the morning is relatively minor.

Abu Qatadah: The wars in Iraq and Afghanistan cost the USA billions of dollars. They're one of the main reasons America's been in crisis for the past few years. Just take a look at cities like Detroit or whole states that are bankrupt. Places where people are fighting the government or the city about whether drinking water is a right, whether it should cost money or not. Where families report that they live in tents because their homes have been seized by the banks. All these things can be traced back to the billions of dollars the government used to fund the wars. And now that Germany is starting to get involved in the war in Afghanistan—it's equipping the Kurds and more military operations will follow—the gap between the rich and the poor in Germany will also keep getting wider. Sooner or later, people in other countries as well will have had enough and get hostile—they'll find a scapegoat. That's what Hitler did with the Jews. It'll be the Muslims next. Did you see what happened with the Muslim woman who was stabbed to death in the courtroom? [In 2009, Marwa el-Sherbini was stabbed to death by a German in a Dresden courtroom.] Every day there are more and more attacks on Muslims that end with stabbings or some other violence. You've seen how many attacks there have been in Belgium and France. Not to mention England. It's getting worse. If people start falling on hard times because of these wars, things are going to start unraveling very quickly. And it's the Muslims who will suffer.

JT: Let's change the subject. What role are the Kurds playing in this war?

Abu Qatadah: Basically, they're the Western troops on the ground. Ten years ago, the PKK was still on the list of terrorist organizations. But now they need them as foot soldiers. The FSA, the Free Syrian Army, is, as Obama has said, a bunch of bakers, butchers, and farmers who have no idea how to wage war. You can press the most amazing weapons into their hands and they have no idea how to handle them. Most of them don't understand anything about war. So their corruption is incredible. We buy all the ammunition we need from the FSA. So of course you ask, how can that be? Isn't this ammunition coming from the Americans and the Western powers? Well, that's the problem. They're lining their own pockets. Western politicians and Western governments have done a great job of showing them how to do that.

JT: Are you getting a great deal of ammunition from the FSA at the moment?

Abu Qatadah: We just go and buy it. Not weapons but ammunition. The weapons, we seize in war. And that's how it is. You'll soon see that I'm right, because you'll see the first IS fighters running around with G36 weapons, with G3 rifles, and other pieces of German equipment because the Kurds are doing exactly the same thing as the FSA.

JT: They're also selling on weapons?

Abu Qatadah: Yes, of course. It's all a question of money.

JT: I thought the Kurds and the FSA would use the weapons they're getting from the West to fight against you—not that they would sell you their weapons or their ammunition.

Abu Qatadah: Of course, some of them are going to do that. Until January, the so-called Islamic Front was being equipped by Saudi Arabia and Qatar to fight IS. The FSA was being equipped by France and a few other states, by the Americans and countries like that. In

January, we began to fight them. When you take a look at the area still under their control and the area that has come under our control since then, you'll soon figure out that the battles they fought there couldn't have been very fierce. They lost a lot of ground. They've only got a couple of villages left under their control. They've completely withdrawn from the city centers, and they've totally said good-bye to Homs. They still have a few areas in Idlib and Latakia, and that's it.

JT: So the FSA doesn't pose a military threat to you?

Abu Qatadah: We are the muhajirun, the people from other lands. [The muhajirun were Muslims who followed Muhammad when he emigrated from Mecca to Medina.] We have come to establish an Islamic state, to seek the martyr's death. The Syrian in the FSA started to fight so he could have a nicer life. His basic motivation is completely different from ours. Thanks to American and Western money, his life has become more comfortable. If he can then be just a little bit corrupt and hawk weapons and ammunition for a good price to get even more money, his life gets even better. Why should he jeopardize that to fight against people who are happy to die?

JT: When's the last time that you fought?

Abu Qatadah: Oh, that's a while ago now.

JT: If I come to visit you, how would I even get across the border? I'll be captured right at the border.

Abu Qatadah: You mean by the Turks?

JT: I don't know. Perhaps by everyone who's listening now?

Abu Qatadah: (Laughs.) You must clear things with the German authorities yourself. Unfortunately, we can't help you there. As far as the border crossing into Syria is concerned, naturally we have people who can look after that.

JT: And how about the guarantee? Will the letter say you promise by Allah we will return safely and nothing will happen to us?

Abu Qatadah: I think we can put that in the letter. But we are in a war. Tomorrow, if a bomb falls on the house where we're staying, then you will die and we will die. We can't do anything about that.

JT: Send me the letter. As soon as I have your invitation, with the guarantees we've discussed, I'll look for someone to accompany me and film everything. I hope I can find someone who'll come along. Journalists are quite fond of life. As am I.

Abu Qatadah: Your companions will, of course, get the same protection as you. I think that should be clear. Of course, we're going to need to know in advance how many people that will be.

JT: Finally, one more question on IS's strategies in war. What does it look like? Earlier you engaged in guerilla warfare. Now you have modern tanks. Do you attack like a modern army now, or do you still fight as though you were guerillas?

Abu Qatadah: If you've got the means, you use them. We don't just call ourselves a state; we also act like one. And that includes having a real army. Everyone who comes to us is also a soldier. It's not like in a Western army where only chosen people belong to the army. By now we've seized about two hundred tanks in Syria and Iraq. And we've used them, of course.

JT: Do you even have that many tank drivers?

Abu Qatadah: Unfortunately, that is a problem. We have more tanks than drivers, and more planes than people who can fly them. Still.

JT: How many planes?

Abu Qatadah: We seized ten, fifteen jets, so when it comes to aerial warfare, we are vastly superior to the Iraqi army. We lack pilots, unfortunately. There just aren't that many of them.

JT: In the meantime, have you discovered whether the attitude of IS toward the German government has changed since the Germans have been supplying the Kurds with weapons?

Abu Qatadah: Yes! Yesterday, al-Adnani, the spokesperson for IS, released a new official speech. It contains a call from the Islamic State to Muslims in Western lands to attack people living there.

JT: So that means you also intend to attack in Germany.

Abu Qatadah: That is the consequence of some of these countries getting involved—Germany as well. They are all part of the allied group.

JT: That could mean, for example, that German Salafis will now be treated harshly in general. Because of suspicions that your friends are among them. Even if these Salafis expressly reject violence.

Abu Qatadah: That's exactly what I was just talking about. It's only a matter of time before the government cracks down even harder and the shadow of suspicion falls over every Muslim. And the whole thing blows up. We'll see what happens. For some time now, we've been expecting an escalation in the war of words against Muslims. In the end, each person will have to decide for himself. As Bush put it so well, either you are with the Americans or you are with the terrorists. Our emir approved of this maxim. There is going to be no in-between anymore. Then so-called moderate Muslims in Germany go and do something as absurd as to hold a candlelight vigil against the Islamic State! What should we say in response to that? You are against a state that operates according to the Quran and the Sunnah [the Sunnah and the Quran make up the two primary sources of Islamic theology and law], according to our moral practices and customs? That is apostasy! All the so-called Muslims who took part have turned their backs on Islam.

JT: Does that mean there will now be attacks by your people in Germany?

Abu Qatadah: I don't think anyone will go back and carry out attacks there. But I think people who are still there will do something. I doubt whether there will be plots, bombings, or anything like that. It's more likely to be isolated incidents.

JT: Now you're threatening everyone who respects Islam and considers Islam to be a great religion. These people are going to think, this just can't be right. For example, for years, I've been pointing out that until now not a single German has been killed in Germany as a result of so-called Islamic terrorism. Thanks to your call to action, now every Muslim in Germany is under general suspicion. Every Turkish student or pickle merchant will be subject to even harsher scrutiny than they were before. You are creating a huge problem for many people. What you're doing is really destructive.

Abu Qatadah: Sooner or later, people have to decide. I mean, the pickle merchant or the so-called moderate Muslims, they decided a long time ago. For them, it would be no big deal to say, actually, we don't really have anything to do with Islam, we've just been pretending all this time.

JT: Most of the Muslims I got to know in Germany were very dedicated Muslims.

Abu Qatadah: What were they dedicated to?

JT: Perhaps not to the same Islam as you but to the belief in one God, the belief that you should do good and avoid evil. That, as a Muslim, you have certain duties. There are many people I admire for the strength of their beliefs.

Abu Qatadah: If a person like that strives to do good and to do nothing bad and maintains he's doing this in the name of one God and so on and so forth but, in the end, votes or encourages people to take part in democratic elections or submit to democracy, then this person has clearly committed apostasy and betrayed Islam. This person is no longer living according to a belief in one God, but giving someone else the right to make laws. But this right is Allah's alone. That is apostasy against Islam. These people are no longer Muslims. As I said, most people decided long ago which side they belong to.

THE MOTHER WHO CRIES

IT'S A GRAY afternoon in October. Freddy and I are standing on the banks of the Rhine in Düsseldorf. A nondescript little car drives into the nearby car park. A fraction of a second is enough for me to recognize the driver is Mrs. E., Abu Qatadah's mother. Her sad eyes speak volumes. She recognizes me immediately as well. I wave and walk up to her.

She is in her early sixties. Her curly blond hair is going gray. She looks exhausted. You can see by looking at her that the past few years have been hard on her. We decide to walk along the Rhine. After two hundred yards or so, we sit down on a park bench. Mrs. E. doesn't just look exhausted. She is exhausted. Both physically and mentally. If she was in better shape, she might have visited her son a long time ago, she says without hope. Perhaps she would have stayed with him for a while. Because, like every mother, she worries about him and wants to know how he's doing. But he says a journey would be too dangerous right now. And Mrs. E. says she is not healthy enough to travel without being a burden to others.

HERE IS HER story. I'm telling it just as she told it to me. In her own words. Mrs. E. tells me that over the past years and months, she has often been contacted by journalists who know that Christian is in Syria fighting for IS. She blocked them all. She doesn't want to betray her son; she wants to protect him. Apart from that, the family has been through hard times. When it became known that Christian was in Syria fighting for IS, the family received threatening letters, hate mail, and their car was scratched up. People called them names on the street or when they went shopping. Mrs. E. calls her son Christian. For her, he is not Abu Qatadah, the name he now carries as a jihadist. For her, he will always be Christian.

Although Mrs. E. usually declines all requests for interviews, something had prompted her to meet with us today. Her gut told her: "This is good. Go and meet them." Of course, she had written to her son as well. He reassured her in an email that she could more or less trust Freddy and me, and that's why he had given us her email address. For four hours we sit on the banks of the Rhine and talk about Christian. Mrs. E. weeps many times during our conversation. As a mother she finds it all extremely difficult. She will always love her son, no matter what.

Since early childhood, Christian had always been extremely thirsty for knowledge. He would ask questions like, "What is death, Mama?" When he asked questions, she often had to think long and hard about the answers. When he was young, they spent a lot of time reading. Books like *Was ist was?* (a popular science book for children) were in great demand. If you didn't know something, you could learn about it in books. His teachers and his Protestant minister also noticed how many questions Christian asked. But Christian never got answers to the questions he asked in church. Christian was so disappointed that shortly before his confirmation, he decided not to take part in the ceremony. And he decided not to accept any of the gifts either. He preferred to continue looking for answers.

Mrs. E. always encouraged her son to broaden his horizons. Christian was highly gifted. So gifted that he was sent off to an elite school, where gifted children were encouraged to develop their talents.

One day, Christian witnessed another pupil being thoroughly pummeled in the schoolyard by an older pupil a couple of years above him. Christian threw himself between them and began to beat up the older pupil. Even though Christian got a beating as well, he was expelled from the school. He had to go back to a normal school.

Wherever he went, Christian was a leader. He had a way with words and was a good communicator. Above all, though, he always stood up for others. This got him into a lot of trouble.

Once, when the school principal threw a Muslim classmate's cell phone out the window as punishment, Christian got extremely upset. Why was this boy being punished more severely than his fellow students? Christian told the teacher he had to throw Christian's cell phone out the window too, along with the cell phones of the other students. After all, the Muslim boy was not the only one who used his cell phone in class. When his Muslim classmate was thrown out of the school because of the altercation, Christian insisted that he be thrown out too, as he was the one who had given the teacher the most grief. So he left the school as well.

The way he stood up for other people also earned him lots of friends. He enjoyed parties, he loved to go to barbecues, and he brought groups of friends home with him. There they spent hours with his mother discussing God and the world.

Despite his popularity, Christian was often unhappy. A few years ago, he came to his mother one evening and said: "I love you, Mama, but sometimes I feel so dreadfully alone." All those years he had been missing a positive father figure. Someone he could swap ideas with, who would encourage him, and who could be a model for him to follow. Christian did get to visit with his father often, but his father was emotionally distant. He gave him presents, but he didn't really care about him.

In his youth, Christian was very athletic. For years, he played sports competitively, and he played ice hockey for Neuss. He had grand ambitions. He wanted to turn professional, and it looked as though he could make it. Until, at the age of seventeen, he almost ripped off his thumb playing hockey. The tendons and ligaments were shot. His career was over. Christian fell into a deep, dark hole. He gave up sports completely and lost interest in doing anything.

One day his best friend, Melek, was going to be deported back to his homeland. The authorities were looking for him, but at the last moment, Christian came to his rescue and took him back home with him to his mother. "Mama, we've got to help him!" His plan was to smuggle Melek to Sicily. He was to sit tight there for two years. But just before they could leave, the police showed up at the door. They took Melek with them and deported him.

A few years later, Christian broke up with his first great love. He and Sabine (not her real name) had been together for years. When she ended their relationship, he spent two days and nights with his mother crying. He had hit rock bottom. His mother explained that was the point when everything changed. As far as Christian was concerned, his whole small world had been shattered. She had never seen him so unhappy. "If he had still been with Sabine, none of what was to come would have happened."

After his career in sports and his relationship with Sabine ended, Christian changed totally. He asked his mother to order him two copies of the Quran. In Arabic. She had been spending time with a Muslim girlfriend and had told her son: "If you want to read the Quran and really understand it, you must read it in Arabic."

Christian immediately began to learn Arabic. Very successfully. He soaked the new language right up. Soon he could read the Quran in the original language. Christian began to get more and more interested in Islam, and he began to go to the mosque often. Then he decided to go to Alexandria to study Islam at a university for foreigners. When he returned after more than six months, he declined a well-paid job with an insurance company. He preferred to go into business for himself, and he began to sell computer hardware and software. Then he was accused of shady financial dealings. He claimed innocence and got off lightly.

Mrs. E. began to get seriously worried about her son. He began to sink ever more deeply into his new beliefs. He grew a beard and changed how he dressed. He began to wear only black clothes or traditional Muslim garments. His new girlfriend just couldn't deal with it all. When he finally had to decide between her and Islam but couldn't make the decision, she called it quits.

IN 2011, CHRISTIAN wants to go with his buddy Robert B. to England to attend a meeting of the Muslim Brotherhood. Apparently, it takes place there every year.

When they arrive at Dover, they are both arrested. Supposedly, they're planning attacks. Files on Christian's laptop are cited as proof, articles about jihad and about building bombs. Christian swears he only read them because he was curious. He isn't a terrorist. Both are convicted of possession of radical writings and instructions on how to build bombs. Christian gets sixteen months in jail.

This marks the beginning of a difficult time for Christian's family. Nighttime raids on their home. Everything stripped bare. Cell phones, laptops, USB drives—all taken away. They are harassed from all sides. It gets so bad that Mrs. E. has to move from her neighborhood.

When Christian is deported from England a short time later and put on probation for the rest of his sentence, he increasingly withdraws into himself. Other than sleeping late and going out to meetings at night, he doesn't do much anymore. He gives up work. He wants to do something completely different. What, he doesn't know. Everything still revolves around Islam. War begins in Syria and the dreadful pictures are shown on all the television channels every day. As Christian doesn't have anything else to do other than "look for work," he has plenty of time to look at the pictures.

One day, without saying a word, Christian disappears from Germany. No good-bye, nothing. After a few months, there's a rumor he's in Syria. A few weeks pass before a friend confirms he is indeed in Syria.

After a year, Mrs. E. can't stand it any longer. She begins to look for her son on Facebook. She thinks about what name he might be using. She searches using his Muslim name and the name of the friend who was deported. She finds someone by the name of Abdul Melek who appears to be in Syria. For a few days, she watches his

Facebook page, then she summons all her courage and writes: "Is that you, Christian?" The answer comes a couple of days later: "Yes, Mama."

They've written to each other a few times since then. "Just come home, Christian! Come home!" That is what Mrs. E. wants more than anything else in the world. She wants her son back. She has not seen his face since he left. "If only I could hold him in my arms once again. If only I could say good-bye to him properly."

When we accompany her back to her car, she is crying.

V

Planning a Journey into the Heart of Terror

A FEW DAYS LATER, on October 23, 2014, I called Abu Qatadah once again on Skype. We exchanged only a few words about our visit with his mother. I didn't want to make any extra trouble given our fears that someone might be listening to every word. Here's a summary of my final conversations with Abu Qatadah before my journey to IS.

JT: You're not often online these days. We won't make any progress that way. That's a shame.

Abu Qatadah: Yes, it's all taking a bit longer than planned.

JT: It will soon be freezing cold in Syria.

Abu Qatadah: You're right, but during the day it's still really pleasant, twenty-five degrees [seventy-five degrees] or so. Did you get the letter?

JT: Frederic's got it. I wanted to tell you once again: I'm really interested in coming. I'm interested in finding out if you're just a terrorist guerilla group or if, as conquerors, you really are trying to found a state. These issues are rarely debated in public. But I need credible guarantees. The only option I see is that you publish the invitation along with the guarantee. So that you're bound publicly around the world. I don't have any particular mistrust of you. We've spoken together for a total of about eight hours now, I met your mother, Frederic met your mother. But despite that, I still don't feel sufficiently protected. And that means I won't be able to get a good journalist to come with me. So, what can we do?

Abu Qatadah: The problem is we no longer have any official media outlets. Twitter keeps blocking our accounts. We've tried to switch to other social networks, but basically the same thing happens with them as well. They're deleted daily, sometimes even hourly. Right now, we don't have any channel where we can make an official announcement about your visit.

JT: Would it be possible for you to give the invitation and the guarantee to some recognized Muslim personality? They don't need to share your opinion about absolutely everything.

Abu Qatadah: For example?

JT: I'm thinking of someone who knows IS, who you can deliver the letter to, and who could publicize it in the event of a crisis.

Abu Qatadah: In the meantime, you have a letter from the highest authority, the office of the caliph. The caliph has personally authorized your visit. We will honor this contract. Even if a bomb falls on me. I mean your friends, your family, surely they know they could make this all public in the media around the world so that we could not benefit from it. [Translation from Arabic of the guarantee of safety: "Islamic State—in the name of Allah, the Merciful, the

Gracious, praise be to Allah, the Lord of the world—peace and blessing to the imam of the mujahideen, our Prophet Muhammad and the members of his family and his companions. This is a guarantee of safety for the German journalist Jürgen Todenhöfer, so that he can travel safely in the territories of the Islamic State with his worldly goods and his traveling companions. Therefore the soldiers of the Islamic State will respect this guarantee and allow him free and safe passage until he has fulfilled his mission and left once again. And may Allah richly reward you—20 Dhu al-Hijjah 1435 (October 19, 2014)—Secretariat of the caliph—stamp of the caliph."]

JT: The main problem remains that no one can prove the authenticity of this document. The whole thing could be a forgery. You've got to come up with something more convincing. After all, it's my neck on the line here.

And I have a couple more factual questions. First, how many men did you have when you captured Mosul? My estimates put the number at around two thousand. But I'm being heavily criticized in public because apparently this number is way too low.

Abu Qatadah: Two thousand? Never! One hundred and eighty-three men took part in the capture of Mosul. Many people can't imagine that. We don't need large armies. Only the belief in something much bigger. In Allah. It's difficult for you to understand that. You talk about worldly things. We talk about spiritual events. I can tell you stories that are absolutely inconceivable for you. For example, how we advanced on Anbar. The Iraqi army tried to stop the brothers. They fired on them heavily. Our fighters wanted to take shelter somewhere. The only thing they could see was a couple of houses. They ran toward them at full speed to take cover. And the Iraqis? What did they do? They thought: "They're charging us!" They became afraid, and they ran away. Allah was with us all the time.

JT: The second question has to do with our last conversation. You said then that Shias have the opportunity to convert to Sunnism. If they don't, they will be killed. What happens to Christians who don't want to pay the jizya?

Abu Qatadah: The same.

JT: They will also be killed?

Abu Qatadah: Yes.

JT: And the same goes for Muslims who don't convert to your interpretation of the Sunni belief system?

Abu Qatadah: Islamic law makes a distinction here. Shias are considered apostates of Islam. Because of how they associate others with God, how they worship at graves, and other odd practices. They do not have the option of paying jizya. Unlike the Christians and the Jews, the Shias have only two choices. Either they accept Islam and demonstrate that they repent of their own free will for what they have done or they will be killed.

JT: And what happens if you're a Muslim in Germany? You leveled the criticism that Muslims in Germany mix their religion with democracy and secularism. They, however, consider themselves to be true Muslims. If they were to say to IS: "Your belief system is too strict for me," have they then forfeited their lives and will they then be killed?

Abu Qatadah: That's right! It's quite simple. So, if someone says: "I'm a Muslim, but I also believe in democracy," then that person is not a Muslim. To be Muslim means to be devoted to Allah. One of Allah's ninety-nine names is al-Hakam. That means that he is the one who makes the laws. If Allah has authority to do something, that authority belongs to Allah alone. If someone usurps the role of Allah and makes laws, then he has taken one of the characteristics of Allah upon himself. That is apostasy! How can someone claim he is a Muslim if he takes upon himself the godly attribute of laying down laws? As soon as he does this, he has committed apostasy. That is a very simple principle. Without much need for philosophy.

JT: When I'm in the "Islamic State," will I have the opportunity to discuss these questions with people who are competent to talk about them?

Abu Qatadah: Of course! It's good you want to address this. The best thing to do would be to jot down a short outline of what you'd like to do, who you'd like to meet, and which institutions you'd like to visit, and so on. Then I'll pass that on before you visit, and we'll see what we can do.

JT: What is the nationality of the head of your media department?

Abu Qatadah: I can't tell you that. (Laughs.) But I can say the leader of our media department is not Abu Talha al-Almani [a German] as stated on Wikipedia. I cannot give you any more information than that.

JT: Once I'm in the "Islamic State," can I walk around the streets by myself?

Abu Qatadah: I think you'll have people with you for your protection. We don't want someone who knows who you are and who has heard you're in town to get ideas of his own and mess up our arrangement. So, you'll always have a couple of people with you. Of course, they won't be right behind you. But when you go out, they'll probably be around.

JT: But I want to be able to talk to people on the street without someone standing right next to me holding a submachine gun under their noses!

Abu Qatadah: Yes, of course. You can talk with people on the street. You already saw that on Vice News. He went into the mosque to talk to people, as well.

JT: There was another instance of people from IS talking to Western media without your consent. There was even an interview.

Abu Qatadah: Yes, but that was not officially sanctioned. Someone had a conversation with the BBC. Via Skype. I don't know if you saw that. Unfortunately, sometimes people get involved with things they shouldn't. That is a problem. But they will all be punished.

JT: Will it be possible for me to stay in a hotel? So we're not too much trouble?

Abu Qatadah: The thing is, we don't have hotels anymore. We had some, but they've all been repurposed, as administrative buildings or apartments.

JT: How will I find the right border crossing?

Abu Qatadah: You have to go to the Turkish town of Gaziantep. By taxi or bus. We'll look after everything else. We'll come to collect you.

JT: I need to address the issue of Kobane again. That's a hot topic in the media here right now. They're saying you control only thirty percent of the town.

Abu Qatadah: In a few days, *inshallah,* they'll be amazed. When we take the whole town. It could be that the Americans will bomb the living daylights out of everything.

JT: But why are you focusing so intensely on this town? You are losing many fighters.

Abu Qatadah: The Kurdish Peshmerga have been allied with the USA since Saddam Hussein's time. And, geographically, Kobane lies right in the center of our territory. The Kurdish PKK has very raw fighters. So, we said to ourselves: "Okay, now we've chased all the Nusairis [Alawis] out of our territory, we'll do exactly the same with the PKK, and then we'll move on to the next group."

JT: I don't understand your decision from a strategic point of view. It's unusual for a guerilla group to concentrate so many fighters in a place where they can be heavily bombed.

Abu Qatadah: That's just another example of Western hypocrisy. The PKK and their Syrian offshoot the YPG [Yekîneyên Parastina Gel or People's Protection Units] are allies of the West. Even though the world officially designates them as terrorist organizations. Even the Germans and the Americans. And despite that, they get shipments of weapons and equipment and who knows what else.

And we've just got our first hand grenades, our first MG36s, the spoils of war! And a few MILAN launchers [*missile d'infanterie léger antichar*, a guided antitank missile]. Your deliveries of weapons always benefit us in the end. Feel free to throw more weapons our way. We're happy to seize them.

JT: So, that's it for today already. We've discussed the most important points. Make sure we get a guarantee that can be verified as authentic. Everything has to be done in a totally professional manner. I'll get back to you. As you can see, I'm already growing a beard.

A FEW DAYS later, on November 2, 2014, we spoke to each other again.

JT: Where are you?

Abu Qatadah: In Raqqa.

JT: My computer says you're in Turkey.

Abu Qatadah: That's possible.

JT: But you're not about to conquer Turkey now, are you?

Abu Qatadah: Ah, that's still in the future.

JT: But they're supposedly your secret allies.

Abu Qatadah: How can they be our allies when they associate with the Americans?

JT: The Turks don't do that of their own free will. They're forced to do that. Basically, they don't want to allow any Peshmerga across the border.

Abu Qatadah: They've just allowed PKK fighters across.

JT: Yes, because the pressure was too intense. Pressure from America. Turkey is a member of NATO.

I've sent you an email in response to your suggestion about how we could prove the authenticity of your invitation. Now I'd like to hear your response.

Abu Qatadah: I've spoken with my superiors about it. The media outlets you mentioned, al-Jazeera and al-Arabiya, are a nonstarter. What we can offer is to publicize the invitation over our affiliated Twitter accounts.

JT: But your Twitter accounts are always changing. So you could say someone wrote that on Twitter but it wasn't us. What if I give the letter to al-Jazeera and they publish it?

Abu Qatadah: Why does it have to be al-Jazeera or al-Arabiya? In our view, they cannot be the primary sources. We will not work with them, because they are terrible liars and have too much influence over a certain segment of the Arab population. Other news agencies or television stations are no problem. We're happy for them to publish the letter. Or you could do it on your Facebook site.

JT: Can I speak with other members of IS and not just you? I'm not interested in a superficial treatment of your organization. I'd like to report what's really going on. Are there others who are also qualified to give me their perspectives?

Abu Qatadah: For certain areas you can meet good people to talk to. But as for approaching Abu Bakr al-Baghdadi or al-Adnani, I don't think that's going to happen.

JT: Why not?

Abu Qatadah: Because we see absolutely no advantage for us in such a meeting. Or in an interview. What we want and what we are doing is clear, and you will be able to see it. There is no need for interviews with leaders to flesh out the picture.

JT: I believe there are many politicians who have explained things in interviews that the world didn't understand before. And so the interviews were very effective. Will there be the possibility of observing combat missions up close?

Abu Qatadah: If you want, yes. Perhaps you can travel to Kobane and look at the situation there more closely if things are not completely resolved by then.

JT: You can just drive there?

Abu Qatadah: Yes, of course. It's in our territory. On our side, everything is free and everything is open. You can go as far as the front lines if you want.

JT: How far is Raqqa from Kobane?

Abu Qatadah: I don't know exactly, but 200 kilometers [120 miles], I think. You need to allow about two and a half hours by car.

JT: So far, very few people know I'm traveling to IS, but those who do keep telling me two things. First: "You won't be able to talk freely and you'll never get a straight answer." And second: "What do they want from you? They must want something. How can you even think of going there?"

Abu Qatadah: Of course you will be able to speak with people without having someone standing right by your side or pressuring the person you're speaking with. Once you're here, you'll see very quickly that there are a lot of muhajirun—that's to say, foreign fighters—in town. Even if you were out there alone, there would always be one of us nearby.

JT: I also have questions about the accommodation.

Abu Qatadah: We've prepared an apartment. It has everything you'll need. In any case, it's all prepared. As I mentioned before, unfortunately, we no longer have hotels here. They're all being used for something else. The terrorism industry, uh, the tourist industry is dead.

JT: What did you just say? The terrorism industry is dead?

Abu Qatadah: No, the terrorism industry is booming.

JT: So, you don't have many tourists at the moment?

Abu Qatadah: No, not many.

JT: That's not too difficult to understand. Do you have any objection if I'm in contact with the outside while I'm with you?

Abu Qatadah: I don't think there's anything stopping that. There are Internet cafés all over the place here.

JT: How many fighters do you have at the moment? Different numbers are being mentioned. Is the number thirty-five thousand still correct?

Abu Qatadah: Honestly, I can't give you an exact number. What we've noticed from our own personal experience is that the organization Human Rights Watch always has really accurate numbers. Throughout the whole conflict in Syria. I don't know exactly how they get these numbers. But as far as the dead or wounded are concerned, their numbers are always correct. I don't know if they've mentioned numbers of fighters as well.

JT: So now we need to fix a date. You said in an email that Raqqa was bombarded heavily a couple of days ago. Does that affect the journey?

Abu Qatadah: Not really. They bombed two buildings. They weren't too far away from the place where I'm staying. But it means we've lost a lot of time. Mostly due to security concerns. The situation now isn't much different from before. Assad was bombing us. Now he's stepping back a bit and concentrating on Aleppo. Now the Americans are bombing us for him. The situation is pretty much the same as it was before.

JT: Is there something I should watch out for so that I can't be located?

Abu Qatadah: By the Americans?

JT: Yes. It's no fun when they can accompany me wherever I go. It's also not good for your safety.

Abu Qatadah: I don't think that there's anything you need to be aware of, no idea. We don't have any cell phones or a cell phone network here.

JT: So you have to go to an Internet café?

Abu Qatadah: Yes. I don't think the Americans are going to be randomly bombing Internet cafés.

JT: Incidentally, IS is getting criticized more harshly every day. Politicians and the media are appalled by your beheadings, they are talking about forced marriages and rapes. Are there forced marriages, and how does the leadership of IS react if there are rapes?

Abu Qatadah: The question, as always, is what does this mean? The politicians and the media are talking right now about sex slaves, beheadings, whatever. There are definitely beheadings. Depending on what crime a person has committed, either his head or his hand is cut off. I think those are things you already know about from other countries that were allies at some time or perhaps from history books or from other sources. And there's slavery in Islam again as well.

JT: With you too?

Abu Qatadah: Yes, of course. We consider ourselves to be an Islamic state. We exercise a certain amount of power over our territory and the territories we capture. All laws prescribed by Islam are enforced. And under certain circumstances, Islam allows non-Muslims to be made into slaves. This right has been exercised with the Yazidis, for example.

JT: They have been made into slaves?

Abu Qatadah: Yes.

JT: Christians, too?

Abu Qatadah: Christians have the opportunity to pay jizya and accept Islam or they are simply killed. Then their women are enslaved.

JT: Enslaved or forcibly married?

Abu Qatadah: Not forcibly married, that doesn't happen. But at the moment this is how it goes: in Raqqa most Christians pay jizya.

JT: What does that mean in practical terms when you're a slave? That you don't get paid or do you get a few rights?

Abu Qatadah: It's just like it used to be. There are certain rights, and there are also certain duties a slave must perform. Of course a slave doesn't get paid, someone owns this person after all. And must look after his slaves' upkeep, food, accommodation, clothing, and so on. He also has the option to free his slaves. If the owner commits certain offenses, a judge can also force him to free his slaves. I've been told that in Iraq many slaves converted to Islam. Apart from that, owners who are involved in a lot of fighting and don't have much time let almost all their slaves go free.

JT: And what happens if there's a rape somewhere? Is the rapist punished?

Abu Qatadah: What do you understand by rape?

JT: Forcing a woman to have sexual relations.

Abu Qatadah: (Laughs.) That's always relative. What does "force" mean? What does it mean to force someone if this person is a slave who belongs to you?

JT: So, in your opinion, the rape of a slave is not a rape at all. And what happens when you capture a village and one of your fighters rapes a woman there? Unfortunately, that happens in war.

Abu Qatadah: If the perpetrator is caught in the act, that is considered fornication and whoring. If he's married, he'll be stoned to death. If he's unmarried, he'll get one hundred lashes. But if she was his slave, then that would of course be a different story.

JT: What is your policy about Germany at the moment? In Germany, all the security services—the BKA, the BND [German Federal Intelligence Service], the Federal Office for the Protection of the Constitution—are talking of a high risk of an attack.

Abu Qatadah: You know what al-Adnani has to say on this issue. And you have perhaps followed what has happened in countries such as Canada, the Philippines, and Algeria, as well, where they killed a Frenchman. Those are all reactions to al-Adnani's call to the people to take action.

JT: So you are expecting attacks in Germany?

Abu Qatadah: We're at war and in war things change every day. At first, I thought nothing at all would happen in Germany. Then came al-Adnani's speech where he called for attacks against every country that is part of the coalition. Now we're hoping something big will happen, maybe a bombing or something like that. When war rages on one side, it's only a matter of time before it breaks out on the other side as well.

JT: Who would carry out these attacks? There are, after all, at lot of Salafis in Germany who reject violence. So they would be out of the question...

AT THIS POINT, we lost our connection again. After a number of not particularly friendly emails about the terms and details of the journey, we spoke again via Skype on November 13, 2014, a Thursday.

JT: Hello? Abu Qatadah? Yes, now I can hear you fine. You write really tetchy emails! I cannot accept such a tone. There's nothing I can do about the difficulty of traveling to your country. It's not like we're talking about a pleasure trip! And I'm not coming on my own. Some journalists have their own wish lists and conditions, and I'm just passing those on. So, I'm going to reiterate my own personal position for you. I would like very much to trust you. You personally. What it comes down to is the only thing I have as a guarantee is what the two of us have agreed to personally.

Abu Qatadah: That's right.

JT: I can see myself coming in about a week and a half, two weeks. So you see: I trust you.

Abu Qatadah: (Laughs.)

JT: You really shouldn't be laughing right now. Probably you're pleased I trust you. Later, I'm going to get asked: "How come you went to the 'Islamic State.' Wasn't your life in danger?" So I must be able to make it clear to my family and friends that we negotiated the conditions thoroughly. So there's no need for you to be as unpleasant as you were in your last email and the one you sent today. There's no excuse for that. And it doesn't reflect well on you.

Abu Qatadah: Okay. All that wasn't something I decided all by myself. I'm getting flak. And instructions about what to write. Personally, I want you to come and write a fair report. The report can show us as we really are. You're already quite popular with some Muslims in Germany and perhaps in other countries as well. It's just that all this is not my decision alone. I have an employer who tells me what I can and cannot do.

JT: I'm going to say it just one more time: I've always been pleasant to you and you should be pleasant, too.

Abu Qatadah: I'll try to do that from now on.

JT: It would be good if we could settle the details on Sunday. Exactly how we will meet up and things like that. And you can also tell me then exactly what you're going to put out on Twitter. And when. I should know that as well.

Abu Qatadah: I'll publish the letter we sent you and add one or two sentences.

JT: If the "Islamic State" doesn't denounce the invitation, then I'll assume it's genuine and authentic.

Abu Qatadah: Okay!

JT: Do you know the Soufan Group?

Abu Qatadah: Doesn't mean anything to me. No.

JT: It's an American think tank. They've published a thirty-three-page report about IS, which I've read. Very interesting. They must have access to a lot of detailed information. Much of what they've written backs up what you've told me. At the end, they write that there has never been anything like the "Islamic State" in modern times. That's what's being written by an organization that reports directly to the American government. They get their briefs mostly from the U.S. government. I found that interesting.

A completely different question: Is the caliph still alive? Apparently his convoy was attacked in Iraq. Supposedly, it sustained heavy damage.

Abu Qatadah: He's still alive.

JT: Wounded?

Abu Qatadah: Not, he's not wounded either. If you follow the Iraqi news, you should know that they're always lying. Not only that, but it was a rather foolish news story. What kind of an IS leader would drive around in a convoy in the first place and then drive through an Iraqi control post? It's odd the American government, or rather the American media, would have picked up a story like that. Normally they're not taken in by that stuff.

JT: And Kobane? The Kurds say they're making progress.

Abu Qatadah: I don't know what they mean by "progress." The latest news I got was that they had advanced but were then pushed back again. That it's back and forth. I really don't know what the Kurds think they're doing. I mean, the Americans did a thorough job leveling the center of town. Even if we lose the battle, there's not much left of the town for the Kurds to take. But we'll have the longer staying power, like it was back in Iraq, when we had to withdraw for many years. Even if we have to wait another one or two or three years. That's not an issue for us. There's no such thing as a retreat for us anymore.

JT: You've said you are expecting fair reporting from me. But I cannot guarantee that you will like what I have to say.

Abu Qatadah: That's a different issue. As long as no lies appear, that's okay. You'll see the truth for yourself. For example, if someone writes that *al-Dawla al-Islamiya* killed five people in Raqqa because they committed the crime of fornication, that's fine by us. Even if that makes us look bad in the eyes of the West. If you make things up or spread lies, that's quite different.

JT: We've talked many times about the fact that I'm highly critical of IS. But I can guarantee you, I have no interest in spreading fabricated stories about IS. I've never done that. You know I spent time with the Taliban. And you know I was with the Iraqi national resistance forces during the American war with Iraq. And that, by the way, was when I met your predecessors. At that time, they called themselves the Islamic State in Iraq, ISI.

Abu Qatadah: Who invited you then?

JT: No one. At that time, my biggest problem was how to get through the American lines. In Ramadi, I stayed with an Iraqi resistance fighter, a young student. I wrote a book about him. It's called *Warum tötest du, Zaid?* [Why do you kill, Zaid?]. Zaid had no desire to be a resistance fighter. But he lost one of his brothers because of the Americans, and then another. He had to spend the whole night watching helplessly through the kitchen window as his brother bled to death. That was when he became a resistance fighter. He blew up an armored personnel carrier. I stayed with these people for a week.

My son will probably come with me when I visit you. He'll film. We're looking for a third person to join us. But it's hard. No one believes that we're going to come back alive.

THE NEXT SUNDAY, November 16, 2014, we spoke again.

Abu Qatadah: Hello! Can you hear me?

JT: We can hear you. Frederic is here as well.

Abu Qatadah: Can you see me?

JT: Yes! What's the weather like?

Abu Qatadah: It's a bit colder here now.

JT: We're still flying to Gaziantep?

Abu Qatadah: Yes, I think we'll use that border crossing and bring you over there.

JT: How far is that from the airport?

Abu Qatadah: I have no idea. Between Gaziantep and the border, there's one more little town, Kilis. I figure it's about an hour to the border by car.

JT: Will you be coming over as well? To the Turkish side?

Abu Qatadah: Not me personally but other people.

JT: You won't be there?

Abu Qatadah: That would be too dangerous. I'll pick you up on the other side.

JT: Will it be possible to go to Mosul?

Abu Qatadah: Theoretically speaking, it's possible. I don't know how much time you want to spend.

JT: Mosul interests me because I know the town. So it would be easy for me to compare how it was then with how it is now.

Abu Qatadah: That's not completely out of the question. The road to Mosul is open. It's about five hours by car. That shouldn't be a problem.

JT: You know there are many things we don't agree on. I am a Christian and you are a Muslim. Despite that, I had hoped you would have

let mercy prevail in the case of the convert IS executed today. That person was, after all, a convert to Islam, an aid worker. There's no way you can justify an execution like that.

Abu Qatadah: What was he called again? Peter, I think. I've forgotten his name. The reason for his execution is simple. To be a real Muslim, you must fulfill certain conditions. For example, you must know the professions of faith: no one other than Allah has the right to be prayed to and Muhammad is his messenger. You have to fulfill these conditions. This Peter was never a true Muslim, and right from the beginning we didn't consider him to be a Muslim. It was a Western media campaign to keep claiming he had accepted Islam after he served in Iraq. In order for his apparent conversion to Islam to be accepted, he would have had to officially distance himself from his actions in Iraq. He never did that. And, therefore, we considered him to be an unbeliever.

The French government paid for their hostages. Then they appeared on television and said: "While we were in jail we acted as though we were Muslims. We tried to trick ISIS." What the French did not know was that they were busted early on. The prisoners exchanged news in the bathroom. We discovered that because the bathrooms were monitored. They wrote to each other: "We will accept Islam so that they don't do anything to us." To put it politely, they tried to make fools of us. The French were lucky their government coughed up so much cash. But the others were left in the lurch by their governments. And after that, their citizens were simply executed.

JT: What was the accusation against the aid worker?

Abu Qatadah: There was no accusation against him specifically. But in Islam, the blood of an unbeliever is basically not protected except in a few exceptional cases. The first is if he lives in an Islamic state and pays jizya. A couple of hundred American dollars a year. The second case is if a Muslim personally grants him protection. Or third, if he accepts Islam and so his blood and his property are then protected. None of them met these conditions. None of them had an effective protection agreement. They even tried to play this game with the NGO man, Peter Kassig, when they claimed that an Islamic charity had granted him protection. The mistake there was that the Islamic State did not exist at the time and no protection can be granted in a war zone. In war, no protection agreement is valid, even if it comes from a Muslim. Because he is not in a position to provide protection.

JT: That's a strange line of argument. You're saying a guarantee of protection is invalid the moment one cannot provide effective protection. But after the creation of the "Islamic State," you could have granted Kassig protection. So what's your guarantee of protection for Frederic and me worth if you argue like that?

Abu Qatadah: I said the possibilities for protection are a) if a protection tax is paid in an Islamic state, or b) if a Muslim grants protection, which is the case in your situation. You will get protection from us in the Islamic State, protection from the office of the caliph. And for us, that means everything is in order.

JT: But there's a war on. Is your promise valid in war?

Abu Qatadah: Definitely. We consider our territory to be territory of the state. In that sense, there's no war here anymore. The only war being waged in our territory are the air strikes by Assad and the Americans. We told you: for our part, you can be one hundred percent certain that nothing will happen to you. If a bomb falls, we can't do anything about that. It will hit us, but it could also hit you. Of course, we won't take you to a military base that's known to the Americans.

JT: Despite that, there is a war going on. Air strikes are enough. Can the Americans find out where I am?

Abu Qatadah: I don't think they can find out. As long as you don't have a GPS on you. Of course, you can bring all the technical equipment you need for your work. You probably know better than I do what the Americans are and aren't capable of. We see that in their attacks. They're not hugely competent. Most of the buildings they've targeted have been empty and we hadn't used them for months. And not nearly as many of them went up in smoke as the Americans would have liked.

FREDERIC: I have another question. The English prisoner John Cantlie, who makes this television broadcast for you every week, is he going to keep doing that? Or will he be set free one day? Or are you going to execute him during his last broadcast?

Abu Qatadah: (Laughs.) I can't answer your question for you. I don't know what they have planned for him. I don't think he's going to be executed. The fact is, as he mentioned in the first episode, he is a captive and he has been sentenced to death. With this television series, he can reveal certain things, and we've asked him to do that. That way, he can prolong his life. Whether he'll be executed in the end or not, I can't answer that.

JT: If you killed him, you would destroy everything you intended his appearances to achieve.
     Perhaps one more technical question. You say we're invited by the office of the caliph. Does that mean we're invited by someone in particular? So, for example, by you? Or by the person who signed the letter? Might someone later claim he didn't have the authority to sign the letter?

Abu Qatadah: Many people were involved. An important principle in Islam is that we try not to play tricks on people. If something is based in Allah's law and we have made a promise, we will do everything we can to not break this commitment. You are the first to receive such an agreement under the new caliphate, that is to say, from the new Islamic government. So naturally, it's very important to us that it doesn't all go down the drain and the media then gets to say: "Hey, look, they agreed to something in writing in the name of the caliph and Allah, and then they just reneged on the agreement."

JT: Is it possible to get the original letter?

Abu Qatadah: That would be very difficult, especially at such short notice. Unfortunately, we don't have a functioning postal system to send packages across the border. I can give you the original when you get here. That's not a problem.

JT: Finally, I wanted to tell you that you will play an important role in the book I'm writing. We've discussed a lot of issues.

Abu Qatadah: (Laughs.) We'll talk more when we see each other in person, and you can write about that, too.

JT: I just wanted to let you know one more time so you're prepared. We'll email you. Things will happen fairly quickly now.

ON THE MORNING of November 27, 2014, our telephone rings off the hook. The BBC, CNN, France 2, and other foreign broadcasters are calling us. Apparently, IS has let it be known on Twitter that I am either in or have been in the "Islamic State." The release of this information wasn't discussed with us. It's all starting to happen.

Freddy checks Twitter. He does indeed find a few tweets. The first one seems to come from one RamiAlLolah. An enigmatic individual. He appears to not only be very close to IS, but he also keeps publishing confidential information from the intelligence services. He claims to have "leaked" information about many Israeli air strikes.

Shortly before eight o'clock in the morning, he publishes the following on Twitter: "ISIS claims they have allowed the German journalist Jürgen Todenhöfer and his team to report from Iraq and Syria, and they will protect them..." In a later tweet he writes: "Very reliable ISIS sources have confirmed this news. However there is as yet no official statement from either Todenhöfer or ISIS."

Malicious comments follow very quickly. Many hope they will soon see me in the next IS beheading video. "I hope he never comes back." "Will they allow him back in one piece?" another asks. The general tenor of the comments is that it's a brilliant trick: invite me, screw me over, and then cut off my head.

RamiAlLolah and others who publicized the announcement on Twitter find their accounts inundated with articles I've written about IS sent by my opponents in IS. "Have you seen what Todenhöfer wrote in January about Assad, ISIS, and Nusra?" They send many links to the Assad interview as well. "Do you have any idea who you have invited? Todenhöfer is an enemy to terrorists and a friend of Assad." For the moment, it seems no one at IS is dealing with the Twitter controversy. We can't reach Abu Qatadah.

Frederic is furious. He warned me many times that IS was going to trick me. From the beginning, he thought a journey to the "Islamic State" was a crazy idea. Now he's giving me hourly updates on the worst commentaries from the Internet. While all this is going on, television networks are calling every couple of minutes. Shortly before our journey into the "Islamic State," Frederic reads me a disturbing Twitter message. A female IS fan in Syria wrote that she had dreamt a Western VIP was going to be taken captive. Now she's waiting for her dream to come true in the near future.

I write Abu Qatadah an angry email. And on November 30, 2014, we succeed in having another Skype conversation.

JT: I thought you'd been wiped out by an American bomb. Or perhaps a Syrian one.

Abu Qatadah: No, thank goodness. Not yet.

JT: Is Raqqa getting bombed heavily at the moment?

Abu Qatadah: Right now Assad is bombing Raqqa heavily. Every day. Three days ago, it was quite intense. About nine bombs. On other days, it's one or two. But at the moment, it's really heavy.

JT: All hell's let loose here as well, unfortunately. You went ahead and published our trip on Twitter without running it by us. That's caused us a lot of trouble. I've written to you about it. Now the media knows about my trip and I can't even step out onto the street. How can I travel without attracting attention? I've got not only the media but also all the Western intelligence agencies on my back. And if that wasn't enough, I can't find the original Twitter announcement.

Abu Qatadah: I've already tried to find who was the first one to write about it. I told you before that we no longer have any official Twitter sites. Only people who broadcast our news. Sometimes there are glitches.

THE CONNECTION IS broken and resumes later the same day.

JT: There seems to be huge interest in the media. I could do without that right now. CNN, BBC, *Bild, Der Spiegel,* they're all calling. French television called my kids at three in the morning.

FREDERIC: Unfortunately, my father has enemies as well. When you go into war zones and talk to both sides, something he does all the time—in Afghanistan with the Taliban and the president, in Syria with the rebels and the president—sometimes the other side gets downright nasty. Now there's a whole bunch of people saying: "What? That Todenhöfer, you've invited that jerk? But he went to Assad and talked to him." Just to be clear, so that after our visit you don't say: "We had no idea!"

Abu Qatadah: Rubbish. We know all about that. I personally—and my superiors as well—naturally, we looked into your father. It's clear to us that we don't always like what he writes. We've hashed that out already. We simply want him to report the truth.

JT: But the point is—we have to speak openly with one another about this—I have strongly criticized IS. You know that, right? So I am asking you that specific question one more time.

Abu Qatadah: Yes, of course, I know that. I am familiar with what you've published. Your critical side. But I think many Muslims consider you to be a reporter who sticks to the truth. And that is one reason why we've accepted you. You can report whatever you see. You've already referred to this Twitter site: "Raqqa is being slaughtered silently." They have people who live in Raqqa. They take photos and write reports. And even though they are on the spot, they make up lies. I'm thinking you don't want to come to fabricate stories. And we don't want that either.

JT: We could make up stories in Germany as well. We wouldn't need to make the effort to come and visit in order to do that.

Abu Qatadah: That's the whole point. We understand you can't report from our point of view. There are, quite simply, things that non-Muslims cannot understand. Why would someone get into a car and blow himself up? A non-Muslim would never be able to understand that. And that's why you'll never be able to report things the way we want them reported. But it's a matter of reporting the truth. From your point of view.

JT: That's what I've always tried to do. When I visited the Taliban leadership, we discussed suicide attacks. I told them I couldn't understand them and my opinion of them was completely different. They accepted that. They respected my critical remarks enough to invite me back again later. I reported on them fairly. They accepted I couldn't understand something like suicide attacks and I never would understand them.

IN THE BACKGROUND, we can hear loud explosions. Abu Qatadah sounds as though he's getting nervous.

Abu Qatadah: I'm sorry, but I must wrap up our conversation right away. Perhaps we can talk again later or tomorrow? We've got company here again. There are a couple of airplanes flying around quite close to us.

JT: Okay! Then just quickly. How's it going with the plans? When can you pick me up? When can we leave?

Abu Qatadah: You can leave right now. We should be able to pick you up the same day you arrive in Turkey and get you across the border.

JT: So that could all happen anytime from tomorrow?

Abu Qatadah: Yes. All you have to do is check in with me either by phone or email and let me know you've arrived and you're ready to cross the border. We'll pick you up there.

JT: So I don't need to tell you when I'm flying? Basically, all I need to do is give you a call after I've landed? How many days do you think we should plan on?

THERE'S AN ENORMOUS crash in the background.

JT: Go somewhere where you'll be safe.

Abu Qatadah: Okay. Good-bye.

VI

Entering the Nightmare

THE DIE WAS cast. There was no going back. For seven months, I had debated with myself. Was my plan to travel to the "Islamic State" a reasonable one? Almost every day, I either saw or read about new barbaric atrocities perpetrated by IS. Before I fell asleep, I often had the feeling someone was drawing the edge of a blunt knife across my throat. Most times when I felt that, I got out of bed, went to the living room window, and stared out into the night. Would we ever come back? How much is the word of a terrorist worth? I knew from Iraqi friends in Anbar that there had been negotiations with IS. With the express promise of free passage. No one from the delegation of Sunni tribes ever returned.

Yet I had an enormous curiosity to find out the truth about IS. This curiosity about the truth has driven me my whole life. Thanks to our Skype conversations and the guarantee from the caliphate, we had created a situation in which our capture or death would have hurt IS. After all, it wanted to be taken seriously as a state. Apart from that, as odd as it sounds, I trusted Abu Qatadah. I trusted the positive side that he still had. Or that he once had.

What impressed me the most was that my thirty-one-year-old son was coming along on this hara-kiri expedition. The whole family had begged me not to take him. If something happened to me, he would be the only male left in the family. They needed him. Most of all, his youngest sister, Nathalie. This girl is as pretty as a picture. But the invisible yet ever-present Damoclean sword of multiple sclerosis hangs over her.

The day before our departure, when I asked Frederic once again to stay with the family, he answered: "You know I'm against this journey. Totally. If you get killed, you will have destroyed everything you've spent decades fighting for. For the respect of the Muslim world. People will take your death as proof that you were wrong. The journey is madness."

"Perhaps," I said. "And that's why I'm asking you to stay here."

Frederic looked at me angrily. "I will not let you go there alone. We'll see this through together. You cannot leave me behind. If they kill you, I will have to live my life knowing I helped set up your fatal journey. You can't do that to me. That's not fair. And apart from that, if you leave in secret, I'll cut off all your Internet and Skype connections. You won't be able to find anything or anyone. I'll erase all your contacts."

I didn't stand a chance. Frederic wouldn't budge.

OF COURSE, I had taken precautions in case IS went back on their word. I know a few influential politicians and intellectuals in the Muslim world. I contacted them well in advance of our departure. They promised me that in case of emergency they would get in touch with their governments, who would then intercede on our behalf with their contacts in IS, for example with the Iraqi tribes. At least, perhaps. And the office of the chancellor in Berlin was to be informed, once again, explicitly and in writing the moment I entered the "Islamic State."

Apart from that, I knew from individual fighters that they often carried poison pills with them on dangerous missions. If they were captured or threatened with torture or excruciating execution, they could take them so that sadistic murderers could not toy with them for their amusement. In the summer, in the back room of a drugstore in the Kurdish section of Erbil, I had provisioned myself with four doses of a medication that is deadly if taken in excess. The pills looked perfectly innocuous next to the Imodium and aspirin in my medicine kit. I am against suicide. But that was not what was at stake here. What was at stake was the opportunity, when facing inevitable death, to avoid torture and a humiliating public execution. If I had to die, I didn't want my death scripted by IS.

The day before our departure, I told Frederic about the medication. He stared at me in surprise, but he nodded. He seemed almost relieved. Suddenly, we were not surrendering ourselves quite so helplessly to IS. We had a weapon we could fight back with. Unfortunately, it was fatal.

Then we wrote to Abu Qatadah to say we would set off the next day. And we began to pack our luggage. The most important thing after the medication was our sleeping bags.

TUESDAY, DECEMBER 2, 2014

MY ALARM CLOCK rings at 7:00 AM. I have not slept well. But now it is just a matter of following my pre-trip routine. Get up, get ready, check all the documents and bags one more time, and leave. Despite the routine, today everything is different. I don't feel as if I'm embarking on a journey; I feel as if I'm preparing for a serious operation at the hospital. Under general anesthetic. I've got the smell of disinfectant in my nose. It's a strange feeling to have before a long journey.

A little before ten, Frederic turns up at my apartment with his old school friend Malcolm (not his real name). Malcolm has been pestering us for weeks, and Frederic has decided at the last minute to bring him along. Malcolm will record our journey in writing; Frederic will record it on film. My oldest daughter, Valerie, is here as well. She has brought us copies of the guarantee of safety from the caliphate. Each of us gets one. We fold them in half and stick them into our inside jacket pockets. This piece of paper is our only guarantee that we will come out of the "Islamic State" alive! Unless it's just a trick to get us captured.

I ask Malcolm to buy fresh ginger cookies from a little store next door. As gifts for our hosts. Valerie has also packed gummy bears, chocolate candies, and milk chocolate. Frederic takes the bag. He asks if you're even allowed to give gifts to terrorists or if that is a punishable offense. Supporting a terrorist organization. I tell him that politeness is never an offense. Only the gummy bears are taken out. They are made of gelatin, which is made principally from pork products. Then there's a long intimate hug. Valerie is very brave.

ON THE WAY to the airport, my cell phone rings. It is an agent from the federal criminal police office. They've discovered that I intend to visit IS. I am strongly advised against the visit. The foreign office has a travel advisory in place. A couple of officials would like to visit me and discuss the matter. I let the agent know that, unfortunately, I don't have the time. I thank him and politely say good-bye.

At the airport, everything proceeds wonderfully smoothly. We plan to take Turkish Airlines as far as Istanbul and then, after a short layover, proceed to Gaziantep. No one tries to stop us from leaving, and the security people don't ask us any questions. So far, so good. Malcolm and Frederic joke that the German state knows better than to stand in the way of my trip to IS. There's no better way to get rid of me. Even the Turkish officials don't seem to take much interest in us.

Our plane to Istanbul is, unfortunately, somewhat delayed. That means we can forget our connection to Gaziantep. We hurry to the departure gate in Istanbul anyway. As it turns out, the flight to Gaziantep has been cancelled because of bad weather. However, there should be another delayed flight around midnight to Adana, which is only a two-hour drive from Gaziantep. Realistically, we won't get to bed until around four in the morning. That's too late for me. So tonight, we'll stay at a hotel near the airport.

WEDNESDAY, DECEMBER 3, 2014

THE NEXT DAY at lunch, Malcolm brings up the question of possible sources for ransom money. So who will pay his ransom? His family can't afford it. He's assuming I will pay it. I explain to him that I don't even know where my own ransom money is going to come from. I tell him there's still time to turn back. Malcolm becomes pensive. He hesitates. Then he summons up another ray of hope. Perhaps the German state will get him out? "Dream on!" I say. But Malcolm doesn't want to hear any more talk about turning back. Then he buys himself a thick notebook that from now on will be the official record of our journey.

Today's six o'clock flight to Gaziantep is also cancelled because of bad weather. I sprint to the counter for the flight to Adana, which is about to close. With a great deal of trouble, I manage to rebook us. Frederic and Malcolm have already forged plans for a sightseeing visit in Istanbul. But Adana is okay, too.

There's a whole class of schoolchildren on the plane. The atmosphere is cheerful. Even though Adana lies really close to the Syrian border. And there's a war going on there. Despite that, the young boys and girls seem happy. Two girls who must be about eighteen years old are excited to tell me how beautiful their town is. You just need to live on the right side of the border. They beam as we step out onto the runway at Adana. It's foggy and smells of burnt wood, diesel, and generators. A town in smog.

I rent a car and a driver who will take us to Gaziantep. For less than US$100. Our driver's name is Erdogan. During the drive, he tells us most of the foreign IS fighters cross into Syria at Hatay, Urfa, or Gaziantep. From Gaziantep, you have to cross the border by way of Kilis.

Farther north, near Kahramanmaraş, is where the German Patriot missiles are stationed. No one really knows what they are protecting. Syria doesn't punch in the same weight class as Turkey, which is a member of NATO. And so, it seems, future IS terrorists cross the

Turkish border protected by German missile defenses. Pilots in the antiquated Syrian air force will be careful not to attack IS fighters in this area. One inexpertly flown arc, and they would be in the firing line of the German missiles. So basically our "patriots" are ensuring the stream of terrorists eager to join the "Islamic State" can pour across the border undisturbed.

When we arrive at the hotel in Gaziantep at about 11:00 PM, we have to chuckle at the pompously kitsch foyer. The obviously well-heeled gentlemen sitting around in the lobby looking like Mafiosi regard us with suspicion. We can only guess how many of the guests here, about an hour away from the border, have some kind of connection to IS. But we sleep peacefully anyway. Things aren't really going to get going until tomorrow.

THURSDAY, DECEMBER 4, 2014

ABU QATADAH HAS still not made contact. Yet again. We settle in for a long wait. In the afternoon, we decide to drive down into the old town center. We'll stroll through the market a bit, find something tasty to eat. We're already weighing our options if Abu Qatadah doesn't get in touch in the next few days. The Turkish border town of Kilis comes under consideration, but a few foreigners have been abducted there recently. We're not very keen on that. We could, of course, hire a reputable security agency. But do such things even exist here?

We go into a romantic out-of-the-way mosque to pray. I love the often-mystical atmosphere of Turkish mosques. Later, we walk through the market, buy a few raisins, pistachios, and bananas. People are at work, hard at work, in many of the small workshops. Huge metal bowls are being beaten into shape and hammered with ornate designs.

Frederic suddenly notices on his cell phone that Abu Qatadah is online. He writes that he can Skype with us now. Half an hour later, we are talking to him. According to Abu Qatadah, the security situation is stable in Raqqa at the moment. Assad hasn't ordered any bombing of the town for the past few days. On account of the bad weather. Assad's pilots can't drop bombs when the weather's bad. With their old planes, they have to fly low below the cloud cover, where they are in danger of being shot down. And they are not in a position to hit their targets precisely. Which explains why there are so many dead civilians. It's different with the Americans. They are more dangerous, but even they cannot see if it's fighters or civilians gathered in the buildings they target.

We want to discuss our accommodation and when we will be picked up. But Abu Qatadah still doesn't have clear answers to most of our questions. We agree to speak again the following afternoon at three. The crossing into Syria won't take place until late afternoon, or at night, anyway. However, we should prepare ourselves for the possibility that everything will be a go for tomorrow evening. Or the day after tomorrow. Apparently, time is a flexible concept for IS.

We talk to Abu Qatadah about the ever-increasing Twitter commentary, which is repeating my criticisms of IS in remarkable detail. Abu Qatadah repeats they don't have any problem with that. Our guarantee of safety is valid and nothing can change that. Unless one of us takes it into his head to insult God or the Prophet while we are in the "Islamic State." In that case, not even the guarantee of safety can save us from the death sentence. But he doesn't say where he draws the line when it comes to blasphemy. "Pretty early on," Frederic suggests later. My undiplomatic conversations with extremists fill him with dread. I have never minced words, not even in Afghanistan.

AFTER THE CONVERSATION with Abu Qatadah, we drive back to the old part of town so that we can eat at least one more good Turkish meal. We find a traditional old kebab house. We order everything we recognize: a variety of lamb kebabs, chicken kebabs, and a few appetizers, *lahmacun,* or "Turkish pizza," salad, and other delicacies. As we dig in to our meal, we discuss whether we should announce our journey on Facebook before we cross the border. Along with a copy of the caliph's guarantee. There are pros and cons. The biggest consideration against publication is that I cannot run the risk of being publicly criticized in the days following the crossing. So finally, we decide we won't confirm the trip until after our return. If we're taken captive, Valerie will publish the caliph's guarantee.

Before we turn in for the night, we want to watch a little television. But the al-Jazeera reports about fifty dead in Iraq, skirmishes with IS in Syria, and yet more kidnappings dampen our mood. We turn it off.

FRIDAY, DECEMBER 5, 2014

THE NEXT DAY, we wait for a call around 3:00 PM—in vain. It reminds me of Somalia. Years ago, I waited a week with a television crew and a journalist from FAZ [*Frankfurter Allgemeine Zeitung*] for a meeting with then-president Siad Barre. When the meeting finally took place late one evening, the television crew was nowhere to be found. Off in some nightclub. Only the FAZ journalist, Günter Krabbe, had loyally stuck by me. Frederic and Malcolm are just as patient. They are in no hurry to journey to the "Islamic State."

WAITING, WAITING, WAITING. Off to eat again in the old part of town. But then Abu Qatadah makes contact after all. He gives us a telephone number to call. Things are getting serious. I dial. Someone who speaks good German comes on the line. I tell him we are ready. He promises to call back in fifteen minutes. And he does indeed call back in a quarter of an hour to tell me that tonight the border isn't passable. Everything is pushed back until nine o'clock tomorrow morning. We're to call him again then. I begin to get impatient. Why is it all so complicated? Are there problems?

بسم اللَّه الرحمن الرحيم

الحمد لله ربّ العالمين والصلاة والسلام على إمام المجاهدين نبينا محمّد وعلى آله وصحبه أجمعين...

وبعد:

فهذا كتاب أمانٍ للصحفي الألماني المدعو (يورغن تودن هوفر) يدخل فيه أراضي الدّولة الإسلاميّة آمناً على نفسه وماله مع الوفد المرافق له، فعلى جنود الدّولة الإسلامية الالتزام بهذا الأمان وعدم التّعرض للمستأمن ومن معه لحين إنهاء مهمّتهم وبلوغهم مأمنهم... وجزاكم الله خيراً.

١٤٣٥ /ذو الحجة/ ٢٥

1 Our guarantee of safety—document from the office of the caliph. "This is a guarantee of safety for the German journalist Jürgen Todenhöfer, so that he can travel safely in the territories of the Islamic State with his worldly goods and his traveling companions. Therefore the soldiers of the Islamic State will respect this guarantee and allow him free and safe passage until he has fulfilled his mission and left once again."

2 The first few yards inside the "Islamic State." A diverse group of smugglers are waiting behind the olive trees to collect us and the others who are "entering the country."

3 IS fighter wearing an explosive belt around his waist as a defensive weapon for less fit fighters.

4 A young fighter in a reception center for new arrivals.

5 Black IS flags in Syrian territory. You can no longer find portraits of Syria's president Bashar al-Assad anywhere in this part of the country.

6 A Syrian jet shot down by IS troops. The black flag has been raised even here.

7 The "gateway" to Mosul. This city, which once had 2 million inhabitants, is controlled by five thousand IS fighters.

8 Brochures on subjects such as how to treat slaves or be a good IS fighter arranged in a display case at "IS Publishing."

9 Religious or moral police on evening patrol in Mosul.

10 A conversation late in the evening on a lively street in the center of Mosul. The man in the ski mask is a European IS fighter. He pulled on the mask before the picture was taken.

11 We are greeted by IS fighters at the entrance to a hospital in Mosul. As a state, IS manages hospitals as well.

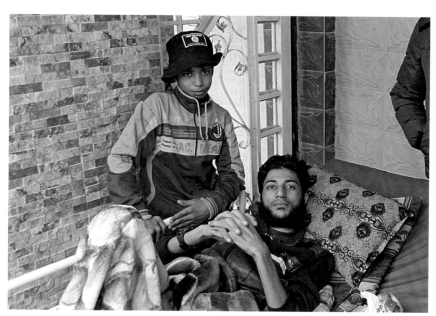

12 A wounded IS fighter is eager to shake our hands. A boy wearing an IS hat and an A.C. Milan sweatshirt stands beside him.

13 A double-amputee IS fighter is waiting for his prostheses. "As soon as I can walk again, I will fight until my last breath."

14 To our surprise, the doctor in the hospital speaks German. In order not to cause trouble for his family, he will only allow us to film him wearing a mask.

15 History was written in the Great Mosque of al-Nuri. But IS did not allow us, as non-Muslims, to enter.

16 The al-Hadba minaret leans more than the Tower of Pisa. The black flag now flies from its highest point.

17 In July 2014, the caliph of IS, Abu Bakr al-Baghdadi, gave his famous sermon from the minbar of the Great Mosque of al-Nuri.

18 As we were not allowed to enter the interior of the mosque, one of our escorts took photographs for us.

19 The IS logo—"Caliphate of the Islamic State"—is emblazoned on this black license plate.

20 When this little boy sees his nose in between my fingers, he touches his face in surprise.

21 People in Mosul have adapted to the presence of the new rulers—an everyday scene at a fruit and vegetable stand.

22 There are FC Bayern fans even in IS-controlled Mosul. After some blank looks, we managed to communicate our delight in seeing this Ribéry sweater.

23 The local traffic police in Mosul manage cars and passersby with Kalashnikovs.

24 A fifteen-year-old as IS policeman. "We are here to help."

25 Members of a special unit of the IS police. "We want people to see that law and order are in place here now."

26 A crossroads in Mosul. It's all about visibility.

27 A local police chief in Mosul is convinced that "after years of anarchy, we are loved."

28 An IS judge explains that it's always the hand that did the stealing that is amputated. And the former judges were all killed.

29 An old man in a jail cell. His crime—possession of a large quantity of sleeping pills and antidepressants.

30 To serve the "Islamic State," they follow us wherever we go—young men with beards as local "guards."

31 A tank graveyard in a former military base in Mosul. "That's what it looks like when twenty-five thousand soldiers flee from IS."

32 Standing in front of a gold-painted U.S. howitzer, an Egyptian IS fighter explains why he is against elections.

33 An IS fighter shows off his looted American vest. Astonishingly, he wears the "U.S." emblem with great pride.

34 An IS fighter and his American sniper's rifle with its telescopic sight.

35 This Kurdish fighter has a U.S. weapon as well.

36 Interview on a traffic circle with one of IS's Kurdish prisoners—"They want a prisoner exchange."

37 Not exactly giants: both IS fighters were among the first to capture Mosul in the summer of 2014.

38 Abu Qatadah, AKA Christian E., in Mosul. After this photograph, I was allowed to interview the bearded German on camera.

39 According to Abu Qatadah, those who do not convert will be killed. "One hundred and fifty million, 200 million, 500 million. The number doesn't make any difference to us."

40 A man at the market in Mosul explains: "Now we are ruled according to the laws of Allah. Who can complain about that?"

41 Talking about soccer is always an icebreaker. We list all the Muslim soccer players we can think of.

42 In the wrong hands: even German weapons end up in the hands of IS. People are happy in anticipation of new weapons shipments to the enemy.

43 What they can't buy on the black market, they win in war. The German government delivered this German MG3 to the Peshmerga.

44 IS forbids personality cults. That's why Cristiano Ronaldo and Lionel Messi have lost their faces.

45 Friday prayers in Mosul. Hundreds of people are praying in front of a mosque that is filled to overflowing.

46 IS has obliterated the old Sykes-Picot border and wants to define its own borders—using the symbols of the "Islamic State," of course.

47 A screenshot from an IS video: the Japanese hostages Kenji Goto and Haruna Yukawa with their executioner, Jihadi John.

48 Frederic and me in Mosul, looking like locals.

VII

Ten Days Inside the "Islamic State"

DAY 1, SATURDAY, DECEMBER 6, 2014

IT'S 8:55 AM. My alarm goes off. I look at the piece of paper beside my bed, pick up my cell phone, and dial the number. It rings. Once. Twice. Then someone answers. "Did you sleep well, Mr. Todenhöfer?" I say yes and ask when we'll set off. "I'll call you back in five minutes," says the voice at the other end of the line. "I'll give you exact instructions then."

A few minutes later, my phone rings again. I'm told we are to get into a taxi in an hour or two and call a particular telephone number. Then I must give the person I've called a password ("Ali") and hand the phone to the driver. He will be told exactly where he must drive to. We'll be picked up there. Our contact speaks extremely politely and cheerfully. That's somewhat unexpected. But they can't all go racing around shouting furiously as though they were throwbacks to a bygone age.

I inform Frederic and Malcolm that it's all going to start happening within the hour. Finally. We eat a quick breakfast, bring our bags down, and check out. We get into the first taxi that comes along. On my cell phone, I dial the number I've been given. No answer. I dial again. Again, no answer. Again. "Yes? Hello?" someone answers in Turkish. I cover my mouth with my hand and repeat the password, "Ali!" several times quietly but clearly. Then I say, "I will pass the phone to the driver now," and I press my cell phone into the driver's hand. He nods a couple of times, gives me my cell phone back, and drives off. It is 10:44 AM. We drive for about five minutes. Then we stop by the side of the road near a small mosque.

A short while later, a white minivan appears. There are three young men in the van. They look as though they are from eastern Europe. So, we're going to be smuggled in with new recruits. We fall into conversation with the young men. They want to know where we're from. One of them is from Azerbaijan; the other two are from Turkmenistan. They are twenty-two, twenty-four, and twenty-eight years old and at first glance don't appear to be the brightest bunch. One of them is constantly giving updates into his phone or taking calls. At some point, the three of them find it odd that Malcolm keeps writing in his notebook. They're getting nervous.

Malcolm tries to explain that he is writing a diary. None of them appear to believe him. All three begin frantically phoning. The atmosphere in the vehicle is suddenly extremely tense. Almost aggressive.

I dial our contact's number and ask him to explain everything. Then I hand the phone to one of the young men. After a few minutes, the atmosphere in the van changes completely. All okay. Now they're nothing but smiles. We get a thumbs-up from one of the young men.

AFTER ABOUT A ten-minute drive, we stop. Another young man and a large young woman with blue eyes and a light complexion climb into the vehicle. She is German. She is wearing a black cloak, an abaya. Her wrists are slightly swollen. We drive a couple of hundred yards and stop again. There are two old taxis parked in front of us. Another young man and two older men are waiting beside them.

We climb into one of the two taxis. Frederic sits in the front so that he can film us when we cross the border. But the driver looks at him, points to Frederic's short beard, and asks him to sit in the back. To draw less attention. Now it's very cramped in the back.

We set off all squished together. Then a couple of minutes later, we stop yet again at a nondescript crossroads. The other car has been stopped by the police, the driver tells us nervously.

Then suddenly, he drives off. Without saying a word to us. Showing great presence of mind, Frederic calls our contact. He explains the problem. Our driver was going to take us across the official border. Now he's grasped that it's a smuggling operation. Off to the illegal crossing point. In the meantime, the second taxi has caught up with us.

There's almost no traffic on the road to Kilis. After a few minutes driving down the highway, suddenly we're driving along a bumpy farm road. Our two taxis are now racing toward the border! I can only imagine what this must look like from above. There couldn't be anything more obvious. In front of us, the Turkish flag is flying on a hill . . . Is that the border already?!

We suddenly turn right and drive into a farmyard. Everyone has to get out right away. Now we take off again over ruts and stones, this time lying on the floor or crouching down in a minivan without seats. We're no longer driving down tracks through fields but through the fields themselves. It's so bumpy, we all fall on top of each other. The woman keeps looking at us. Does she know me from somewhere? My face looks familiar. No idea, I say pleasantly.

One of the men in the front of the van turns around. In broken English, he tells us that soon, on his command, we are to get out with our bags and run. Shortly after, the minivan stops. The side door slides open. All of us leap out and start running.

A hundred yards in front of us a man is standing at the border fence. He's nervously holding up the barbed wire so that we can all squeeze through. Everyone keeps running as fast as they can. But it's difficult to run across fields when you've got luggage. Frederic is carrying my suitcase. I'm lugging my backpack and the German woman's backpack. A few hundred yards farther on, five vehicles are hidden behind the trees. We are greeted by five masked men.

The veiled woman comes from Berlin. She must be in her mid-thirties. She tells me she converted to Islam and then traveled to Mecca. After that, she was on the intelligence services' watch list. In the end, they took her six-year-old child away from her. After Mecca, she didn't stand a chance. Now she's set all her hopes on the "Islamic State." She never wants to go back to Germany.

I say, somewhat nonplussed, that means her child will be lost to her forever. "I've already lost everything," she replies. "I can't lose any more."

Our conversation is interrupted. For some reason, Malcolm, Freddy, and I must be brought to safety right away. We climb into a white pickup truck. Two armed men from IS sit up front. The driver has a long black beard. Over his shoulders, he's carrying a Kalashnikov and a rifle. We pile our luggage into the truck bed and climb in. The driver roars off. We drive through a barren landscape. Occasionally, we pass through country villages. We chat with the two men from IS. The icebreaker, as usual, is soccer. We list off all the Muslim soccer players we know.

When we make a brief stop at a house, a grim-faced man carrying a Kalashnikov asks us if we are from the BBC. Frederic says no and shows our guarantee of safety for the first time. The man reads it in amazement. Then he gives it back and says, almost reverentially, that everything is in order. All the women in this place are completely veiled. Children are playing soccer in the street just as they do the world over. Before we drive on, the driver gives each of us an apple—a token of hospitality.

WE GET OUT in front of an old house. We are led through a room where people are praying. We are to wait in the next room. It reeks of diesel. A dark green board on the wall suggests this used to be a school. There are little hand grenades on a shelf. Behind the desk, a stash of Kalashnikovs. On the desk, a PlayStation console.

The people here are very welcoming. One of the people we speak to is Moroccan. We talk to him in French. The friendly IS fighter explains there are now about fifty thousand foreign fighters in the "Islamic State." He doesn't know the exact number, but it's got to be over fifty thousand, he says. From all over the world. His job is to register the newly arrived fighters.

It's important to him that we get the story straight. There's enough rubbish being said about Islam in the West, he says. Tomorrow, we can visit all the towns we want, to see for ourselves what's going on. The Quran is difficult to understand. Many Muslims don't really understand it. You need a teacher. *Al-Dawla al-Islamiya* (IS) is true Islam put into practice—Islam lived as it should be lived. The West is waging a war against Islam. "Our religion is peaceful," he tells us.

IS propaganda videos are meant to be shocking. They are meant to make the enemy afraid. They are the answer to the equally brutal wars the West wages against Islam. All that luxury in the West is only possible because they plunder the raw materials of the Third World. Arabs have to sell their oil at much lower prices than the Russians, he claims. "We aren't madmen. We just want to live. In the Western war against Islam, America is the butcher and the Muslims are the sheep. Over fifty countries have banded together against us. But they cannot defeat us. Our strength is not our weapons, our money, or our fighters but the fact that we are following the right path." In this region, there are only occasional air strikes, so we don't have to be too worried.

The presidents in the Arab world are not Muslim presidents but Western presidents. They might have a lot of money, but they are following the wrong path. To a certain extent, I can understand Arab resistance, I reply. But IS's atrocities make it difficult to defend oppressed Muslim populations, because it sounds like a defense of IS. I'm completely against force; therefore, I abhor the way IS celebrates its killing. Gandhi would surely have found more successful strategies in the Arab world. Without resorting to violence. Where is it written that you can achieve legitimate goals in your life only by resorting to violence?

The friendly Moroccan replies they always abide by divine laws. In the West, we are morally corrupt and on the wrong path. With drugs, whores, war, and the rampant desire for money.

I tell of the kindness and gentleness with which the Kurdish Arab hero Salah ad-Din (Saladin) treated the Christians after the conquest of Jerusalem. Our Moroccan explains they also will be kind and gentle once they win the war. They live according to sharia and the Quran. Therefore, they are fair and just.

He repeats we are safe here only because they live according to sharia and never break laws or agreements. We have been promised protection, and this promise will be kept. There are Christians living in Raqqa and even in Mosul. They can live completely normal lives without restrictions. Our friend will never return to Morocco. If he went there, he would go to jail.

A BOY CARRYING white paper bags enters the room. Grilled chicken, potatoes, Syrian flatbread, yogurt flavored with garlic, Pepsi, and a salted yogurt drink called *ayran*. Everything is first-rate. We eat sitting on the ground. On thin mattresses. The chicken is unbelievably good. Someone removed the labels from the Pepsi bottles before they were brought to us.

OUR SITUATION IS a little clearer now. So far, we've been well treated. For the time being, it doesn't look like there's a kidnapping in the cards. On the contrary, everyone seems to be concerned about our welfare and is constantly offering us something. Covers, cushions. "Should we make a fire in the stove, something more to eat perhaps?"

In the next room, IS fighters are praying. Six fighters in a row. One stands up front and leads the prayers. All have oriented themselves in the direction of Mecca, as required by the Quran. After prayers, we fall into a conversation with three of them. They are in their mid-twenties and they come from Frankfurt. "What are you doing here?" we want to know. They are surprised and happy at the same time. Mostly because we're not here as fighters but as journalists. They are impressed that we are traveling with approval right from the top. This is completely different from what they've been seeing in the IS propaganda videos.

A somewhat corpulent IS fighter enters the room. He's got a pistol hung over one shoulder and a Kalashnikov hung over the other. Around his waist he's wearing an explosive belt. The young Moroccan shows us how to handle the belt. Those who are less fit and might not be able to run away from the enemy in time wear them whenever they go into action. That way they can blow themselves up at the last moment and take many enemy lives with them. The Germans estimate the belt will kill anyone in a hundred-foot radius. Particularly courageous fighters in special units also wear the deadly belts. When they are surrounded by the enemy, it is their ultimate weapon.

I try on the brown belt. And I'm surprised by how light and inconspicuous it is. It weighs no more than a few pounds and fits snugly around my waist. You'd never notice it under a sweater. I had imagined the thing would be much bulkier. Frederic gets quite nervous as I carefully fumble around with a short black cord and want to know where the detonator is. Even the IS fighters are mildly alarmed. When I take the belt off again, everyone is visibly relieved.

WE GET READY to leave. We believe we're going to drive to Raqqa to meet Abu Qatadah. Two young men pick us up. However, they don't drive us to Raqqa but to a house about forty minutes away. We are to spend the night there and get picked up tomorrow. Man, do these people have time on their hands! We've been traveling for almost a week now.

We pick up our bags and go with our two new escorts to a black SUV and get in. At least there's more room here than on our last drive. The two IS fighters sit up front; we sit in the back. It's downright comfortable. They turn on the radio. So-called *nasheeds* are being broadcast. These are religious and sometimes military a cappella chants. They don't sound brutal at all. With their many different harmonies, they are quite beautiful and sometimes almost hypnotic.

Freddy and I talk to each other in German. But both the IS fighter who looks like a young bin Laden and the somewhat more corpulent driver, whose face is completely hidden, understand not only English and French but also some German. IS really is a multinational force, Frederic says. But perhaps it's just that our drivers have been cleverly chosen. The young men don't want to tell us where they're from, nor where they learned all those languages.

IN THE MEANTIME, darkness has fallen, so we don't know where we're going. Now and then, we can vaguely make out a traffic sign or a small place name. But we can't really read anything. At some point, we stop. To our right, we see the wall of a building that must be about six or seven feet high. A door opens. A young man comes out and signals to our handlers. We get out, collect our luggage, and enter the inner courtyard, which is only about 25 feet by 25 feet. The imposing house we've entered with such anticipation turns out to be an unfinished shell.

There's nothing in our room except for a diesel heater and a couple of thin black rubber mattresses. It seems we are to sleep here for the night. The gangly young "Osama bin Laden" shows us the dugout toilet next door, the washroom, and a sort of kitchen. Opposite our room, there's another one, but we're not allowed to enter it. That's where the IS fighters who live here sleep. It's all very Spartan and takes a bit of getting used to. I don't even want to talk about the toilet. But basically, none of this matters to us. There are situations where comfort isn't important.

After we've sat down on the floor of our room, the young OBL explains that first they're going to search us and then they're going to search our luggage. It's purely a routine safety check. I think of my special medication and hold my breath.

I chat with the young IS inspector about God and the world. Very controversial. Frederic whispers to me somewhat nervously that I shouldn't forget Abu Qatadah's warning about blasphemy. None of us knows exactly when blasphemy starts for IS. For the IS fighter, America is not a superpower, God is. And he is fighting on God's side.

That's why he is not afraid to die. God will decide the exact time of his death.

After a while, the other, more corpulent fighter asks me to stand up, and we take a few steps to the other end of the room. I lift my arms up as you do at airport security checkpoints and let myself be patted down. I have never been patted down so thoroughly. But I know he won't find anything. I have to empty out my pockets. He unfolds every piece of paper, investigates every package of gum, opens every pen. Every inch of my bag and its contents are patted, tapped, and investigated. My pills don't set off any alarm bells.

"Are you looking for anything in particular?" I ask.

"Spying devices, GPS, and stuff like that," he answers in English.

Okay! Lucky that Frederic was unable to find any GPS devices small enough to hide before we left Munich. We wanted to bring them along in case we were kidnapped. So that we could always be located. Thank goodness we hadn't found any such mini devices. Or we would have a lot of explaining to do right now.

While we and our luggage are being searched, the conversation continues. Here are a few of the fighters' statements.

ON NONBELIEVERS: "ALL nonbelievers are on their way to hell. It is our duty to wake them up. For unbelief is the greatest sin of all. So we are doing a good thing. It's like when someone wants to jump off a cliff. We want to save that person."

On freedom: "The West doesn't know what freedom really means. There is a huge misunderstanding about this between us. In the West, freedom means doing whatever you want. Without listening to anyone else. For us, freedom means being free from worldly desires. That's why we can live so simply. Because we are free from the desire for material things."

On the future of the West: "The greatest civilizations all went under after a while. That's exactly what will happen to the West."

On IS punishments: "The punishments IS imposes are also a blessing, because they prevent further punishment in hell."

On Shias: "Shias are not Muslims. They are not monotheists, because they pray to their imams for help and consider Ali [Ali, cousin and son-in-law of the Prophet Muhammad and regarded as the first imam] and others to be saints. But the first rule in the Quran is: 'You should pray to no other God.' Idolatry is a crime punishable by death."

On Syrians: "At first, the Syrian people did not view the Islamic State in a positive light. But they are now changing their minds in view of the bombings by the West and Syria."

On the daily new arrivals: "People who have lost hope in their homelands. For them, this is their last chance."

On Turkey: "They will be the next to fall."

On their own time zone: "We simply kept to summer time. We don't follow. We lead."

AFTER MORE THAN an hour of painstaking searching, one of the IS fighters brings a number of paper bags into the room. Sweet treats, Pepsi, and freshly pressed fruit juice from kiwis, bananas, and oranges. The young man could have been an American. At least, he speaks with an American accent. Only a few words, it's true, but enough to understand where the accent comes from. Appropriately enough, he's also wearing American military pants and army boots. With a dark-blue hooded sweatshirt and a black ski mask over his face. He puts the bags down and disappears out of the room. A cheerful French-speaking IS fighter brings in another couple of bags. Bread and lamb kebabs. Even though we are no longer hungry—there'd been that IS roast chicken, after all—we each take a piece of flatbread. We put one or two pieces of kebab on top, add some parsley and onions. Then we roll the whole thing up. It tastes delicious. If things keep going like this, we're going to put on a lot of weight on this trip.

The IS fighter with the French accent explains that although food like this tastes good, it's rarely served. If they ate like this all the time, they wouldn't be able to fight very well. Good food makes you tired.

Malcolm pulls a long face. He had just begun to enjoy himself a bit on this trip.

I move on to talking about the brutality and ruthlessness of IS, using just those words despite the critical glances Frederic is giving me. I ask how that fits with the Quran, whose surahs usually begin with the words: "In the name of Allah, the Beneficent, the Merciful." Where is mercy in IS? How can IS, with all its cruelty, claim it is doing God's work? This question will be a recurring theme on our journey. The young OBL has a simple answer: "You can only be merciful when you have power. Whoever is weak must be like the wolf."

The somewhat corpulent IS fighter talks to me about the work my foundation is doing in Afghanistan, Syria, Iraq, and the Congo. He says he's sorry that even though we're doing good deeds, we will not be rewarded for them when we reach the other side. If we don't die as Muslims, there's no way we can be saved. Even good deeds on this side don't count. We will only be rewarded for our good deeds in this life. With things like good health and good luck and so on. But nothing later. I explain to him we don't want any reward and the obvious thing to do with money if you have it is to spend it. How you treat people is much more important. The conversation gets us nowhere.

Then he tells us it's not just individual fighters who are now coming to the "Islamic State," but entire families. Every fighter who has a family can bring them with him and he will get a house of his own to live in. There's also a fixed wage. Fighters and state officials get free hospital visits. So many things are better than the Western media portrays them to be. Much of life is normal. Sometimes it's almost like an ideal world. Some families apparently only come here on vacation to visit relatives. Then they go back home.

If it were up to the young OBL, IS would reclaim the greatness of Arabs in Andalusia and become a bastion of scientific and religious thought. Of course, that's not his decision to make. But he thinks it will happen. Somehow this OBL is the least typical IS fighter I can possibly imagine. He used to go skiing in Austria, and he's a great soccer fan and knows the sport well. Basically, he has a lot in common with us. With one important difference: he works for a ruthless terrorist organization.

Our hosts take their leave around midnight. For security reasons, we are given the choice either to surrender our laptops and cell phones or to let a fighter sleep in our room. IS wants to be sure we don't contact anyone. We surrender our electronic gadgets. We don't yet know that from now on, communal sleeping arrangements will become completely normal. And we will acclimatize very quickly.

DAY 2, SUNDAY, DECEMBER 7, 2014

IT IS 4:00 AM. The fighters are getting ready for morning prayers. I can hear footsteps and voices. Later, they prepare their breakfast in the kitchen. It's way too early for me. I stay in bed and sleep on. Five hours later, we get up. There is a knock on the door so loud that Malcolm thinks the GSG 9 (German counterterrorism and special operations group) has arrived. Completely terrified, he sits straight up in bed. The door opens and the IS fighter with the American accent asks in English: "You guys need anything? Some eggs? Tea?" Room service IS style. Sure, why not?

When he does in fact reappear ten minutes later with scrambled eggs, canned tuna, jam, flatbread, and tea, we're quite amazed. "There you go. Typical IS breakfast," he says as he turns to leave after bringing us, apparently, a typical IS breakfast.

Frederic asks him, "Are you from New Jersey?" His accent reminds Frederic of a friend he has in Franklin Lakes, New Jersey. He's almost sure of it.

"What makes you think that?"

"You sound like you're from Paterson, Jersey."

"Close." He doesn't say any more than that. He just laughs and leaves to join the other fighters.

On the way to the washroom, I see five people from IS sitting in the sun in the courtyard chatting. Three seem to be in their early to mid-twenties, the other two perhaps in their late thirties. Somehow, the whole picture is really surprising. We are with IS and we're being treated really well. Right in the middle of a war zone. A few days ago, none of us would have thought that possible. Was something awful awaiting us just over the horizon?

WHILE WE SPEND the morning waiting in the courtyard enjoying the sun, we can hear bombs going off in the distance. But the noise doesn't seem to interest anyone here. The fighters sit down beside us and want to know what we have in mind. We want to know exactly the same thing about them. But the young men of IS have made up their minds, and they don't want to reveal their real identities under any circumstances. Treading cautiously, we discover snippets about their former lives. They are very eager to talk about the future and less eager to talk about the past. However, the breakfast American does admit he's from New Jersey. He used to work in Hawthorne, twenty minutes from Paterson. Frederic knows the area like the back of his hand.

From the young man from New Jersey, we hear sentences such as: "If the Americans come to *al-Dawla al-Islamiya,* they'll find themselves in a second Fallujah." Or: "Muslims have been oppressed for hundreds of years. That's why we're going to fight on to the end now to protect the weak. We'll protect the Christians as well, if they want to live amongst us." Over and over again, he tries to explain to us that Christians don't have any problems in IS. All they have to do is pay a small protection tax. And this is the only tax there is in the "Islamic State." He doesn't think much of Jews. But, he apologizes, that is a personal issue. He has this feeling left over from his time in the USA. He says, "I like the accent. It's difficult to lose it." Frederic tells him about his Jewish friends in New York. But he cannot get him to change his mind.

The American IS fighter is delighted with the prospect of being in direct contact with America again. He wants America to finally send in ground troops. To fight against them would be the best thing ever. He laughs. They'd shit themselves as soon as they started rappelling down from their helicopters. His friend, the one we've discovered in the meantime is from Lebanon, laughs along with him. "We've got some of their equipment already. We'd love to have the rest, and their other weapons as well."

Malcolm stays with the guys in the garden. Frederic and I go up onto the roof. And talk to two fighters about Iraq under Saddam Hussein. I tell them about the national resistance I observed in Ramadi in 2007. It seems one of the two IS men fought for a very long time in Iraq. He says he was with the national resistance forces at the time. However, now IS offers the only right answer.

We would love to leave the building and visit the village that lies about five hundred yards away. But our IS fighters say they've been ordered not to let us off the premises for now. They don't want to draw any undue attention to us. In the background, we can hear gunfire and bombs going off.

AT 3:00 PM, the door to the courtyard opens. The young OBL finally has the news we've been waiting for. It's time to go. We need to get our bags. Five minutes later, we go outside.

And there he is! Abu Qatadah. Almost as wide as he is tall. With a thick reddish-brown beard. Christian E., AKA Abu Qatadah. He's wearing a blue Arab robe and a red scarf on his head.

To greet us, he opens his arms wide and gives us the traditional Arab welcoming hug. "So here you are at last!" Frederic greets him with mock formality. Abu Qatadah plays along and laughs: "Yes, here I am."

We load our bags into the bed of the white pickup Abu Qatadah and his driver arrived in. Finally, we are going to Raqqa. The driver's head and face are so thoroughly wrapped with a large charcoal-gray shawl that only his eyes and the contours of his nose are visible. He murmurs a greeting in English in a strikingly rhythmic accent.

For security reasons, we can't use the main roads and we have to drive the long way around. The drive takes more than three hours. Abu Qatadah claims business is booming in IS. Almost all the stores are open and lots of goods are being sold, above all at the markets. Life, meanwhile, is almost normal. We notice there's a lot of new construction. "In places that are not being bombed, life goes on as normal. Even in Raqqa," Abu Qatadah tells us.

He explains that we were staying in al-Rai, the "armpit of the world." Right at the western edge of the "Islamic State." In Aleppo Province, about 125 miles from Raqqa. They've held power in this region since last May. Then he gives us a short lecture on the "Islamic State's" version of sharia that is downright cynical at times.

FOR THEFT OF goods worth more than US$40, a hand is cut off. US$40 is the price of a gram of gold.

Christians have to pay jizya, a protection tax. It comes to about US$300 a year for poor people and $600 for the rich. But then that is the only tax. Christians are among the more prosperous inhabitants of the country. All they have to do is sell a couple of sheep to raise the money to cover the tax.

Muslims pay a zakat, or religious tax, based on their assets. Rich Muslims pay more tax than Christians. Poor ones pay less. The money is used for social programs. In Raqqa, for example, IS runs three hospitals.

At the moment, IS finances itself mostly through assets seized in war, sales of oil, and the zakat.

The fighters of IS get to keep four fifths of their looted assets; the state gets the remaining fifth. This is the reason the fighters are paid only a small fixed wage. Abu Qatadah gets $50 a month from IS for his work in the media division. Plus a place to live. That is enough for him.

In reality, there are no slave markets the way we imagine them. Slaves are part of the spoils of war and therefore either go to the fighters or are sold. A Yazidi woman is worth about US$1,500 at the moment. About the same price as a Kalashnikov.

WE DRIVE THROUGH a landscape reminiscent of Tuscany. Only much more barren. Huge IS flags are painted on the sides of some of the buildings. IS flags appear everywhere else as well. There is even one hoisted over a downed Syrian fighter jet sticking out of the ground at an angle.

Thirty miles from Raqqa, we're stopped at a checkpoint. A boy who looks to be about fifteen waves us through with his Kalashnikov.

Our heavily swaddled driver doesn't say a word. He objects just once when Frederic takes a photograph of a fruit stand. We had stopped to buy drinks and a bite to eat. Sprite, Mirinda (a brand of fruit-flavored soft drinks), Pepsi, and Snickers—those were the travel provisions Abu Qatadah had selected for us and for himself.

It is already dark when we arrive in Raqqa. But there is still some activity in the streets. We drive by a circular plaza we recognize from media reports. It's surrounded by an iron fence. This is where the heads of decapitated enemies are impaled and put on display. I had imagined the eerie plaza to be much larger. Frederic was not allowed to take any photographs. The decision of the masked driver, who evidently has a lot of say. Abu Qatadah murmurs apologetically that we'll talk more later about this and other details of the journey.

According to Abu Qatadah, Raqqa is definitely not the capital of IS. That is just media hype. For IS the city has nothing that makes it stand out. Mosul, with its population of about a million, is more important.

We stop at a kebab kiosk to get something to eat. We look around. It looks as though life in Raqqa is completely normal. It's difficult to imagine that a terrorist organization runs this place. That here we are in the heart of terror. But then again, we weren't here when the heads were impaled on spikes and people were crucified.

Frederic asks what they did with the bodies of the hostages they killed. James Foley and all the others. "They were buried individually, or rather, tossed into the ground. Somewhere," Abu Qatadah answered impassively. Incidentally, IS chose beheading for the death penalty for political reasons. The decision was made right at the top.

I speak to Abu Qatadah once again about the concept of mercy in the Quran. And I start to tell him about Salah ad-Din. But Abu Qatadah doubts the truth of the story. It's probably got to do with the translation, when something got distorted. Often when history is recorded, reports about jihad or sharia are left out or censored. For political reasons. From the time of the Prophet until today.

Just when I'm about to say I have my doubts about this, a column of honking vehicles drives past. In the first vehicle, a young man is leaning out of the window and waving. In the next vehicle, we see a man with a camera filming the vehicle behind. In that vehicle, we see a bridal couple. A wedding! Back in Germany, probably no one's going to believe this. But when you have 200,000 people living together, from time to time you're going to have a wedding.

We keep on driving. We stop in front of a nondescript apartment building with multiple floors. In this part of the city, there's almost nothing but buildings like this. Our apartment is on the third floor. There is no electricity. So our driver takes off to find flashlights and candles. And we need bedding as well. It looks as though we will be sleeping on the floor once again. In small cold bedrooms. The apartment even has a "living room" right off the entrance, a small kitchen, a bathroom without running water, and another fairly dirty toilet. Everything is very simple. But with a good sleeping bag, every night is a good night. And we do have good sleeping bags.

WE SIT DOWN in the living room to discuss a few matters and eat our kebabs. The apartment is pitch dark. It's getting colder and colder. The windows don't close properly. Abu Qatadah finds his chair far too narrow, just like the chair in his office. He's going to get a new one soon. He's arranged to get it from the U.S. consulate in Mosul. The spoils of war. Then he looks down at himself and laughs heartily at his impressive bulk.

Abu Qatadah explains that I've been invited to visit because some of my books have been translated into Arabic. That has won me a certain measure of trust. In addition, I made contact with IS very early on.

Then we go through my wish list. We won't be able to meet with well-known jihadists such as Deso Dogg (German militant Islamist and former rapper who was added to the U.S. Department of State list of specially designated global terrorists in 2015) and similar "terror stars." IS doesn't approve of the personality cults that have developed around certain people, and in the future, they want to try to keep fighters out of the media spotlight. So that individual life stories and the fates of individual fighters don't get raised to the same level as IS's own narrative. IS no longer likes it when fighters upload photos and videos on their own initiative. Then Abu Qatadah begins to talk. Malcolm, who mostly sits discreetly in the background, writes it all down as quickly as he can.

CALIPH ABU BAKR al-Baghdadi will likely never appear in public again. There are a few reasons for this. One is the security risk. If I were to interview him, the CIA would know where he was, at least at the time of the interview. Apart from that, IS wants to avoid a personality cult around al-Baghdadi as well.

The caliph's public appearance in the mosque took three months to plan and prepare for. That's just too time intensive. Especially when IS is at war with sixty different nations.

The West's "campaign of lies" never ceases to amaze everyone here. So al-Baghdadi's ex-wife and son were never captured in Lebanon as reported by the Western media. And, as he explains to me for the third time, the supposed attack on al-Baghdadi's car convoy was pure propaganda. "Do you really believe al-Baghdadi would be stupid enough to drive around in a convoy to attract the maximum possible amount of attention?"

The office of the caliph has the authority to organize everything. However, the caliph personally reviews all the really important decisions. He was the one who made the decision to allow us into the "Islamic State" and to guarantee our safety while we are here.

There are only a few Christians left in Raqqa. Their churches have been repurposed. Not by IS but by the other rebel groups who wielded power here before IS arrived.

Assad's air force only drops bombs during the day and never at night. His planes are outdated. When the weather is bad, Assad cannot order any bombing raids. The Americans bomb day and night.

Jabhat al-Nusra and the FSA are apostates. Despite that, if they were to repent publicly for their actions, they could join IS.

Now there will definitely be attacks in Germany as well. Al-Adnani, the spokesperson for IS, has publicly called for these attacks. German politics is slippery. They do a lot of things using their secret service, so the German public is kept in the dark. For example, the German secret service is said to have helped build a border fence in Saudi Arabia. To say nothing of training the Saudi intelligence service and the Saudi police, and the enormous shipments of arms. Support for the Kurds and support for the American war against IS are further reasons IS now definitely views Germany as an enemy of Islam. Add to that Merkel's praise for the cartoonist Westergaard, arms shipments to Israel, and much more. "There are countries that keep out of all these wars, that do not take part in these murders. There will never be any attacks in these countries."

NOW WE COME to the planned comprehensive interview with an IS fighter. We've thought this over and we tell Abu Qatadah that in order to spare his family, we don't want to interview him. That would be too difficult for his mother. We would ask Abu Qatadah not only about the Quran but also about killing. But it's all the same to him. "She'll survive. That's just the way it is." We look at him in silence. "What do you want me to say?" says Abu Qatadah, irritated. "Don't worry about my mother. You can't interview just anyone here. The time for that has passed. The person you interview must be competent and know exactly what is correct and what is not."

Tomorrow we're supposed to be going to Mosul. Just as I had expressly requested. Because I know Mosul from Saddam Hussein's time. And I want to make comparisons. Abu Qatadah still has custody of our cell phones, and we're not getting them back yet. Anyway, there is no connection in Raqqa since Assad shut it down. And there's no connection in Mosul because IS shut it down. Because our iPhones have built-in GPS systems that cannot be disabled, they would pose a security risk in Mosul. Under no circumstances are we to be locatable. Therefore, the phones are going to stay right here. We won't be able to retrieve them until we leave.

Abu Qatadah explains that at the end of our journey, all our video and photo files will be reviewed. That's normal procedure in wartime. We look grim. That was not what we agreed to. We try to negotiate a compromise. But our driver, still completely disguised, who clearly has more authority than we first realized, repeats the requirement brusquely, emphatically, and clearly. With stinging coldness. And in his striking British accent, an accent I will never forget. Then, jutting his head forward, he looks us right in the eye and asks if we finally understand. His right eyelid seems to droop a little. But perhaps he's just trying to look cool and determined at the same time.

An icy silence fills the room. The tone and atmosphere have suddenly changed. No trace remains of the hearty welcome at the IS recruitment camp. I know from now on everything will be deadly serious. For the driver, we are enemies. Deadly enemies. The situation is precarious. But right now, we don't have many options. So at first I simply don't answer the driver's gruff question. Abu Qatadah seems to find the whole situation rather uncomfortable.

AFTER A GREAT deal of persuasion, Frederic is allowed to send one last email from Raqqa. From an Internet café. Under the supervision of Abu Qatadah. The Internet café is around the corner. Abu Qatadah goes quickly inside, gives Frederic a code he enters into a cell phone, and he's online. "You have two minutes," Abu Qatadah tells him. Freddy sends a quick update to his mother, his sisters, Malcolm's family, and the few other people in the know. He tells them he will check in regularly in the future.

On the way back, Abu Qatadah explains the Arabs are very lazy and they have many problems with them. He doesn't think much of the Arabs. "Are you well liked here?" Frederic asks him. "Not really," Abu Qatadah replies, laughing. "We're foreigners, after all. Many people don't like us. But they'll soon get used to us."

A short while later, a wiry fighter who looks about twenty-five bangs on the door to our drafty apartment. He has a short beard and glasses and long dark hair. With his black Turkish-style pantaloons, his blue hooded sweater, and his pointed black cap, he reminds me of a minstrel or balladeer from the Middle Ages. His battle name is Abu Loth. "Where does the name come from?" I ask. "Loth fought against homosexuals. I don't know if you know of him. I applaud what he did and what he stood for. He was against depravity, against homosexuality, and that's why I decided to adopt this name."

Malcolm and Freddy have to make an effort not to laugh. Does he always introduce himself like this? Loth (Lot), I tell him, is a well-known figure in the Old Testament and in the Quran. He fled Sodom and Gomorrah shortly before God punished both cities. Only his wife didn't escape because she turned around one last time while they were fleeing, even though God had expressly told her not to.

Abu Loth is German with Moroccan roots. Right now, he lives in Raqqa. Before that, he was in Aleppo for a long time. It was very intense there. He tells us that here they sometimes get to play PlayStation or billiards. Jihadists from the Maghreb prefer to play soccer. In summer especially, there are a lot of soccer games in some places. He jokes that perhaps they'll take Qatar soon so that they can host the World Cup in 2022. Although IS doesn't yet have a national soccer team. "But that will happen."

DAY 3, MONDAY, DECEMBER 8, 2014

WE GET UP around 8:00 AM. Abu Loth and Abu Qatadah slept in the living room while we slept in the next room. At night, our paths occasionally crossed on the way to the toilet. Someone obviously had a bit too much freshly squeezed fruit juice. Abu Qatadah has fetched a variety of pizzas and flatbread for breakfast.

Now we must review plans for the next few days, he says. He seems excited. Our request for a completely free rein reporting without any censorship has been categorically denied by his superiors. The security risk is clearly too high for them. A drone only needs a single photograph of an individual to be able to target that person and kill him.

I say I cannot accept censorship. The Western media would jump all over me if I did. Of course I know IS's stipulations are not unusual in a war zone. But I think: nip this in the bud. If I don't protest vociferously right now, IS will come up with more and more restrictions later. So I say if they don't restrict censorship to a few clearly exceptional cases, then it would be better if we just left.

The argument escalates. Abu Qatadah lets us know we're no longer allowed to go out and about in Raqqa. We have to stay in the apartment until we leave for Mosul. Now we can see only Mosul and nowhere else. I was the one who absolutely wanted to travel there, he reminds me. I ask if before we leave we can at least see the British hostage, the journalist John Cantlie, or the famous executioner Jihadi John. Abu Qatadah's answer is a resounding no. What on earth is going on now?

THE DOOR OPENS. Abu Loth appears along with our "driver," whose face is still hidden behind a large shawl. The masked one with the English accent immediately takes charge of the conversation. "You are free to leave!" he snarls at us. Basically, he doesn't trust journalists, and if we don't want to accept that, then we can go. "Do you think it's smart to let somebody come, someone you don't know, to invite him to your state, the state everybody is fighting against. And then you don't control him?"

He suggests a compromise. On this trip, he'll show us a couple of things we want to see. If we prove ourselves to be trustworthy, we are welcome to come back and visit another time. Then all restrictions would be lifted. As it was, we had already achieved a great deal and could count ourselves lucky. We are the first non-Muslim journalists to come here without having our heads cut off. "We even tell you, you can come again."

I am getting increasingly angry. I reply, "This is not what we arranged. I have never allowed myself to be censored, and I won't agree to it now. I always say what I think, and free reporting means just that—free reporting."

Why are we so interested in this "Jihadi John, as you call him" and John Cantlie, the masked one wants to know. Why aren't we interested in Muslims who are suffering in this country? Why are we focusing on these two individuals when there are so many more important issues?

Despite his protestations, the theme of John Cantlie seems to interest him a great deal. He suddenly makes a baffling suggestion. He can arrange a visit with John Cantlie under the following conditions. John Cantlie has written a letter to his mother and another one to David Cameron. John Cantlie would give me these letters. We could take this opportunity to speak with him in person. We would, however, not be allowed to take any photographs or film the meeting. The meeting and the handover of the letters would be filmed by IS and made public.

I know I cannot agree to this proposal. Obviously, I will not appear in an IS propaganda show. I would lose all credibility. Much as I would like to see John Cantlie and help him. Therefore, I propose that neither side film the event.

For some reason, the masked driver seems to be remarkably flexible when it comes to John Cantlie. He wants to speak with his superiors again to find out if we might be able to visit Raqqa after all and whether a meeting with John Cantlie might be possible, even without cameras. Abu Qatadah follows him out. He seems optimistic. He whispers to me that he believes we'll be able to find a reasonable solution.

Abu Loth thinks both of them are basically behaving normally. Our visit is an experiment for IS, and there are many things that could go wrong. The Internet reporting by the Muslim reporter from Vice News was arranged by the local IS media department in Raqqa. Our visit, however, has been arranged by the central media department and by the caliph's office. So no one wants to take any chances.

Then Abu Loth tells us why he was drawn to jihad and now lives and works in IS. Here are some of his main arguments.

"A MUSLIM NEEDS sharia the way he needs air to breathe."

"The way the Prophet and the first four caliphs lived is a model for the way we should live."

"In the West, you have the wrong idea about freedom. For you, it means freedom without restriction, without guiding principles. That is not good. A Muslim can't live like that."

"Value systems in the West are disintegrating... playing down homosexuality... living to excess... This causes problems for Muslims all the time."

"Democracy conflicts with Islam. You are not permitted to put human laws above God's laws."

"Theoretically, of course, it's possible to live a God-fearing life anywhere. But everyone needs a community. For me, living in the caliphate is a dream come true."

"Most acts of aggression in our world happen against Muslims in Muslim countries. Every Muslim woman is my sister. I have to defend her. It is the duty of every Muslim to help when Muslim blood is spilled."

"We are living in a time of Islamic awakening... a retreat from democracy... a return to our origins."

"It doesn't matter how few fighters we have. We know that in the end we will prevail."

"In a year or two, we'll negotiate a peace treaty with the West. Then the West will crumble. That is what the Prophet Muhammad prophesied."

PROMPTED BY THE word "Muhammad," I argue that if he were alive today, Muhammad would have been a great reformer who would preach the virtues of progress. Just as he did in his own time. Abu Loth tries to explain that the laws of Allah, handed down more than 1,400 years ago, are valid for all time. Therefore, there is no need for reform. All you have to do is obey God's laws.

ABU QATADAH AND the "driver" return. Both look extremely sullen. Have their proposals been rejected? The "driver" sits down again on the armchair across from me. "Mosul or Turkey. That's it!" he snaps at me disagreeably. And he sticks by his original proposal in the matter of John Cantlie. I am completely mystified by his message and his sharp tone. Is he serious? He can't talk to me like that. I stand up and tell him that very clearly. He needs to treat us with more respect. What's gotten into him?

But the masked driver just repeats even more forcefully that he will not discuss the matter further. Either we travel to Mosul tomorrow or we go back to Turkey right now. He is very worked up. Abu Qatadah is too. The two of them must have received a severe telling-off from their superiors. Until now, they cut the heads off journalists in the "Islamic State." Now they let one in and he has the gall to lay down conditions. The masked man ups the stakes. There will be restrictions in Mosul as well. His tone is once again very surly and aggressive.

I've had enough. I tell him calmly but very firmly that the ban on leaving the apartment is completely unacceptable. Such a thing has never happened to me, not even when I visited the Taliban. "We aren't the Taliban," the masked man snarls back. The only part of his face that is visible is that one eye with the half-closed lid. Meanwhile, Frederic is staring at the Englishman with a horrified look on his face.

I take the invitation from the caliph out of my pocket and say: "You gave us a formal invitation filled with grand words. Instead, you're treating us like prisoners. If we're not allowed to leave this room, then we are your prisoners."

"You are not prisoners," the masked man yells at me in his rhythmical accent. "Prisoners don't get to choose what they want for breakfast."

That's it. I am not going to put up with this any longer. "Change your tone right now," I yell at him so loudly he jumps.

But there's no point continuing a discussion with someone who is so furious all of a sudden. The way he's looking at us, there's nothing he'd like better than to cut off our heads. Where has this sudden aggression come from? Does the caliph's guarantee of safety still mean anything at all?

We must try to extricate ourselves from this conflict without losing too much face and most importantly to return to a position where we can negotiate. So I tell the Englishman as calmly as I can that we are now going to return to our room to decide whether we wish to drive on to Mosul or turn back. We will let them know of our decision at the appointed time. Frederic is still staring at the masked man with a stunned expression. He has noticed something. Then we leave.

Malcolm is of the opinion that if we end the journey now, there's a good chance IS will change their minds and see a greater advantage in kidnapping or beheading us. That would be no worse loss of face for them than if, on our return, we describe how IS's word isn't worth the paper it's written on. It's all too complicated for me. I don't want to break off the journey because of a breach of etiquette. Apart from that, film and photos are also censored by Western states in war zones for security reasons. Therefore, we decide to continue with the journey but to insist on changing the tone of our exchanges.

AFTER A WHILE, Abu Qatadah comes into our room and asks if he can bring us anything. He obviously wants to smooth things over. Thank goodness. He's going on a quick shopping trip and he could bring us back something to eat. Unfortunately, we can't go with him. He doesn't always understand some of his superiors' decisions, he says, "but that's just the way it is."

When he leaves the room with Malcolm, Frederic sits down next to me, white as a sheet. He whispers almost inaudibly: "I'm not absolutely sure because I can't check anything here without my computer. But I think the masked Englishman is Jihadi John. The half-closed eyes, the strongly curved hooked nose, the rhythmical, guttural British dialect. I listened to his voice in Munich half a dozen times. I will never forget it. What should we do now?"

My heart almost stops. The executioner who beheaded James Foley and others, too. He's our chaperone? "Don't say anything to Malcolm. We won't be able to check your suspicions until we get home. First, we've got to get through this." I hide my dismay. But I have that feeling again of being pushed into an operating theater reeking of disinfectant. A room I don't want to enter, a room I want to escape from. Everything has gone so smoothly until now. We sit together in silence for a long time just looking at one another.

WHEN WE GO back into the living room, we let our IS team know we want to continue. However, we expect to be treated differently. Without saying anything, the other three acknowledge our decision. Abu Qatadah and Abu Loth try to lighten the sour mood by telling us more about the "Islamic State." The following points are noteworthy.

SMOKING IS FORBIDDEN in the "Islamic State." Apparently, the ban was not imposed from one day to the next but gradually. First the sale of cigarettes was forbidden. Then, a couple of weeks later, smoking in public. Finally, it was completely forbidden. According to Abu Qatadah, IS cannot, however, control what people do within the four walls of their own homes. "So if you want to smoke at home that is your business. IS doesn't check up on you. Whoever is caught smoking in public gets thirty lashes as punishment."

Music is also forbidden. Abu Qatadah tries to explain to us that there are studies that prove certain music influences mood and can make people sad and depressed. He understands the law, even though he used to listen to music himself, of course. Mostly hip-hop and German rap by groups such as Deichkind and Fettes Brot.

The Syrian people are very nationalistic. IS has been here in Raqqa for a year now. Despite that, they are still looked down on as outsiders. Some even consider IS to be an occupying force.

Smugglers charge Syrians at least US$600 to get them to Europe.

Generally, it's important for IS to take good care of the people here. They even allow female students from Raqqa to attend university in areas controlled by Assad. Many girls take advantage of this. IS must make it possible for people to lead normal lives. Financial considerations are hugely important. Money opens every door.

The largest source of income for IS at the moment is the oil business. IS sells oil for US$12 a barrel. There are natural gas fields, too. But most of the natural gas goes to people who live in their territory.

The future currency of IS will not be tied to the U.S. dollar. It will be tied to gold. They are preparing their own gold-based currency. Apparently, the first gold coins are already in existence.

IS arose in Iraq in 2006. Since then, it has been accepted by the people who live in Iraqi areas. "People know they can live their lives without interference as long as they don't contravene the laws of Allah."

In Syria, IS consists of 70 percent foreigners and 30 percent Syrians. In Iraq, it consists of 30 percent foreigners and 70 percent Iraqis.

The first thing every IS newcomer must do is go to training camp. There are two parts to the training. In the first part you learn sharia, the basis of Islam. The course lasts two to four weeks. There the newcomers are taught what is good and what is evil and how to abide by Allah's laws. The second part covers military training. Here they are trained to be fighters. The newcomers are quick to learn how to fight and handle weapons. After all, it's not that difficult. The determination of the new IS fighters is a huge advantage. Every one of them wants to learn, and every one of them wants to help IS as best he can. Every one of them wants to fight. "One year fighting on the front lines is equivalent to sixty years spent in prayer."

Not everyone has to die. For example, if a well-trained specialist were to insist on getting himself blown up in battle, the caliph would not allow it. That person must continue to carry out his important duties.

Many women also work in the service of the "Islamic State." But not as fighters like Kurdish women do. In contrast to the PKK, the Peshmerga are such "wimps" that even women have to fight on the front lines.

IS teaches children three main things in school: the Quran, law, and fighting. These are the three main branches of the school system.

At the moment, the PKK is the strongest enemy with the best ground troops. But if it hadn't been for the American air strikes, IS would have taken Kobane as well. The USA destroyed Kobane so completely there was nowhere for the IS fighters to hide. The town looks like Nagasaki after the atom bomb was dropped. If that's the

American anti-IS strategy, then the Arab world is facing hard times. Abu Qatadah estimates about five hundred IS fighters were killed in Kobane. And numerous civilians. Mostly as a result of air strikes.

Yazidis must accept Islam or be killed, because according to Abu Qatadah, they believe in the Devil and they even pray to him. Many Yazidis in Sinjar have converted to Islam. The majority of their women have been enslaved.

UNTIL THE END of 2001, Abu Qatadah was a "total USA fan." After the September 11 attacks, he even signed a condolence book. But a little while later, he began to question everything. Why was America attacked? Malcolm wants to know what he thinks of the conspiracy theories about 9/11. Abu Qatadah chuckles and says: "Yes, we have our doubts, too. Totally."

I shake my head. The world loves conspiracy theories. There are even some people, I tell Abu Qatadah, who claim the IS beheading videos are fabricated. He counters that the videos are purposely edited to allow room for speculation. IS wants to spare the West the actual beheading. Moreover, according to Abu Qatadah, even Muhammad would have beheaded James Foley. Before Muhammad it was not the custom to behead people. It was Muhammad who decided the head had to be severed from the body.

The Prophet—who is not here to defend himself after almost 1,400 years—is responsible for everything as far as IS is concerned. If IS were to conquer France one day, they would no doubt claim the guillotine was an invention of Muhammad's as well. "The reason we cut people's heads off," says Abu Qatadah, "is to put fear into people's hearts."

Abu Qatadah continues. Abu Mohammad al-Julani, the leader of the terrorist group Jabhat al-Nusra, embezzled US$10 million. But that was only one of the reasons they split from him. The youthful photo making the rounds in the media really is al-Julani.

Abu Qatadah approves of the radical Pakistani Tehrik-i-Taliban. In contrast, he calls the Afghan Taliban a "disaster." Mullah Omar is a "complete washout." Apart from that, he can never be the emir of a caliphate because he isn't a member of the Quraysh tribe. "He has absolutely no Islamic credentials." But he's made history because he didn't expel Osama bin Laden.

IS fighters who return to Germany are considered to be apostates. If they don't repent, they can expect the death penalty. When I ask him again about the possibility of attacks in Germany by those who return there, he just laughs. "Who knows? But they haven't really done anything here either."

Abu Qatadah claims the forty-five UN peacekeepers from Fiji who were supposedly abducted by Jabhat al-Nusra had, in actuality, been kidnapped by the FSA. However, it would have been difficult for the FSA to ask for ransom money from the UN because of their Western sponsors. Therefore, they handed the hostages over to Jabhat al-Nusra and divided the loot.

FOR DINNER, ABU Loth has procured a huge plate of rice with chicken. Along with some yogurt and Pepsi. Malcolm absolutely wants more fresh fruit juice. Freddy and I try to talk him out of it. After all, there is only one toilet. But he won't be dissuaded. He says he has an iron stomach.

Because our "house arrest" will be over tomorrow, the mood is somewhat brighter. Abu Qatadah and Abu Loth take great pains to gloss over the incident with the masked driver. And they don't protest when, despite the ban on being outside, we go out onto the small balcony to get some idea of what life is like in the streets of the city.

Today, I take my leave early and crawl into my sleeping bag. Frederic stays up with Abu Loth and Abu Qatadah. Poor Malcolm keeps making trips to the toilet.

AROUND MIDNIGHT, WE hear an extremely loud rattling sound. Gunshots. Very close by. Abu Qatadah, who was fairly nervous at first, is certain after a few anxious moments that these are shots let off for joy. Someone is celebrating out there. Abu Loth goes outside to find out more. A little while later, he returns beaming from ear to ear and tells us IS has taken an important zone near Deir ez-Zor airport and the brothers are now celebrating.

Shooting and celebratory fires are not allowed by IS, even for such happy events. Especially not in areas where there are families with children. Later, when Abu Loth also fires a few shots into the air, an IS police official confiscates his Kalashnikov. He'll get it back in a week.

DAY 4, TUESDAY, DECEMBER 9, 2014

AT 8:20 AM we are sitting in a small minibus in front of our house. It's going to Mosul. Freddy, Malcolm, and I haven't really woken up yet. But that's normal for us. None of us sleeps really well here. Our driver, completely wrapped up in his scarf as usual, warns Frederic he can't take any photos from the vehicle here in Raqqa. We can't take photos or film anything until we arrive in Mosul.

Once again, we drive by the plaza where IS sometimes displays severed heads. It's called Dawar Naeem. We feel as if we're in a nightmare. Will we really leave this country alive? One small piece of paper protects us from the deadly Damoclean sword that hangs over us, despite all the promises we've been given. The chilling performance of the masked man yesterday, who seems completely uninterested in being helpful, still resonates with Frederic and me. So far, no Western journalist and his team have left the "Islamic State" alive. Why should it be any different with us? Yesterday's confrontation created considerable doubt about our safety even in my mind. The driver now seems to view us with an ice-cold fury.

NOT MUCH IS happening on the street. Because people fear Assad's bombers, they arrange their lives around the flight schedules. When the weather is good, people rarely leave their homes. They feel safe only once it gets dark. Except that's when the Americans start their bombing raids. Apparently, the schools are open. Supposedly, there is a girls' school with eight thousand pupils. That's a big girls' school. And there are a lot of private schools as well. But many children have to support their families. Instead of going to school, they go to work.

It's amazing how many construction sites there are in Raqqa! Most of them must surely have been started under Assad. Will they ever be finished now? We see many villas. Who on earth lives there?

The driver asks if we still have any iPads, tablets, or cell phones on us. I still have an iPad. Strictly for writing. "Hand it over," says the masked one. Frederic gives me an almost pleading look. It says, "I'm begging you. No altercations with the driver." We stop briefly and give the device to the young IS fighter.

While we take this opportunity to stretch our legs a little, an old woman comes up and spreads her freshly baked flatbread out on the dusty ground to cool. Her daughter helps her. Every bread is laid down individually in the dust and then turned over. Abu Qatadah asks if we want some of the bread. But this morning we have little appetite for dusty bread, and we drive on.

Between the fruit and vegetable stalls, we can see the destruction left in the wake of bombs. Some buildings lie completely in ruins. Others are just missing their upper floors. "That's from Assad's bombs. When the Americans bomb, the whole house disappears." We drive by a Shia mosque. It wasn't bombed by the Americans or by Assad. IS destroyed it. And is very proud of that. Only a façade decorated with frescos still stands.

Even though there is supposedly a functioning garbage service in Raqqa, there are piles of garbage everywhere. Some of them are burning. According to Abu Qatadah, this has nothing to do with the IS garbage service but with the local people's lax behavior.

We are stopped at a checkpoint manned by armed IS fighters. Our driver shows a document and we are allowed through. We continue on into the desert in the direction of the so-called Sykes-Picot line, which the English and French used after the First World War to divide Iraq and Syria between them. After a few miles of desert, a second checkpoint appears. Particularly large numbers of IS flags are flying here. Again, we get through with no problem.

WE FIND OURSELVES on the road to al-Hasakah. There is nothing to see in the desert other than a few herders with their sheep and, here and there, a few clay huts. After about an hour, we take a right turn onto another desert road. IS has already put up a few road signs of their own here. We continue on to al-Shaddadah, where we want to get out for a bit. But we're not allowed to. "For security reasons," the driver murmurs, and he goes to get us something to drink. By now, Abu Loth doesn't understand what's going on either. But he thinks it's better to follow orders. Frederic thinks the driver could at least be pleasant. After all, we haven't done anything to him. Abu Loth replies that the driver is just in a difficult position. We shouldn't take it personally.

But getting out of the vehicle has now become a personal issue. I find it all too stupid. I get out and disappear behind an old shack. The driver can get as mad as he wants. Frederic and Abu Loth follow me. After we've relieved ourselves, we get back into the vehicle. I thank the driver profusely for our cold drinks. He looks at us perplexed. Clearly, he had been ready to get nasty again.

THERE MUST BE a great motorbike salesman in al-Shaddadah. The streets are full of motorbikes. Things are really humming here. It's the liveliest part of the "Islamic State" we've seen so far.

Apart from Abu Loth, no one in the car is talking to us. Especially not our masked driver. Neither is his co-driver, who has hidden his face behind a black ski mask. And Abu Qatadah is either tired or lost in thought. It's a bumpy ride and we're all very uncomfortable. We drive by a large auto repair shop that has been totally destroyed. Apparently, it has been bombed by American planes: "So IS can't repair their vehicles so easily."

Again and again, we see rusted metal barrels with black smoke coming out of them. Next to each one, in a dark oily puddle, stands a man black with dirt. Every couple of hundred yards. One-man oil refineries, says Abu Loth.

While Abu Qatadah seems to be deep in thought, Abu Loth tells us about the people who join IS. The youngest German fighter was sixteen years old. He's dead now. He was German with Bosnian roots. He was still a schoolboy. He was shot at a checkpoint by the FSA.

Burak, another German IS fighter, played on the German national youth soccer team. The son of a famous English banker is also fighting for IS. A "brother from Texas" is there as well. His father is with the American military. A handful of Israeli citizens are also fighting for IS. Arab Israelis with Israeli passports.

Our driver turns the steering wheel over to his co-driver. Fifteen minutes later, there's a loud "wham." We've crashed into a truck. "He just slammed on his fucking brakes," curses the co-driver from behind his ski mask in an even stronger English accent than our surly main driver. "You are British?" I ask him. At first, he doesn't answer, then he says in Arabic that he's from New York—there's no way he's from there—and gets out to inspect the damage. The right bumper of our vehicle is hanging down. We put our backs into it and, using all our strength, manage to break it off. Off to Mosul. There the vehicle will need to be repaired or exchanged. We drive on before too large a crowd gathers around the site of the accident.

Half an hour later, we reach the Sykes-Picot border. There's not much to see anymore. The proud buildings that once stood there to mark the border have been completely destroyed. Everything lies in ruins. The IS flag flies from a flagpole. An Iraqi flag painted on a rock has been painted over with the symbols of IS.

FOR A WHILE, we drive along the base of the Sinjar Mountains where the Yazidis fled this past summer. The landscape is always the same: barren, almost empty, just a few small villages from time to time. Suddenly, we come across a lot of burned-out, shot-up cars lying at the side of the road or a few yards away in the fields. It's as though the IS propaganda video was shot here, the one where IS shot up one car after another until all the occupants were dead. Later, more and more destroyed buildings are the defining feature of the landscape. Frederic still can't take any photos. The order is still: "Not until Mosul."

Now we learn that Abu Loth emigrated from Solingen, along with Abu Qatadah and eight other young men. Two of them are now dead. One of them was Robert B. Abu Qatadah was in jail with him. Abu Loth and Abu Qatadah both think highly of Robert B. He was courageous and completely committed. He absolutely wanted to take part in a "martyr operation." He had to wait patiently for many months before it was his turn. There were 160 other martyrs already on the waiting list. That's how great the rush is, according to Abu Qatadah. On his "martyr operation," Robert B. took 50 people with him.

The list has become longer since then. Back in Aleppo, Abu Loth says, there were more than six hundred names on the waiting list. He asks me whether we had spoken with Philip B. a few months ago. He also blew himself to bits. That would have been sometime this past summer.

IT'S ANOTHER THIRTY-SEVEN miles to Mosul. Another checkpoint. Again, no problem. We're waved through. We can see the outlying suburbs. We drive by a large prison. One of the walls has been destroyed. This is where IS conducted a "martyr mission and freed all the prisoners," Abu Qatadah explains to us proudly. This is the first time he and Abu Loth have been to Mosul. Accordingly, they're full of anticipation, even though they don't really want to show it in front of us.

We drive by an oil refinery. It seems to be in operation. Security guards are stationed at the entrance. You can see people on the premises. The region is full of oil fields. You can smell them as well as see them.

We also drive by a refugee camp. Countless people are living here in tents. Where do they all come from? Why did they flee to IS? We're told they come from war-torn areas or places that have been destroyed.

TWO MORE CHECKPOINTS and then we've arrived. Mosul! A large dark gateway arches over the multilane road. The arch advertises its loyalty to IS: it's painted black with white lettering and the IS flag. Finally, Frederic is allowed to film.

So now we are in Mosul, city of millions. In the heart of the "Islamic State." Five thousand IS fighters control this city, which once had a population of 2 million. Fewer than 400 men was all it took to rout more than two divisions of Iraqi soldiers, 20,000 of them. Abu Qatadah tells us it was only 183 men.

Mosul looks damn normal to us. Just like other big cities in the Middle East. Nothing looks as though it comes from the "IS Stone Age." On the contrary. Mosul is a vibrant, lively city with lots of traffic and countless people on the street. Did we just drive by an IS traffic cop? I'm not sure, but that's what it looked like.

Of course, as I look around, I don't forget that countless Shias and Jews have been murdered in this city or driven out, and a zillion Christians have fled. Mosul is now a completely Sunni town. You can't see the misery of those who were murdered or driven out.

We turn off into a side street to meet someone from the media department who is going to explain what will happen next. We're led through a glass door into a small shop. This is where "IS Publishing" conducts its business. The books and brochures piled up here will soon be distributed to mosques all over IS territory. The latest flyers and brochures are laid out in a display case. A sampling.

How to Handle Your Slaves
How to Swear Allegiance to the Caliph
How Women Should Behave and Dress
How to Look After the Poor
How to Be a Good IS Fighter

Also on display is the first book officially published by IS, *Fiqh al Jihad* (Understanding Jihad). The author is Abu Abdullah al-Muhajir, Zarqawi's spiritual mentor. He was the one who convinced Zarqawi suicide attacks were not only acceptable but the proper way to go. Abu Qatadah thinks if this book were found on me in Germany, I would be sentenced to at least seven years in jail.

We have them explain the brochures to us as best they can. The book, too. I ask for, and I'm given, one copy of each. I'm offered IS flags as well. They come in different sizes.

Frederic and Malcolm are hungry. We decide to come back later, and we drive on toward the center of town to get something to eat. In Mosul, there are even hotels. Although the better ones have closed since the capture of Mosul. There's not enough electricity. Of course, we are not allowed to stay in a hotel. IS doesn't want to let us out of their sight. After numerous unsuccessful attempts to persuade them otherwise, we give up.

The restaurant we visit looks from the outside like a glamorous version of an American fast-food chain. But only two tables are occupied. We—Abu Qatadah, Abu Loth, an Iraqi driver from Mosul, Freddy, Malcolm, and I—go up to the second floor. Right away, Abu Qatadah randomly orders half the menu. For starters, a variety of small salads are brought to the table. For the main dishes, there's deep-fried chicken, barbecued chicken, lamb kebabs, lamb chops, pizza, fries, and bread. To drink there are the usual choices, the ubiquitous Pepsi, Sprite, and water. Apparently, the food in Mosul is better than the food in Raqqa. Abu Qatadah is not going to let this opportunity pass him by.

Abu Loth tells us what made him want to leave Germany and move to the "Islamic State." Like Abu Qatadah, he often attended the Millatu Ibrahim mosque in Solingen. Everyone was very enthusiastic about the imam they had back then. Mohamed Mahmoud, AKA Abu Usama al-Gharib. After the sermons, they sat down together and discussed things. Was he a Salafi? Abu Loth doesn't like the term "Salafi." Suddenly there was a media frenzy about this imam and his sermons. Many characterized him as a preacher of hate. For a while Abu Loth avoided the mosque because he was afraid of the intelligence service. But he soon realized "what the imam was preaching was the right path!" He went back to the mosque often with his friends. They spent a lot of time together, discussing issues, playing soccer, barbecuing.

Then, in 2012, they all moved together as a group to engage in jihad. They now saw jihad as their divine duty. They were trained in Libya. For almost two months. For the most part, it was religious instruction, but they also got training with weapons and tactical exercises. Abu Loth thinks there are no clear values and no sense of direction in the West. It's getting worse every day. Our Creator cannot want things to be going the way they are going in the West. "All of life is just a test, and you need a clear set of instructions."

I spark a heated discussion when I ask what the Prophet Muhammad would preach today. Whether he wouldn't be far ahead of his time, as he was back then, and advocate progressive reforms. One of the greatest reformers in history surely wouldn't insist on customs and practices that are almost 1,400 years old. For an angry Abu Qatadah, the answer is clear: "Muhammad would live today exactly as he lived then. Because after the Quran, Allah didn't make any more revelations. And Muhammad just did what Allah told him to do. It's not a matter of reform but of following the right path. The path of the Prophet. Muhammad showed us the right way to live."

"The right way to live in his time, over a thousand years ago," I answer. "If we were to live our lives today according to the Old Testament, we would have to kill every day," I say.

"And that's just what you do," replies Abu Qatadah frostily.

The most important message is that you must believe in only one God. Everything else follows from this. Even executions and slavery. To "associate" anyone or anything with God is the greatest sin of all. That is why everyone who accepts democracy and its laws is following the wrong path. They are putting man-made laws above God's laws. There's really no such thing as those "moderate" democratic Muslims I like to talk about so much. They aren't Muslims; they're apostates. For a Muslim, there is no one before Allah. The right to pass laws doesn't lie with any parliament "but with Allah alone."

If God is as great, merciful, and powerful as I believe him to be, why, I ask Abu Qatadah, would he want, above all things, to be prayed to by insignificant beings like us? Wouldn't it be much more important to him if we were to follow his wishes and do good deeds? For me, God is much greater and more ambitious. God can't be as small minded as you imagine him to be, I tell him.

It is clear to me that here I am verging on what Abu Qatadah described before our journey as blasphemy with deadly consequences. But can it be blasphemy if I declare God to be greater than they all think he is? Abu Qatadah looks at me scornfully. The way he sees it, I have simply not grasped the concept of monotheism. "You are wrong," he says. "A bad Muslim who lies, cheats, and kills, is preferable to Allah than a non-Muslim who does good all day long."

The discussion ends here. Over the radio, the driver from Mosul lets Abu Loth and Abu Qatadah know we can leave now. The others have arrived. What others? Our two drivers from Raqqa?

WE DRIVE BACK to the store with the propaganda brochures. Our hosts are saying their prayers together, so we wait in the entryway. A young fighter sitting next to us watches al-Jazeera news. A member of IS enters the shop and greets us pleasantly. He's about four foot nine and looks to be no more than thirteen years old. He says he's twenty-one and comes from Saudi Arabia. He seems to be very popular with the Iraqi IS fighters, who are returning one by one from their prayers. Everyone is happy to see him.

I persuade Abu Loth to go out onto the street with us. "But just for a little while," he says. He seems to have great respect for the English driver. I want to buy a watch now that they've taken our cell phones away. When I wake up, I want at least to know what time it is. It's already dark outside. University Street, where we're walking, is well lit and very lively. Almost every store is open. Selling nuts, raisins, dried fruit, ice cream, coffee, tea, and all kinds of knick-knacks. There's even a stall selling cotton candy. It's not exactly the picture of a terrorist town the way we had imagined it. I find a wristwatch. The cheapest on offer. Abu Loth insists on paying. It costs about ten euros. There's no way that we, as guests, have to pay for anything. "I'll give the watch back to you at the end of the trip," I say. "Don't worry about that at all." Abu Loth laughs. "You're welcome to keep it."

A crowd has gathered on the other side of the street. About fifty people are pressed around a stall displaying a large IS flag. We go over to see what's going on. The latest IS propaganda videos are being shown on a medium-sized television. Scenes of fighting recorded with night vision equipment. There are children in the crowd of spectators. Frederic starts filming. It's quite amazing that people living in the middle of a war zone are happy to watch videos like this. One of the many bearded men in the crowd casts questioning looks in Frederic's direction. After a while, he comes up to him angrily. He wants to know why he's filming here. He gives Frederic a shove. Within a few seconds, Frederic is surrounded by a pack of agitated men. He keeps calling, "No problem," and looking around for Abu Loth. Abu Loth is standing on the other side of the street. "Loth!" Frederic keeps yelling furiously. The whole time, the IS people have been all over us, but now, when we need them, they've lost track of us.

I wade through the pack with Malcolm. The men obviously want to wring Frederic's neck, and we try to calm them down and drag them away. Malcolm throws himself fearlessly into the melee. Luckily, Abu Loth is on the spot quickly as well and explains the situation to the people. We have been personally invited by the "chief" to report on what things are really like in the "Islamic State." We have permission to film whatever we want.

The sinister looks change to friendly smiles and apologies in English. "Sorry, my friend! Welcome..." Now no one wants to make a bad impression. It turns out the ornery man has family in Baghdad and that's why he doesn't want to be filmed. His relatives will get into trouble if someone recognizes him. We reassure him he doesn't have to worry. Frederic will erase the footage he has of him. Just to be on the safe side, however, we go back across to the other side of the street. Crowds are always dangerous.

We meet three young fighters. They are impossible to miss: two of them are blond. A Finn and a Swede with a Kurd in Mosul. That is not the beginning of a joke but real life in IS. The Swede calls Mosul "my paradise on earth. The best time of my life."

When Frederic wants to film my conversation with them, all three pull ski masks over their heads. They don't want to be recognized. But they are very interested in why we are here. When we tell them the reason, they find us even more interesting. They open up more.

They want to explain how amazing everything is here. They want to broadcast their message to the world. We are offered tea from a tea vendor. Very sweet but very delicious.

IT'S ALREADY QUITE late by the time we arrive at our accommodation. Our bargain bungalow is in a vacation spot used by IS fighters as well. The area's laid out like a little village. On vacation with IS. Mind you, the interior is modestly furnished and a bit run down. Two bedrooms, a living room, a kitchen, and a bathroom, this time with a decent toilet.

Before we turn in for the night, Abu Qatadah wants to share something surprising with us. He thinks there will come a time when IS and the West will negotiate with one another. It could even be that IS will suggest to the West that it set aside its expansion for a while. This is foretold in a hadith—one of Muhammad's sayings. So far, all the prophesies in this hadith have come to pass. IS will join the West against a common enemy and conclude a treaty to this end. Naturally, it will be for a limited time. But who could this common enemy be? Russia? Iran? Time will tell. I reply anyone making a proposal like that would be laughed down in the West. No Western government will speak with IS, not a single one. Abu Qatadah gives a knowing smile: "IS will make a proposal. You'll see."

DAY 5, WEDNESDAY, DECEMBER 10, 2014

WE'RE WOKEN UP by Abu Qatadah around 9:00 AM. It's very cold, especially in the bathroom. There's no hot water, so we wash in ice-cold water instead. It's not at all pleasant, but it helps us wake up. For breakfast there's flatbread, Kiri processed cheese, and tea. Abu Loth is the only one to breakfast with us. Abu Qatadah has gone to another bungalow where IS fighters are staying. He seems fairly put out by our discussion.

Outside, it's not only cold; it's also raining lightly. Next to our building, there's a children's playground. We didn't see it last night in the dark. In summer, it must be quite busy here. With three cars and now six armed escorts, including Abu Qatadah and Abu Loth, we set off in the direction of a hospital we want to visit. Frederic sits up front in the passenger seat so that he's in a better position to film. May he open the sunroof so that he can film from the car from this vantage point? He may. He stands up on the passenger seat and after a while he even sits on the roof. Traffic on the streets is brisk. We drive through some quarters that are particularly lively. Lots of people look at us in amazement. An agitated IS street cop yells something after Frederic.

We're greeted by IS fighters at the entrance to the hospital. The building is painted with a lot of IS flags. There's a large IS flag hanging in the entrance. The hospital waiting rooms are full of people. The televisions are playing propaganda videos showing charitable activities undertaken by IS. IS fighters distributing toys and school supplies to girls, food to the poor. We hadn't known about these sorts of IS videos until now. I would never have imagined they existed. But it makes sense. This is not a place where they want to spread fear and terror.

THE FIRST DOCTOR I speak to (unfortunately, he didn't want to be filmed) complains there's a huge shortage of medical supplies. The main problem is Baghdad's boycott on medical supplies. Especially since the government in Baghdad is no longer letting medical supplies through to Mosul. Even before IS took power, supplies were low. But now the situation is almost as bad as it was during Western sanctions against Saddam Hussein. Apart from that, the water supply is getting worse. You can't drink the water from the faucet anymore. He doesn't have a problem with IS. Working together is okay. What else can he say?

In search of a doctor who is willing to speak to us on camera, we come across a wounded IS soldier. He has a fresh bullet wound in his arm. A young doctor with long hair is looking after him. To our surprise, the doctor speaks German. But he doesn't want to be filmed either. He comes from Europe. He doesn't want to say any more. Despite that, I ask him to give us a short description of the situation here. He thinks about this and suddenly grins and pulls on the ski mask of one of our escorts. Now he's ready to talk. Another wounded fighter is rolled past us on a stretcher. He is eager to shake hands with us. There's a little boy with him. Wearing an A.C. Milan sweatshirt. With an IS flag on his hat. A bizarre picture.

The doctor leads us through the hospital and introduces us to many of the patients. One of them is called Ahmed and he comes from Ramadi. He was wounded by a shell from an Iraqi tank. He's lost the lower part of his left leg. His right leg has been broken in so many places and is so riddled with shrapnel it will never work properly again. Ahmed doesn't seem to mind. He's been wounded while fighting, and he wants to return to the battlefield to fight again. For that, he needs prostheses for his legs. He's waiting for them now. They are going to be made of wood. I'm just amazed. "You're going back to fight? Without legs?"

"*Inshallah!* If I get to walk again, I will fight until my last breath, as soon as I can walk, *inshallah!*"

Abu Mariam is another IS fighter. He also has severe leg wounds. He is thirty-two years old and was wounded during one of the Iraqi air force's bombing raids. He used to be a merchant at the market. Now he's fighting for IS to protect his religion, he says. While we are talking to the wounded, there must be about ten men standing around us. That makes it difficult to create the right atmosphere for a casual conversation. But bystanders are always immensely curious. Their motto is: if something is being filmed, it must be interesting. I would have loved to have been able to talk in more detail with the wounded.

The last patient we talk to is a somewhat older man. He's a truck driver. He was severely wounded the previous Saturday in a drone attack. He has cuts and abrasions all over his body. Even his face is a patchwork of tears and scratches, and his eyes are swollen. He was on the receiving end of multiple rocket shards to his upper body, stomach, and legs. Twenty people were killed in the attack. According to him, they were all civilians. And he doesn't even have anything to do with IS, he says bitterly.

A Tunisian fighter we want to speak to doesn't want to speak to us. We are not allowed to film a woman from Holland who is fighting for IS and was injured in an attack. Other than that, everyone here is really cooperative. But Frederic must erase two photos he took of a beggar woman at the entrance to the hospital.

Before we leave the hospital, the doctor tells us about something that apparently happened in Mosul barely two weeks ago. On November 27, a U.S. drone shot at two of the hospital's ambulances. When the emergency doctors tried to flee, they were shot by "gunfire from the drone." All six were killed. They weren't fighters but hospital staff on their way to collect the wounded.

Just as we are going to get back into our car, a large charcoal-gray E-class Mercedes draws up to the front of the hospital. The black license plate displays the IS logo, "Caliphate of the Islamic State." IS now has its own license plates! A young armed man gets out of the car. He asks Frederic to point his camera away while he lets three women out of the car. Then he accompanies them into the hospital. When he comes back, he thanks Frederic for his discretion.

MEANWHILE, IT HAS stopped raining. The sun slowly comes out from behind the clouds. From the hospital, we drive to the al-Nuri mosque where Abu Bakr al-Baghdadi gave his sermon a couple of months ago. The mosque is really quite small. Its leaning minaret makes the Tower of Pisa look positively vertical. Despite its green ornamentation, it is less beautiful by far than other mosques in the Muslim world. But it has enormous significance. History has been written here, even if it's not pleasant history. The black flag of IS flies above the minaret. With the seal of the Prophet on it and the first sentence from the Islamic creed: "There is no god but God." I wonder what God thinks of the deeds of IS?

To our surprise, we are not allowed to enter the mosque. I've already walked in a few yards without my socks when I'm called back. This is the first time in more than fifty years I've been prevented from entering a mosque. I was even allowed in the al-Aqsa mosque in

Jerusalem, one of the holiest sites in Islam. But the highly agitated Abu Qatadah won't listen. "It may well be that some apostate let you do that somewhere else. But a true Muslim would never let you in." What rubbish!

So we stay by the entrance and make our point by kneeling down and praying there. Calmly and for a long time, everyone for himself. While we are doing this, one of our escorts walks through the mosque with Frederic's camera filming for us. During our "visit" to the mosque, we three are the only people praying. Our IS men, it seems, pray only at the prescribed times.

After that, we check out the neighborhood a bit. We observe people going about their daily lives. Everything seems normal. If it weren't for the IS flags and IS murals everywhere, you wouldn't know we were in a city occupied and governed by IS. But isn't that the way it is in all totalitarian states? Isn't mind-numbing normality the order of the day in such places?

Abu Loth explains: "As long as people abide by the law of God, they can do, or not do, whatever they want. People here lead simple, normal lives." Abu Loth, pleasant and often also thoughtful, has become the main person we speak to now that the others have become increasingly silent in our presence.

Lots of people watch us with amazement. We're like beings from another planet. Especially when Frederic is filming. Usually journalists get their heads cut off. How come we're allowed to film? We are happy our IS minders are a ways away for the time being. I see a young boy, about four years old, standing by the side of the road. He looks at me wide eyed. I walk toward him, squat down in front of him, and pretend to steal his nose. When the young boy sees his "nose" between my fingers, his hand goes up to his face in surprise. Luckily, his nose is still there. The citizens of Mosul witnessing this exchange are highly amused.

THE SHOPPING STREET we're walking down is filling up with people. We see a young man with a red FC Bayern jersey. He doesn't understand why we're so glad to see him. Until he learns that we come from Munich. On his back, he's wearing the number 7 and the name Ribéry. Bayern fans in the "Islamic State"!

We speak with two young IS traffic cops. One is twenty-four years old; his colleague is only fifteen. The older one explains their duties to us. He claims the traffic police are highly regarded and well loved because they do a good job. And what are their duties? To manage traffic as well as they can. "We are here to help."

A few steps farther on, dozens of live carp are lying out on a fish stand. They are being constantly spritzed with water to keep them alive. The scene reminds me of the Iraqi people, who have had to suffer so much poverty and misery, from the invasion of Iraq by George W. Bush until today. Some people keep their fish alive; others gut them right away.

Masgouf, carp baked in a clay oven, is a famous specialty from Baghdad. Frederic and I tasted this delicacy for the first time in 2002, on the banks of the Tigris River. Back then, in the days of the sanctions, the restaurant owner was so pleased to see us that he gave us the whole meal for free. Apart from carp and smaller fish, there is another fish on offer here that I have never seen before. It looks like a fat gray eel. Abu Loth laughingly explains the Shias hate this fish because it once disturbed Ali when he was praying by the river. "They hate it. But the Sunnis love it. Now the Shias are gone and the fish is back." I swallow my laughter at the thought of the many Shias murdered in Mosul.

We are hungry, so I suggest we go into one of the small fish restaurants to eat *masgouf.* "Are you sure about that?" Abu Qatadah asks in disbelief. "It tastes amazing," I say. Those of our escorts who are from around here think this is a great idea and point out where, in their opinion, the best and freshest carp are to be found.

We climb up to the second floor of the recommended restaurant. It isn't exactly the cleanest place in town. But as long as the food tastes good, we don't mind. There's water and, of course, Pepsi to drink. Everyone likes the fish, which is indescribably crisp on the outside and wonderfully moist on the inside. Except for Abu Qatadah.

He orders a different fish, which he doesn't like very much either. Even though he eats a good amount of it. "That was a great idea of yours," he says, wiping his mouth and looking at me unappreciatively. He probably never imagined how difficult and full of sacrifice this journey with us was going to be.

When I have to cross a neighboring room on my way to the toilet, I see our two drivers from Raqqa without their masks sitting with two of our local escorts. I apologize and continue on my way. The strongly curved nose of our strict chief driver sticks in my mind. As does his long black hair, which falls down the back of his neck.

WE TAKE THE oldest bridge in the city across the Tigris. A short time ago, there was an American air strike on the other side. You can still make out a few remains of the explosion. And a burned-out police car is still there as well.

We approach a police station. There are at least a dozen IS fighters dressed in black standing on the square in front. Iraqis but also some foreigners. They seem calm and disciplined. Like men who take their jobs very seriously and carry them out with pride and dignity. Is this the new state?

We are taken to the chief of police, who looks as though he's in his early forties at most. He's wearing a new olive-green uniform with a two-tone American bulletproof vest over the top, an ammunition belt with a gun in it, and American army boots. On his head, he's wearing a tight-fitting knitted black hat. His beard makes him look like a young Jamaican in an American uniform. He's declared himself willing to answer our questions. Frederic films the conversation. Abu Loth translates. Another eleven IS men stand behind us for the duration of the conversation. The atmosphere is quite tense. This is all new for people in IS. Why can we move around so freely? Until now, the only Westerners they've seen here have either been in prison uniforms or dead. One of the IS people looks at me with a decidedly fierce expression. He looks the way I have always imagined the fairy-tale figure of Ali Baba. With an imposing build, toned muscles, an impressive beard, and deep dark circles around his eyes. He is wearing two black belts diagonally across his upper body. These belts hold a large number of handguns and a whole bunch of magazines. He's looking at me as though he wants to tear me into little pieces.

The police chief explains in flowery language that the situation in the province of Nineveh and its capital city, Mosul, is calm, safe, and stable, thanks to the presence of IS fighters and the IS police. In its long history, the province has never experienced so much peace. After years of anarchy, people can finally leave their houses safely again. Without fear of being attacked or killed.

There are still some robberies from time to time, of course. But that happens all over the world. The number of robberies has fallen drastically. Sometimes a whole week goes by without a single charge being laid. Thanks be to Allah and the Islamic police.

I want to know more on the subject of robberies. I ask: "So let's say you catch a thief who has stolen something worth more than US$40. Will he then appear before an Islamic court? And how long will it be before his hand is cut off?

The police chief answers in "officialese." "After an order has been issued for the arrest of the person in question, that person must be brought to an Islamic police station in the province of Nineveh. The person will be there for one or two days. No longer. Then the person is brought before the Islamic court, where the case is registered so the proceedings can begin. If the worth of the stolen objects exceeds the minimum level for hand amputation, then the hand will be amputated. As Islamic law dictates." No hand amputations are expected in the next few days. The hand amputations that have been carried out are very frightening. It is no longer worth stealing things.

I ask how the population feels about the police. The police chief thinks after years of anarchy in Nineveh Province, people don't just accept the police; they love them. On those days when they are not visible in the streets, people really miss them. People are tired of the anarchy of the last ten years. I allow myself to register some doubt, but the enthusiasm of the police chief for his troops is unstoppable.

Moreover, he continues, the sons of many families work for the police. This leads to a very strong relationship between the police and the people. Under the old regime, none of these young people would have had a chance. The former police were also un-Islamic. They treated people badly, they yelled at them, cursed them, and even hit them. These times are now gone.

WHEN WE LEAVE his office we pass two cells. I stop to speak with the prisoners. The police chief has given me permission to do this. A young man is sitting in one of the cells. Mid-twenties. He is distressingly agitated. His "crime"? He was caught meeting his girlfriend. To pay for that, he must spend the day in prison. I ask him if she is at least pretty. The young man smiles and nods. Frederic interrupts me. "Stop it, Papa, or you're going to get him into even more trouble!" I follow my wise son's advice. I wonder if the young man loves the new police force as much as the police chief thinks he does.

An old man is sitting in the other cell. His crime is possession of a large amount of sleeping pills and antidepressants. A whole plastic bag full. We're shown the bag as though that will convince us. "And he had cigarettes, as well," the guard tells me. He'll have to be here for a couple of days, and then they'll set him free. Frederic and I feel dreadfully sorry for him. You can tell just by looking at him that he needs his pills. He seems very depressed.

Unfortunately, we cannot meet any Christians. They've all fled Mosul. Apparently, all they had to do was sign the contract for protection and pay the jizya. Then they could have stayed. But the three Christian leaders supposedly decided against that. Al-Baghdadi invited them to a meeting, but they just didn't show up. Then, three days later, they fled Mosul along with the other Christians. Supposedly 130,000 Christians have left Mosul. They didn't want to live in the "Islamic State." We met some of them when we visited the refugee camps around Erbil in August.

When we leave the building, Abu Loth takes Frederic to one side. Somewhat embarrassed, he asks if Frederic can do something to stop me from asking such probing questions. Some important people in the "Islamic State"—the police chief, for instance—aren't used to that. They interpret my constant questioning as rudeness. Frederic brushes him off. Abu Loth will just have to get used to that. We traveled here to do research and get answers. Not to exchange niceties and drink tea. Frederic leaves it at that.

WE ARE TAKEN out on a police patrol. But we get only as far as a big crossroads a few miles from the police station. There's already a large police unit there on a special operation. Dozens of traffic police with Kalashnikovs are checking cars and passengers. Most of them are being waved through. "It's a matter of showing a strong presence from time to time. We want people to see that law and order are in place here now," Abu Loth explains. The police chief emphasizes his men must behave respectfully, even on these kinds of operations. And they are indeed doing that.

We spot a German MG3 machine gun on one of the pickup trucks. It is mounted on the truck bed behind a protective shield. According to the proud fighter operating it, the MG3 comes from the German arms shipments to the Peshmerga. He snagged it personally. And so it is that the German arms shipments end up in the wrong hands anyway. Often in the hands of those who pay the most. The fighter laughs and asks if we couldn't perhaps send the Kurds more weapons. What IS can't seize on the battlefield, they will have to buy later on the black market.

ON THE DRIVE back to our bungalow, we notice there is something up with our "driver." Something must have really displeased him. He's acting as though he's absolutely furious with us again, and our relationship has reached a new low. Probably because I saw him without his mask when we were eating. But to get to the toilet I had to walk right past him. And I only saw him for a brief moment. And why is that such a big problem? Was Freddy's dark guess right after all?

After we're parked, the masked "driver" gives Frederic an unfriendly nod and signals that he should follow him. They take a few steps and then stop. Bent forward slightly in a domineering manner, with his head a little to one side and his eyelid half closed, the "driver" stares hard at Frederic: "I'm going to tell you something now and you will do as I say. Do you understand me?"

"Yes!"

"All right. I am not going to discuss this. You're gonna do as I tell you," he says in a threatening tone. "You will go and get your cameras now, including all your memory cards. You will give them to me. I will look at everything, make a copy for you, and give you your cameras back tomorrow morning. Are we clear?"

Frederic tries to tell him he's not okay with that at all and he needs his original memory cards back. We did not agree that IS would make copies of his material. That is not going to happen under any circumstances.

Our "driver" is on the point of exploding. He is seething with rage. We have no idea why. Frederic sees that the situation could escalate at any time and he shrugs his shoulders. Then he gets his cameras and gives them to our poisonous chief driver before he blows up completely.

Fairly confused, we go to our bungalow. Just before the entrance, Abu Qatadah and I get into an argument because I complain about the behavior of our "driver." Suddenly, Abu Qatadah starts shouting. "We don't give a shit how you are welcomed and treated in other countries in the Muslim world. They are all just kissing your ass. We will not kiss your ass!" he curses, and he holds his fist up in front of my face while he slams his other hand down onto the crook of his arm in a clearly insulting gesture. "You are never satisfied. You are always asking questions. Challenging us the whole time, everything we do. And may I say, you are really pissing off some people here. We will not accept that." Our IS minders are a bundle of nerves. We are too.

Instead of coming into the bungalow with us, Abu Qatadah stomps off to the other IS fighters and leaves Frederic, Malcolm, and me alone for the next few hours. The other bungalow fills up with our squad of escorts and more IS fighters. What are they talking about? Is that it for the guarantee of safety? Where is this ever-increasing level of aggression coming from? We have a very unpleasant feeling about it all.

A FEW LONG hours later, Abu Loth comes to visit us. The "driver" is indeed mad, so mad you can hardly talk to him right now, because I saw him at the meal without his disguise. But why should that be such a huge problem? I didn't take a picture of him. I've never seen such an overreaction.

"Some people just don't want to be recognized. You have to respect that," says Abu Loth. Apart from that, they think I'm extremely critical, and I take every chance I get to challenge how their actions can be reconciled with the Quran. Lots of people here can't deal with that. No one in the "Islamic State" would dare talk to them that way.

Feelings are running high at the moment. However, we mustn't worry. They'll soon calm down and tomorrow is another day. That's how I usually think, too. If only Frederic's suspicion didn't keep running through my head. Why is the man making such a fuss just because I saw him for a few seconds without his mask on? What game is being played here? If Frederic is right, then we have an enormous problem.

DAY 6, THURSDAY, DECEMBER 11, 2014

JUST LIKE YESTERDAY, Abu Loth is the only one who has breakfast with us today. Flatbread and Kiri cheese.

To our delight, the sun is shining. Abu Qatadah comes in. It's hard to read his expression. "There could be problems today. There are drones in the air. We must be more careful today. We'll see if we can get through our schedule. I'm not sure." Then he leaves again. "You have ten minutes," he says without a trace of emotion.

One of our local drivers has brought his nine-year-old son along, so it can't be all that dangerous. Our first stop is the court. Here we want to see how justice works in practice. We turn down a side street in front of a high-rise clad in blue glass. We drive through two security checkpoints before we stop in the parking lot.

There are a lot of people in the courthouse. There's no space left in the lobby. A large IS flag hangs over the reception desk. Fifty or more people are sitting or standing around waiting for their appointments.

We climb a large spiral staircase with a gold-colored banister as far as the second floor. There we meet a judge who is responsible for criminal cases, among other things. He is dressed completely in black and has a long black beard. Because this conversation was later erased from Frederic's camera by our "driver," here are a few passages from Malcolm's travel diary.

JT: What cases do you hear?

Judge: Criminal law, family law, debts, inheritance.

JT: Are you busy?

Judge: Yes. I'm working about thirty to forty cases right now. Also appeals, if necessary.

JT: Where did you study law?

Judge: In a variety of different mosques.

JT: In mosques?

Judge: Yes. I was a preacher at a mosque before IS came here.

JT: Are there also judges working here who were judges before the take-over by IS?

Judge: No. They were all killed. They put the laws of man above the laws of God. Apart from that, many of them were corrupt. People are happy with the new laws and judges. We use only sharia. We don't interpret; we just apply what is written. And, therefore, all cases are also dealt with more quickly.

JT: Are there any executions, lashings, or hand amputations planned in the next few days?

Judge: No.

JT: **Which hand is chopped off? Is there a rule for this?**

Judge: Yes. It's always the hand that did the stealing.

JT: **Does that happen often?**

Judge: I myself have only had to have a hand chopped off on two occasions. In the whole province, there haven't been any other cases in the past four months. Right now, there's a case of whoring. The condemned women will be stoned. Believe me, that deters people. And now that bribing judges is no longer an option, people think twice before they commit a crime. It used to be you could buy your freedom. Today, that's no longer possible. It's the same law for everyone.

ABU QATADAH SAYS if we want to attend an execution that can be arranged. There are enough prisoners whose crimes fit the bill. "You just have to tell us. We don't have a problem with that. I can even do it for you myself. What would you prefer? A Kurd or a Shia?" He smiles while he offers us amputations or executions. I turn him down fairly brusquely. Frederic is completely shocked. What a cynical attitude! We go outside.

WE DRIVE TO a former Iraqi army base. It's been turned into a base for IS. Mosul was overrun from this point. This is where thousands of Iraqi soldiers fled from the IS fighters. They left everything behind. Our local driver doesn't have any sympathy for them. They tortured him. For a week, he was subjected to electric shocks, which left scars on his legs. After that, he sat in the prison at the airport for many months, until he could buy his freedom for US$5,000.

At the entrance to the former military base, we wait for another car. We notice an airplane in the sky. "Americans," our driver says. He thinks it's just a reconnaissance flight. How reassuring! We keep driving around the base. The base now also serves as a training ground, prison, and weapons depot for IS. The base is enormous. We stop at a tank graveyard. That's what it looks like anyway. There are at least fifty to one hundred tanks here. Old, new, Russian, American. I'm losing track a bit. An apocalyptic sight. On one tank, someone's drawn some graffiti: "I'm sorry!"

Apparently, we're soon going to see fighters training and perhaps prisoners as well.

But suddenly, above us we hear the humming of drones. Our group is too large for the Americans after all. We have to break off the visit. We drive off in different directions in order to make an attack more difficult. The atmosphere is tense. The IS fighters keep in constant radio contact. Our driver steps on the gas. As we drive by, he points out entrances leading to secret jails. We drive by a soccer pitch, then a completely ruined barracks. There's not much left here.

Then we're at the entrance gate again. Half a dozen men and a few children wearing red caps and dressed in black are standing here. They are all armed with machine guns, American M16s, and Russian Kalashnikovs. They belong to a special police unit. While I talk with them, Frederic keeps getting jostled by a guy in uniform. He pushes him away. It takes some effort for Abu Loth to mediate the dispute. Some of the fighters seem very stressed out. IS's anti-Western propaganda is clearly working. The youngest three in the unit are apparently twelve and thirteen, but they look much younger. They claim they have already taken part in the fighting. But they are not getting paid for fighting or for the work they do each day. They are doing it for honor. Two of them attend school nearby. We cannot get into any more details. The drones are still flying around. The police call after us that they are not afraid of drones or airplanes. They fear nothing but Allah. "We'll visit Obama at his house," is the phrase they use to say good-bye.

We drive on to another base. There's a gold-painted American howitzer standing out in front. With an IS flag on top. We get out to a friendly welcome. One of the IS fighters looks like George Clooney. He's wearing a green vest over his camouflage. It has "U.S." in big letters on the shoulder. Amazingly, he wears the American emblem with great pride. Most of the fighters here seem to be equipped with American M16s.

I do a brief interview with a fighter standing in front of the howitzer.

JT: Where are you from?

Fighter: Egypt.

JT: Where were you during the Egyptian revolution?

Fighter: I was working in Mecca.

JT: What do you think of the "Islamic State"?

Fighter: The Prophet, peace be with him, came with the religion of Allah. He established the religion through jihad and not through elections and consultations where everyone can say whether he agrees with Islam or not. Elections mean unbelief and war against Allah and his prophets.

JT: Is that why you are fighting for the "Islamic State"?

Fighter: Yes, because followers of IS regard Allah as the Creator. They distance themselves from those who fight Allah and his prophets.

ONE OF THE fighters, who has been watching the interview with interest, proudly shows me his American sharpshooter's rifle. We look through its telescopic sight to a ruined building about five hundred yards away. From here, you could shoot the spoon right out of someone's hand.

WE DRIVE TO a restaurant. While we eat lamb kebabs, rice, and bread, Abu Loth tells us he doesn't believe IS can be defeated. He personally has given up all his worldly goods and left his family so that he can die here in IS. The pull is just that great. Everyone here is ready to give the shirt off his back. "We go into battle wearing explosive belts. We want to fight to the last shot. You don't." He wants to face the ultimate enemy soon. The Americans. "They cause us so much misery. In jails like Abu Ghraib, in Guantanamo, in Afghanistan, here." Obama is just clueless. All he wants to do is pacify his people. That's the reason for the hesitant air strikes he uses in Mosul, which kill mostly civilians. Every strike is a cowardly murder of civilians. But the bombing raids are a gift that draws more and more people to IS. And a new desire to engage with the Americans very soon.

I ask Abu Loth again about the British journalist John Cantlie. Abu Loth says he's heard he is now praying. Five times a day as prescribed. If that's correct, then he is now in fact a slave and no longer a prisoner. How on earth can I help this man?

FREDDY IS GETTING more worried by the day. Because he can no longer contact our family or Malcolm's family. He promised to keep in touch regularly. But his last email was a week ago. He knows people at home must slowly be starting to panic. For the past few days, our escorts have been coming up with new reasons why we can't drive to an Internet café. Now Abu Qatadah tells us there is no Internet in Mosul.

I ask the owner of the restaurant, and what do you know? Of course there is Internet. Right here, even. We're welcome to use it if we wish. Abu Qatadah is not at all happy about this. He's upset that I didn't take his word for it and that I continue to push. At least the conversation doesn't end with threats, as it did last night. Abu Qatadah promises we can send an email this evening.

It's prayer time. The owner of the restaurant closes the blinds and the door. That is mandatory in IS during prayer time.

After prayers, we drive by the place where two IS fighters broke through multiple checkpoints with their vehicles during the conquest of Mosul. They finally blew themselves up in front of the very hotel where the Iraqi generals were preparing their defense strategy against IS. Six generals died; the others fled. Their divisions in hot pursuit.

We stop at a traffic circle. We have no idea why. Ten heavily armed masked men dressed in black appear. A powerful-looking man leads a prisoner with closely cropped hair and a long reddish-brown beard in our direction. He's leading the prisoner, who's wearing yellow prison garb, by just one finger. The man appears to be completely broken. A loud bang comes from the street. A rear-end collision. The price of curiosity. Hesitantly, we walk to the middle of the traffic circle. "That's a captured Peshmerga. You can question him." Special forces surround us while we talk. Others secure the square. All the cars are stopped. Nothing moves.

The prisoner says, barely audibly: "Thank you for making time for me." His eyes show complete hopelessness, resignation.

JT: When were you captured?

Prisoner: In the summer. There were thirteen of us. One group lived near the dam, the second near Tabadul Square. The third group ran away. We were going to Sitmarkho. We were captured there.

JT: How long have you been a prisoner?

Prisoner: Since June 15, 2014, for six months.

JT: How has IS treated you?

Prisoner: How we are treated is not a big deal for us. We look after our own. At first, we couldn't tell night from day. We had no idea what would happen to us, whether we would be freed or not. All we knew was that we'd survived.

Abu Loth: He asked you how you were treated! Tell him!

Prisoner: Our treatment was fine, no problem.

JT: What was your profession?

Prisoner: Soldier, just a soldier.

JT: Are you Muslim?

Prisoner: Yes.

JT: Have they told you what they're going to do with you?

Prisoner: They've told us we're going to be used for prisoner exchanges. We appealed to the government of Kurdistan, to President Barzani, to participate in this exchange. The government hasn't responded. They aren't showing any interest.

Abu Loth: He asked how you have been treated by IS! Have you eaten well? Have you had enough to drink?

Prisoner: We have been treated well, very well, no problems.

JT: Are you married? Do you have children?

Prisoner: No, I'm not married, but I have brothers and sisters. They are orphans, so I had to look after them.

JT: Does your family know that you have fallen into the hands of IS?

Prisoner: Yes, they've known for six months. We were interviewed on the television. We appealed to the government, to Barzani. And to our families, as well, but with no response. Now they don't know if we're alive or dead! They know nothing about our situation.

JT: What's your name?

Prisoner: Hasan Mohammad Hashim.

JT: Where are you from?

Prisoner: Qada' Khabat, near Erbil.

JT: Did you fight against IS?

Prisoner: There were thirteen of us. We didn't fight.

HIS VOICE CATCHES. More and more onlookers are clustering around the square. I am so terribly sorry for this man and this public display. I have always been shattered by the helplessness of prisoners of war. I want to stop the interview. Suddenly, a drone is spotted. It's the first time I've been happy to see this deadly threat. I shake the Peshmerga's hand long and hard. Then he's taken away. As they walk him away, they put a cotton bag over his head.

We're asked to get into our cars quickly. The traffic starts to move again as though on command. We merge into the heavy traffic and disappear. Abu Loth explains there has already been a fairly large prisoner exchange with the Turks. Forty-nine Turks were released from the consulate in Mosul. He won't give us the exact details. The Turks will say it was a rescue mission. He grins.

So far, there's been no prisoner exchange with the Kurds, but IS is still hopeful this will happen. The twelve other Peshmerga are also to be exchanged. Abu Qatadah imagines the ratio will be one hundred IS fighters for one Peshmerga. As it is for Palestinians and Israelis.

WE DRIVE TO Mashki Gate. Past boys playing soccer. At the gate, we meet IS fighters who participated in the capture of Mosul. They are between twenty-five and thirty-five years old and not exactly giants. At Mashki Gate, I talk with one of the fighters.

JT: You were the first fighters to capture Mosul. Is that right?

IS **fighter:** Yes.

JT: How long did it take you to capture Mosul?

IS **fighter:** More than four days.

JT: How many of you were there?

IS **fighter:** The total number of fighters it took to capture Mosul was not more than three hundred.

JT: How many?!

IS **fighter:** Three hundred! Perhaps less.

JT: And the Iraqi troops, your enemies, how many of them were there? Ten thousand, twenty thousand, thirty thousand?

IS **fighter:** About twenty-four thousand.

JT: What do you think? Why did they run away? Why did twenty-four thousand men run away from three hundred men?

IS **fighter:** Why did they run away from us? Because of the strength of our belief. We do not conquer because of the strength of our weapons. It is Allah, the Almighty, who bestows victory upon us. We have this saying: "The enemy's fear ensures a swift victory."

JT: What weapons did you have? Did you have Kalashnikovs?

IS **fighter:** The most powerful weapon we had·was the 23mm flak!

JT: And what weapons did your opponents have, the Iraqi troops?

IS fighter: There were planes above us, but, thanks be to Allah, they couldn't hurt us. They also had mortars and cannons. A lot of different powerful weapons. But, thanks be to Allah, we weren't afraid of these weapons, and they didn't hold us back. Thanks be to Allah, who helped us!

JT: And helicopters as well?

IS fighter: Yes, there was a helicopter above us to shoot at us.

JT: And the helicopters couldn't hone in on you? They couldn't win against you, against three hundred men!

IS fighter: The helicopters shot at us. But, thanks be to Allah, they missed us. They shot behind us, in front of us, next to us. They had to fly very high and couldn't come any lower.

JT: So you're saying that after four days, you routed the army?

IS fighter: Yes. We fought for four days on the right side of Mosul. But when our martyr brothers blew the bridge sky high, thanks be to Allah, they got frightened. And with the help of Allah, Mosul was captured in less than twenty-four hours and was in the hands of the Islamic State.

JT: They just ran away?

IS fighter: Yes, they ran away from their positions. They even left their heavy equipment behind. Tanks, Hummers, weapons, everything. Thanks be to Allah, we profited from the equipment they abandoned. They even left behind their heavy artillery and airplanes.

JT: And how can you explain that fewer than three hundred people routed twenty-four thousand? How can you explain that?

IS fighter: We didn't kill twenty-four thousand. We killed a bunch of them. But they took fright and ran away. We didn't run away. Allah the Almighty has promised us victory when we fight. And so Allah awarded us the victory. Our enemies do not have a doctrine they are fighting for. They came for financial reasons and to support a tyrant.

JT: Was there a reward? Did you get money after the victory?

IS fighter: We got part of the spoils of war from Mosul. The apostates left a lot of loot, a lot of money behind. So we got part of that. Some money. It came to about the salary of one apostate. One salary. Perhaps even more.

JT: And do you think you will win the war in the whole of Iraq and Syria?

IS fighter: Above all things, we are sure that Allah will help us win and conquer every country. Rome, Constantinople, as well, and America. We will conquer them all. We are absolutely sure of that.

JT: What is your name?

IS fighter: Ahmad.

JT: Thank you!

I HOLD OUT my hand to the young fighter to say good-bye. But he refuses the handshake and gives me a withering look. He and his buddy, who looks like Rambo, want to give me a few more comments for the road. Matters close to their heart, they say. If they come to Germany, we will be the first ones they will kill. They will know how to find us. Then he draws his index finger from left to right across his throat. We are enemies, make no mistake. Even the caliph's guarantee can do nothing to change that.

We go to the car. My "cameraman" Frederic asks Abu Loth to take a couple of souvenir photos of him and me for a change. When Frederic looks at the photos later in the car, he sees that when the photo was taken, "Rambo" was standing behind him with his M16 pointed at Frederic's head.

NEXT ON THE program is the interview with Abu Qatadah. It is supposed to be a somewhat more in-depth conversation about the goals of IS.

We find a spot up on a hill. From here, there's a good view over Mosul. Three of the fighters from Mosul, wearing ski masks and dressed in black, position themselves behind Abu Qatadah and me. The interview takes place under fairly stressful conditions. The air is electric. It would be hard to express repulsion for us more clearly than the conquerors of Mosul are doing now as they take up their positions around us. Casually, they point their machine guns in our direction. The interview, which is later formally released by the "Islamic State," is unedited.

JT: Abu Qatadah, what is the reason you are not in Germany today but here as a fighter in the "Islamic State"?

Abu Qatadah: The main reason I and all the other Germans or Europeans are here is above all Allah, *subhanahu wa ta'ala* [the most glorified, the most high]. To obey him, for it is a command from Allah, *subhanahu wa ta'ala*—and the scholars all agree on this—that the hijra to the Islamic State is our duty. And everyone must emigrate and everyone must support this state. And, therefore, we followed this call and emigrated here. And now we are here.

JT: Were you, as a Muslim, discriminated against in Germany?

Abu Qatadah: I think everyone would agree, or everyone has his own stories, and of course I do, too, about how it is not possible to live with the *kufar* [non-Muslims, in the West, usually mistranslated as "unbelievers"] in Germany. Because the only reason one might possibly live in the land of the *kufar* is if you can practice your religion freely. And the basis of practicing your religion freely is not only praying five times a day or fasting during Ramadan but also the ritual butchering of meat and Islamic weddings and so on. And none of this is recognized in Germany, and so every Muslim is discriminated against and not just me. And, of course, the police and the state authorities also discriminate against us.

JT: What are the goals of the "Islamic State" when Syria, large parts of Syria, and Iraq are conquered? Is that all or is there more?

Abu Qatadah: The main goal of the Islamic State is to establish the sharia of Allah. Whether that's in Iraq, in Syria. We have experienced some gains in Libya, toward Sinai in Egypt, toward Yemen, and on the Arabian Peninsula in so-called Saudi Arabia. And, of course, we say we don't have frontiers, we have front lines. That means the expansion will not stop.

JT: That means one day you want to conquer Europe as well?

Abu Qatadah: No, no, one day we will conquer Europe! We don't just want to do it; we will do it. We're certain of that.

JT: What role do individual religions have in the "Islamic State"? What rights do Christians and Jews have?

Abu Qatadah: Jews and Christians, and, according to some scholars also the fire worshippers [Zoroastrians], have the option of paying jizya in the Islamic State, that is to say, the head tax or protection tax. And if they pay this, naturally they are protected by us and they also have protection in their religion. They can follow all their religious practices. Of course, they cannot convert others. But the fact is they are protected, they can live in peace. If not, then they will all be killed.

JT: Killed?

Abu Qatadah: Yes, or driven out. Like they were in Mosul, for example. They had three days to pay the protection tax, they decided not to do that, and they all fled.

JT: And how about Shias? There are at least 150 million Shias in the world, in Iraq and in Iran, what happens to them?

Abu Qatadah: We regard Shias as *rafidah* [those who refuse], so as *murtadin*.

JT: Apostates?

Abu Qatadah: Apostates. Right. And they have an option. Abu Bakr al-Baghdadi has said to everyone who has fallen into *ridda*, into apostasy. As long as we have no power over him and he makes *tabua*, that is to say if he repents, we will accept his repentance. No matter how many of us he has killed, even if he has killed hundreds of us. We will accept his repentance. We will accept him as a brother, as a Muslim. If he doesn't do that, we will kill him. And for Shias, the protection tax, or anything like that, is not an option. Only Islam or the sword.

JT: And if the Shias in Iraq and the Shias in Iran, 150 million of them all over the world, refuse to convert, that means they will be killed?

Abu Qatadah: Yes, exactly as we ...

JT: One hundred and fifty million?

Abu Qatadah: One hundred and fifty million, 200 million, 500 million. The number doesn't make any difference to us.

JT: Are you going to kill all the Muslims in Europe who don't follow your beliefs?

Abu Qatadah: Whoever doesn't follow our beliefs does not follow Islam. And if he insists on following his misguided path, then of course there is no other choice—other than the sword.

JT: Killing?

Abu Qatadah: Definitely.

JT: Those are very harsh statements you're making.

Abu Qatadah: These are not statements I'm making but the judgment Islam passes on these people, and the judgment of apostasy, and every apostate will be killed.

JT: In Germany, there is a lot of concern, in America and in England as well, that there will be attacks by your supporters. Attacks against German Christians, German Muslims. Is that something that might happen in the near future?

Abu Qatadah: Obviously, I can't tell you if that's a concern. Germany, America, Europe, England, whatever all those countries are, are all fighting the Islamic State. You know about the coalition. All these countries are classified as *Dar al-Harb,* countries of war, and we are at war with them. And they must expect that there will be fighting in their countries as well. Back then, Hitler fought in the Soviet Union, and after that the Soviet Union fought in Germany. That's perfectly normal.

JT: Well, we don't think it's very normal. Are we going to have to deal with attacks from the "Islamic State" in Germany in the foreseeable future?

Abu Qatadah: The thing is, we really don't care whether you consider this to be normal or not. Because you are fighting us. The German state in particular is fighting us. It has made arms shipments to the Peshmerga, and it has equipped apostates in countless governments and things like that. And it has been fighting Islam for a long, long time. Since as far back as Nur ad-Din or the times of Salah ad-Din and so on and so forth. And, therefore, they need to prepare themselves for that. Definitely.

JT: That there will be attacks? Large-scale attacks or attacks by individuals?

Abu Qatadah: As Abu Mohammad al-Adnani, the official spokesperson for the Islamic State, has said. He called on Muslims in the West who live among *kufar* and so on. Consider what you are loyal to and what you are not loyal to. Renounce the *kufar* and declare your loyalty to your fellow Muslims. How can you sleep peacefully over there when the Americans are bombing us over here? And look at how governments are supporting the fight against Islam and so on. Therefore, he says, roughly, take bombs and blow them up or take a knife and stab them to death, and if you can't do that, then at least spit in their faces.

JT: Will these attacks most likely be carried out by those who are returning to Germany from the "Islamic State"?

Abu Qatadah: I don't know whether attacks will be made by those who return. The fact is, whatever happens, those who return must repent for leaving the Islamic State.

JT: So those who return are not your closest allies?

Abu Qatadah: Are they our closest allies...? I don't know their reasons for returning. I hope they haven't renounced the Islamic State and that they're not rethinking their religion. And I hope, as I said, that they will repent for their return, for their departure from the Islamic State. And, of course, we hope they will reconsider and continue to fight for Islam wherever they are.

JT: You are surrounded by fighters who took Mosul in August. There were almost thirty thousand Iraqi soldiers. How many fighters from the "Islamic State," IS, ISIS, were victorious against almost thirty thousand soldiers?

Abu Qatadah: I don't know exactly how many there were. I don't think anyone can say for certain.

JT: Roughly?

Abu Qatadah: We have numbers from 183 to 200, to 300, to 500. Even if there were 1,000 or 2,000, that is still a very, very small number to fight against these people. We don't win because of our weapons or how many men we have, we win because of Allah, *subhanahu wa ta'ala,* and because of the fear in the hearts of our enemies.

JT: Is the caliph fighting on the front lines where you're fighting at the moment? Does the caliph fight with you?

Abu Qatadah: Of course. There are front lines where Abu Bakr al-Baghdadi fights with us. Because we don't have leaders who lie to their people, we have leaders who stand by what they say. And, of course, Abu Mohammad al-Adnani and other leaders, Abu Bakr al-Baghdadi and others, naturally they fight alongside us in battle, even at our most advanced front lines. Because, just like all the other fighters, they want *shahada,* martyrdom, so they can, *subhanahu wa ta'ala,* return to Allah.

JT: You, the "Islamic State," have beheaded people, sometimes in spectacular fashion, and you've filmed these beheadings. You have introduced slavery. You have enslaved Yazidis. Do you think that beheading people and slavery are progress for humanity?

Abu Qatadah: Progress or whatever. I don't think there will ever be a time in human history when these things don't happen. And that is part of our religion, to teach the *kufar* how they should fear us. And we will keep on beheading people. It doesn't matter if they are Shias, whether they are Christians or Jews or whatever else. We will continue the practice. And people should think about that. James Foley and whatever the names of the other ones were didn't die because we started the fight. They died because their ignorant governments didn't help them.

JT: Do you think slavery is progress?

Abu Qatadah: (Laughs.) Definitely. Progress, useful, and so on. There's always been slavery. Christians and Jews had slavery.

JT: But it was abolished.

Abu Qatadah: Only because some ignorant people believe it's been abolished. There's still slavery in the West, and people are well aware of that. There are women who are forced into prostitution and things like that. Under the most awful conditions. Slaves in Islam have rights, and if slaves, for example, convert to Islam or something like that, many of them are freed. And we teach them Islam, and we teach them good things, and we have our morals, and ... we have ... (Pauses.)

JT: Belief?

Abu Qatadah: Not only belief, of course belief as well, but just lots of other things as well, that allow us to abide by the rules. And a female slave, a *kafira*, is better off in the hands of a Muslim than a *kafira* who's simply walking freely around somewhere outside and doing whatever she wants, whoring around and behavior like that.

JT: You used to be a German Protestant. You became a Muslim and now you are here in the "Islamic State." We are here in Mosul, a city you conquered. My question is: Will you return to Germany one day?

Abu Qatadah: Thanks be to God. Allah steered me in the right direction and bestowed upon me the gift of hijra, emigration from Germany. We tried many times. Finally, it worked. To Sham, to the Islamic State. And we are part of the Islamic State in order to build it up. I don't know whether I will ever return to Germany. Only Allah knows. But we will definitely return, and we will not return offering friendship or anything like that but with weapons and with our fighters. And we will kill everyone who doesn't accept Islam or pay the jizya.

SO THAT WAS the interview. Abu Qatadah looks triumphantly over to the other fighters, who congratulate him. Especially the two young conquerors of Mosul who earlier would have liked nothing better than to behead us on the spot and who now beam at him and give him a thumbs-up. For them, Abu Qatadah is a brave German. We, however, are the enemy.

FREDERIC, MALCOLM, AND I are exhausted. Truth be told, since we arrived we've seen quite enough of and heard quite enough about IS. We can easily imagine going back to the Turkish border tomorrow. But unfortunately, our hosts have different ideas. They claim we need another co-driver for the drive back to Raqqa. And that won't be possible by tomorrow.

"You can take Mosul with three hundred men, but you can't arrange for a driver for tomorrow?" moans Frederic. Abu Loth, ever philosophical, says there's no reason to be offensive. We should just accept the situation.

WE DRIVE TO our bungalow. None of us had anticipated being on the road for so long and we don't have any more clean clothes. So we wash our things in the basin and hold them up for nearly an hour in front of the fan on the heater to dry them.

Abu Qatadah and Abu Loth once again leave us alone for hours at a time. Although we are taken along to get dinner. We go into a supermarket and we can look for what we want. But our thoughts are far away. We agree to let Abu Qatadah buy a pizza, which tastes awful. Even the ketchup we get to add to it can't save it.

AFTER MALCOLM AND I have gone to bed, Frederic cleverly stays up to sit with Abu Qatadah for a while. Our relationship with IS is deteriorating dangerously with every passing day. Frederic's trying to do some damage control. Who knows if he'll succeed?

Freddy and Abu Qatadah talk about the accusations of corruption IS has made about Jabhat al-Nusra, the once-powerful rebel organization in Syria. And the "true" story of the U.S. Navy Seal operation in Abbottabad against Osama bin Laden. When the conversation threatens to slide into conspiracy theories, Frederic turns in as well.

DAY 7, FRIDAY, DECEMBER 12, 2014

IN THE MORNING, powerful bombs land very close to us. We are still lying in our sleeping bags. Five loud explosions. The whole bungalow shakes. It was bound to happen. Instead of going home, we're sitting tight here. And the Americans are dropping bombs.

Today is Friday, the day off in the Islamic week. We want to go to Friday prayers. But before we do that, we go to the market again. Hopefully, the Americans won't bomb the market. Between nine and eleven is when it is busiest here. We buy nuts, coffee, and raisins. I talk to a young boy about soccer. A crowd of people gathers around us. We leave before it gets too big. Everyone waves after us and smiles.

Shortly before prayers start, all the stores close their doors and drop their blinds. Everyone makes their way to the large mosque. It's so full many people lay their coats or scarves on the ground so that they can pray on them. Soon, there are several hundred people.

Among them a young man with an FC Bayern jersey. It's number 10, the number of the "unbeliever" Arjen Robben. The world is so small.

A couple of people saying their prayers are clearly disturbed that Frederic is filming. They stare at him questioningly. Abu Loth tells them they should concentrate on their prayers. Frederic climbs up onto the roof of a minibus so that he can get better shots.

The faithful have to listen to a warlike IS sermon. Here is some of what was said.

"WE ARE GOING to conquer Damascus. We are the ones who are going to be living in Mecca and Medina. And we'll conquer Constantinople. Hypocrites have done everything they can to destroy the Islamic State. Because it is clear to everyone that the Islamic State is now coming into existence. Therefore, they have fought this state and its fighters with every means at their disposal. But all they were capable of doing was to start circulating ugly rumors.

Oh Allah, destroy the unbelievers and the atheists and the manipulators.

Oh Allah, destroy America with a strike from the sky or from the earth.

Oh Allah, destroy the American planes.

Oh Allah, sink the American battleships.

Oh Allah, help the fighters who serve you destroy America.

Oh Allah, kill the oppressors and the atheists.

Oh Allah, kill all the unbelievers and do not spare any of them."

AFTER THE SERMON and the ritual Friday prayers, everyone goes their own way again. The colorful choreography of the crowd at prayer dissolves. We look for a juice stand. A young man sits down beside us. His light-brown uniform identifies him as a member of the religious police. He is a friend of Abu Loth's. And he speaks fluent German. So well that, like Abu Loth, he most certainly comes from Germany. But he won't talk about that. He leaves right away, before we can ask him too many questions.

FINALLY, OUR ESCORTS bring us to a once-elegant villa that has been almost completely destroyed by bombs. When it was attacked by U.S. bombers, the only people living here were civilians. Although supposedly there was an IS base nearby. Clearly, the attack hit the wrong house. The next house we are shown was also bombed by the Americans. The people who died here were all civilians as well. Since then, the Americans have changed their strategy. Now they restrict most of their bombing raids to the front lines.

AS WE DRIVE on, the conversation turns to Pierre Vogel. "He's a strange man," in Abu Loth's judgment. Vogel likes to present himself as a Salafi and a true Muslim, but in reality he is neither. He tries to reconcile Islam with democracy. "But that associates the two [a grave sin in Islam]. He should do his duty and emigrate. There is no middle path. There is no Islam with compromises!" Vogel has not understood that yet. Or he's enjoying his role as the best-known German Salafi and would prefer to enjoy the comforts of life in Germany. Abu Loth believes the latter.

Abu Loth, Abu Qatadah, and the others are hungry. They want cheeseburgers. We're not very taken with the idea, but we go along with them. Although the stores should have been closed after Friday prayer, exceptions are made for the fighters. Stores that sell cheeseburgers, fries, and Coke.

"I can't reconcile your American fast-food feast with the lifestyles of the first four caliphs," I quip. Abu Loth smiles but doesn't say anything. "You are what you eat!" I continue. But then I stop myself. The representatives of IS don't seem to be appreciating my criticism very much. Frederic, Malcolm, and I wait outside the store. We don't have any appetite for cheeseburgers.

THAT SEEMS TO be the end of our program for the day. We drive back to our accommodation. I pay our local driver a compliment: he is always very pleasant with us. He is only doing his duty, nothing more, he replies. I ask him what he would do if the Iraqi government regained control of territory conquered by IS.

He'd retreat into the desert with his brothers, he replies. There they would regroup, wait for the right moment, and then come back. That's what ISI, the precursor to IS, did as well. They came back stronger than ever before. They will never give up.

When we meet at our bungalows, our escorts are very agitated. Two U.S. bombers are circling the holiday camp. They are flying fairly low. As though they are just waiting to choose their targets. There is shooting close by. The IS fighters are frantically looking for cover. But there isn't any. The cheap bungalows don't offer any protection. Even Abu Qatadah is creeping around the bungalows. Hugging the walls and keeping his eye on the sky. Then he disappears from view.

The pilots have had their sights on us for a while. As a former pilot of private planes, I know how well you can see things from above just with your naked eye. And those planes up there are equipped with the latest in long-distance viewing equipment. We begin to feel queasy. The phrase: "If you can hear the rocket, you're dead" comes to mind. The pilots descend in ever-tighter circles. Frederic and Malcolm are pale. Even I feel the blood rushing from my face. We're helpless. The bomber crews must certainly have noticed that weapons are being unloaded from our vehicles. What should we do?

On a pitch not far away, younger and older men are playing soccer. They pay no attention to the bombers. They could be our salvation. The Americans wouldn't bomb a soccer pitch, would they? We hurry over to the sports field. We sit down at the edge of the field with a feeling of relief.

But still, one of the bombers circles lower. Directly above our heads. I'm extremely uneasy. I keep looking up at the sky. At the onset of darkness, we return to our bungalow. The noise of the bombers above us is joined by the menacing hum of drones. When will these machines of death call it quits?

IT'S BEEN A few hours since we last had any contact with our IS escorts. Malcolm goes over to the bungalow next door to ask what we should do next. Only Abu Loth and one of the drivers are there.

The others have driven to the center of town. Not a bad idea if you want to avoid getting bombed. But apparently, what they are doing is planning tomorrow's return journey. Abu Loth advises us to stay in the bungalow. Partly because those damned drones are still out there.

The buzz of the drones is so loud it drowns out the noise of the fan on the heating system. And we only turned that on so as not to hear the drones. So out there is a constant reminder that everything could be over at any moment. We feel enormously helpless and defenseless. Some coward in a room full of computers in a land far away has our lives in his hands.

Then Abu Loth comes in and advises us what to do in case of an attack. We should simply not leave the bungalow. Recently, six women were killed when they ran out into the street in panic. The drones immediately located them with their heat-seeking cameras and shot them. Does the Western world have any idea what is going on here?

I ask Abu Loth why such a distance has developed between us over the past few days. They've known from the beginning that I do not approve of what IS is doing. Abu Loth tries to make IS's position clear to us: "What it comes down to is that you are unbelievers. You don't believe in the real Islam. But you haven't made any mistakes or insulted anyone." The barriers of religion, it seems, are much more unsettling than my criticisms. These barriers will always be there. He says he even hates members of his own family because they haven't embraced the true belief. "Love of God is the greatest thing, the most important thing." His father thinks he is a Muslim. But at the same time, he is a firm believer in democracy. "It doesn't work like that. You can't submit to a country's constitution and say you believe in Allah, who demands something completely different from man-made laws."

And, apart from that, distrust is rife in IS. Everyone assumes there are secret service agents out there who are systematically undermining IS. For the most part, they come from Syria. That's why it's difficult to be accepted into the trusted inner circle. You can only advance if someone intercedes on your behalf. Even the people living here sometimes betray IS. Citizens in a suburb of Aleppo joined up with the FSA and suddenly, out of nowhere, started fighting IS. A lot of IS people were captured there. IS has a lot of enemies.

"You're an enemy, too," he tells me. They'd had the opportunity to review the written statements I'd made about IS. It's not easy to come to terms with having the enemy by your side every day, to travel with him, eat with him, sleep on the same ground with him.

Abu Loth would have been a great guy if he had fallen in with different friends and never encountered IS ideology. But as it is, he champions all the ideological junk his friends have talked him into believing. Take women, for example. Although they have some good qualities, basically they are physically and intellectually limited. That's the reason why in IS two witness statements from women equal one statement from a man. Women really should stay at home. That is where they are best protected. And, he reminds us, that's also how it was in the West just a couple of decades ago.

AROUND 8:00 PM, a silent Abu Qatadah brings us roast chicken. He's trying to play the role of the host to the end. No matter how difficult he finds it. Not bad, considering. As he leaves, he tells Frederic he's sent off the email he wrote down on a piece of paper to Valerie. We find out later the email never arrived. At home, panic broke out long ago.

DAY 8, SATURDAY, DECEMBER 13, 2014

THE RETURN JOURNEY starts at 8:00 AM. If all goes well, we could be in Raqqa in five hours. There we can collect our cell phones and my iPad. And then it's off to the Turkish border, which we hope to reach before darkness falls. That's quite an optimistic scenario, but I hope that's how things will unfold. After all, we wanted to be out of here two days ago.

Our departure is pushed back by half an hour because we can't find my left shoe. Yesterday evening, we left our shoes in front of the main door to the bungalow as usual. But one of them is missing.

Frederic and I search the area around our bungalow. The shoe is nowhere to be found. Perhaps a cat has carried it off. Is someone having fun with us? They are my favorite shoes, with special cushioned insoles. Without them, I would never have managed the seven-hour night march through the desert in Libya in 2011 that saved us from Gaddafi's troops. Luckily, I have another pair of shoes with me.

OUR GROUP IS divided up between two vehicles. Freddy, Malcolm, and I, along with Abu Loth and our two masked drivers from Raqqa, are going to go in a minibus. Abu Qatadah and an Iraqi IS fighter are going in a gray all-terrain vehicle. A third vehicle, a small yellow truck, is going to accompany us. To confuse the drones, which are still in the air today, every vehicle takes turns in the lead and then at the rear. We keep changing positions. For the most part, we keep many hundreds of yards apart. We have to be extremely careful. The driver and co-driver keep opening the side windows and looking worriedly up into the sky. It's raining, but that doesn't stop the drones.

Everyone's really quiet. Every once in a while, we chat with Abu Loth. He's surprised the German president himself is calling for more military operations. His message for Joachim Gauck: "If you're thinking of marching in here, you'd better start digging your soldiers' graves!"

To me, he says thoughtfully: "You're right. We are brutal. But we don't hide what we are doing, you do. IS has killed maybe 30,000 Iraqis. Bush killed 500,000."

In Iraq, he says, the people have no problem accepting IS. That's not the case in Raqqa yet. Assad still has more support than IS does. If it were put to a vote now, Assad would win in Raqqa. Cleverly, he continues to pay wages and pensions in Raqqa. Apart from that, people prefer fewer duties and rules than IS imposes. So it's no surprise they prefer Assad. I listen to him completely amazed. I'm glad I've got Freddy and Malcolm as witnesses!

The capture of Mosul, he tells us, is the result of long-term planning. "For years, we carried out so many martyr missions in Mosul that no one in Mosul felt safe anymore." There were attacks all the time. "We even sent suicide bombers to funerals." In the end, the Shias were in a constant state of fear. "That's why we could take Mosul so easily."

Abu Loth becomes serious. "Your invitation was decided at the highest levels. We wanted your visit to open up the door to the West. Perhaps you will soon know why." I make it clear I am particularly unsuited to mediation in their case. Our points of view are just too far apart. In Abu Loth's opinion, that's not a problem at all. All that does is make me even more trustworthy. "For you, perhaps, but not in the West," I tell him. I've experienced this time and time again in earlier attempts I've made at mediation. Whoever talks with the "enemy" is soon labeled a traitor in the West. The latest term for that in Germany is *Feind-Versteher,* "one who understands or is on good terms with the enemy," a term that laces flattery with irony. "From what I've learned about you," Abu Loth says, "I don't think you care."

Later, much to our amazement, the co-driver joins in the conversation. He wants to know why I don't convert to Islam. I'm worse than other Christians because they don't know any better. I, however, know better and still don't choose Islam.

WHEN OUR DRIVER, masked as ever, tries to avoid a traffic jam by taking an unpaved side road, we get stuck in sticky clay. We get out and all push together. It takes more than an hour to free the bus.

On the ramp to the main road, the bus gets stuck again. We try to organize help. An older man calls out in a loud voice: "We are in the Islamic State. Here we all support each other. Together we are strong. We will manage this." Someone else suggests he'd be better off getting a towrope instead of yelling. He does that and soon we're on our way again. But the journey back is dragging on.

OUR CO-DRIVER LOSES radio contact with Abu Qatadah. We wait on the side of the road, but the other car doesn't turn up. We have to go back. Perhaps something has happened to them. The masked driver keeps calling into his radio: "Abu Qatadah, Abu Qatadah!" No answer. He takes out his pistol and releases the safety catch. What's going to happen now? Suddenly, we see Abu Qatadah's vehicle on the side of the road. He has a flat tire. Again, we wait.

Abu Loth tells us about a friend of his who bought himself a slave. "A young Yazidi woman. Not particularly pretty." The brothers gave her a score of no more than four, adequate. Even though she cost so much he had to sell his Kalashnikov to buy her. She cost US$1,500. Because he had invested so much in her already, he sent her to a dentist to get her teeth fixed, and to a beauty salon to have her hair done, and things like that. He put a lot of money into her. And when she'd had her "makeover," he gave her a score of one or two. And what did she do then? "She ran off and left him." Abu Loth's story makes him burst out laughing. Even though the story is both tasteless and sad. "What an awful story!" says Frederic, who is hugely offended by slavery in IS. The only part of the story he finds cool is the slave's reaction. She gave the guy what was coming to him.

Our co-driver wants to talk with the driver of the little yellow truck. But he's tearing along so fast we can't catch up to him. We can't get closer than thirty feet. Our driver tries flashing his lights at him, but the truck driver doesn't react. Whenever we try to overtake him, he pulls his truck out to the left. We flash him and flash him. In vain! After a while, our driver loses patience. He rolls down the window, sticks his pistol out, and fires into the air a couple of times. No reaction. We have to laugh.

Our driver fires a couple more times into the air. Nothing happens. But this time, we almost manage to overtake the truck. As we draw up alongside him, our driver shoots multiple times into the air until the truck driver finally notices who's driving next to him. He listens very carefully to what the pistol-toting driver has to say to him while he races along beside him.

IT'S ALREADY 8:00 PM by the time we arrive in Raqqa. It's too late to continue on into Turkey today. The masked driver tells us we'll continue early, at six o'clock tomorrow morning.

In our apartment, we are greeted by chaos. The doors and windows are broken. There's shattered glass everywhere. What happened here? Abu Loth slaps his hands to his face in horror. Then he runs off to find out if there's somewhere else we can sleep.

A neighbor comes over and offers us bread. We thank him but decline. A couple of minutes later, he returns. This time with the owner of the trashed apartment. He asks us what we're doing here. Our friend will be right back, I say. He can explain everything. But that doesn't satisfy the owner of the apartment. He becomes downright unpleasant. He wants to know if we are Muslims. Malcolm answers: "No problem." But the apartment owner thinks otherwise. "You no Muslim, big problem..." Then he draws his thumb across his throat as though slitting it. The man who lives in the apartment building is now very agitated.

I take our guarantee of safety out of my breast pocket and hold it under his nose. The apartment owner reads the document with care and points reverentially to the stamp. *"Diwani al-Khalifa* (the stamp of the caliph). Ahh. No problem!" He shakes our hands.

Then he explains what happened here. A couple of days ago, the Syrian air force bombed the apartment next door. And completely annihilated it. Two people were killed. We go out onto the balcony so that he can show us exactly what happened. The façade next door is black with soot; the top floor is missing. If all had gone as planned, we would have been here two days ago. We've been lucky. Luckier than our Syrian neighbor.

TWO HOURS LATER, Abu Loth returns. He hasn't managed to find anywhere else. So we're going to spend the night here. Disappointed, we crawl into our sleeping bags. Damp cold creeps into the apartment through the broken windows. Before we fall asleep, Abu Loth tells us how "badass" he thinks 9/11 was. He hopes he too will be able to carry out an operation like that against the Americans soon. Now even I have completely had it with Abu Loth.

DAY 9, SUNDAY, DECEMBER 14, 2014

WHEN WE WAKE up, it's already shortly before eight. Things were supposed to start happening at six. But our driver hasn't checked in. When Abu Loth serves up coffee, beans, and hummus an hour later, we become even more impatient. When are we finally going to be able to leave?

Once again, I ask Abu Loth about the possibility that the British journalist John Cantlie will be set free. Abu Loth promises to speak again with those responsible. Then he reminds me why IS agreed to my visit. I was invited because they wanted to demonstrate the "Islamic State" isn't a state in name only but really is a state. Life here is perfectly normal. The wounded and the sick are well looked after. The state looks after the poor. People are treated justly in the courts of law. "People feel safe with us. Even if some of them don't like us, they like the security we bring. We simply wanted to show you how we live. And show that people can live with sharia and it works."

"For heaven's sake! Where is it written in the Quran that you can cut the heads off innocent people?" I ask. Abu Loth can see I am not convinced.

IN THE MEANTIME, it's now 2:00 PM. We are still sitting in our apartment. Abu Loth heads off to scout things out. Five minutes later Abu Qatadah arrives. We'll be leaving right away. He returns Frederic's camera equipment. Ten out of eight hundred photos have been erased on the final check. Along with the interview with the judge. So as not to endanger the people involved and their families, we're told. Frederic must also take out one question and one answer on the subject of "moderate Muslims" from the interview with Abu Qatadah. Abu Qatadah's statements on this issue were too vague for IS. IS okayed the rest of his statements. Frederic is relieved and agrees. All the important films and photos have survived the censors.

ABU LOTH IS back, completely out of breath. He's spoken with his superiors and he has two important pieces of news for me. If I want to ask the British prime minister David Cameron to make an offer, John Cantlie could be set free very quickly. IS is ready to negotiate. The offer must be fair and realistic. Nothing pie-in-the-sky.

Abu Loth takes me to one side. The leadership of IS might consider exchanging John Cantlie for Aafia Siddiqui. The exchange could happen even without the official involvement of the British government. I should definitely see what I can do. It's an encouraging offer on the part of IS. Abu Loth is very excited. It seems he does have a human side after all.

As for me, he tells me all doors are open as long as I report the truth about the "Islamic State." We can then set up any appointments we want and check out anything we want.

We say good-bye. Abu Qatadah and Abu Loth shake our hands. "Look after yourselves!" says Abu Loth. I press the watch from Mosul into his hand. Abu Loth looks at me with surprise. I have to laugh. Our masked driver is there as well. He's going to take us to the Turkish border.

IT'S ALREADY DARK by the time we stop near the Turkish border four hours later at around 6:30 PM. A man is standing on the street outside the recruiting center. It is the powerful, grim IS fighter from our first day. Our driver tells us we have to get out of the car now and take our luggage with us. In a few moments, a vehicle will arrive and take us to Turkey. He turns around and gets back into the car. Then he gives the powerful IS man our cell phones. He hesitates for a moment as though he wants to tell us something. Then he drives away without saying good-bye.

Within a couple of minutes, a car appears. Our IS man talks briefly to the driver. The result of this exchange is that we can't cross the border today. There are too many Turkish soldiers. It should be okay by early tomorrow morning. In the East the concept of time is somewhat different from in Germany. And this holds true for the "Islamic State" as well.

We're taken to a dreary room where people are already saying their prayers. Our escort tells us to make ourselves comfortable.

Unfortunately, there is nothing to eat. And other than a small cup of tea, he can't offer us anything to drink either. Despite this, we spend a long time talking to the fighter. He tells us about Islam. We listen to him until we fall asleep in our sleeping bags on the cold floor. The last story I hear has to do with splitting the moon (a miracle attributed to the Prophet Muhammad).

DAY 10, MONDAY, DECEMBER 15, 2014

NINE THIRTY AM. We're sitting and waiting. Unfortunately, there's still nothing to eat or drink. Not even a glass of water. Apparently, there are still Turkish soldiers hanging around at the border. No one can get through. Despite this, every twenty minutes or so, a minibus arrives from the other side of the border with new young fighters. They are registered, photographed, and searched. IS immigration control and customs. The new recruits include young Africans, Russians, lots of Turks, and even one German.

We are impressed by a large muscular young man from Trinidad and Tobago. He's wearing khaki pants with ironed creases; a colorful, checked, freshly ironed shirt; and Ray-Ban sunglasses. Just a few weeks ago, he passed the state law exam in his home country and was admitted to the bar. Now he's here. Why? "Too much promiscuity, too many one-night stands. Everyone with someone else. That can't be what life is all about." He finds Western values empty, tedious. And what does he want to do now in IS? "I'll do what is asked of me. If I'm asked to fight, I will fight. If I'm asked to work as a lawyer, then I'll do that. The emir will decide." He's excited about his new life. Finally he is in the "promised land."

OUR IMPATIENCE GROWS. When 3:00 PM rolls by and we still haven't been let out, I go into the courtyard and begin to negotiate with the smugglers. I don't want to sit around here for another couple of days. There must be some way to get us across the border. But most of the smugglers don't dare. Because of the soldiers. I ask the head of the smugglers how much money he wants.

"What are you offering?" he asks.

"Five hundred euros," I answer.

He laughs. "A good offer, but I'll get you out for nothing. You are our guest."

Frederic is mistrustful and upset. I don't even know the man. But the IS people here know him. And they agree.

We get our cell phones back. They are wrapped in aluminum foil. We're told not to unwrap them until we get to Turkey. Then we get into a small, run-down pickup truck. Frederic and Malcolm sit in the truck bed next to two gas cans. The smell is overpowering and the space is really tight. For a change, I'm the one that gets to sit up front. We have our press credentials and passports at the ready. Off we go.

TO OUR AMAZEMENT, we drive just a couple of hundred yards over a bumpy field. Then we turn off to the right and stop under some olive trees. From here we can see an armed Turkish watchtower. That doesn't look very reassuring. Three smugglers behind a tree point the way. We must run over there. We need to get out right now and start running. Our hearts race.

WE THROW OPEN the doors, grab our bags and backpacks, and set out at a run. It's not easy to run over a plowed field while carrying heavy bags. There are reeds to our right. "If they start shooting," one of the smugglers calls after us, "dive into the reeds on your right and keep running." It's about another three hundred yards to the border fence.

The smuggler who is running ahead of us lifts up the barbed wire. "*Yalla, yalla!* (Hurry up!) Keep on coming." Freddy gets stuck, his right arm caught in the barbed wire. He rips himself free. His jacket is toast. Keep on running! In the distance, we see the white van we came in. Faster! No one wants to be shot by Turkish border guards with only a few yards to go. Fifty yards more. The van's doors are wide open. We throw ourselves inside. The driver steps on the gas before we can shut the doors properly.

We made it! We are completely out of breath and drenched in sweat. My heart is racing. A ton weight falls from my shoulders. We've survived the whole mad enterprise.

After a couple of minutes, we're allowed to unwrap our cell phones. Immediately, I call home. Nathalie screams at me in anger. Why didn't we call! Then she starts to sob. My wife, Françoise; Valerie; and Malcolm's mother all break down into tears when they hear our voices, and they can't stop crying. They haven't heard anything from us in more than a week. Now everything's okay again. "We're out! We're fine!"

VIII

A Chilling Thought

A COUPLE OF DAYS after our return, Freddy gives me a call. "Do you recognize this voice?" he asks. The voice I hear is unclear. But the rhythm of the speech pattern seems familiar. "That's our driver. Did you secretly record him when you were filming?" I ask. Freddy replies earnestly: "That is Jihadi John, the executioner. Can I come round?"

A LITTLE WHILE later, we are sitting in my apartment looking at Freddy's laptop. Freddy plays me the video where Jihadi John threatens to behead two kidnapped Japanese nationals. It's as though someone has slapped me upside the head. The rhythmic, driving speech pattern, the mostly half-closed eyes, that piercing stare, the body language—exactly like our "driver." Although the voice in the video has been electronically altered by lowering its pitch, for me there's hardly a shadow of a doubt. We had spent too long with our driver. His gruff interventions, his commands, had left too strong an impression on us. Baffled, I keep shaking my head. Had we really spent days on the road with Jihadi John? Were our suspicions correct after all?

Frederic calls up another video. This time, Jihadi John is speaking while standing next to the handcuffed U.S. journalist James Foley. Shortly before his execution. Again, the same sense of déjà vu. Here again, it is clearly our driver speaking.

Frederic has one more surprise. He's found a YouTube video released by the infamous hacker group Anonymous. Supposedly, in this video you can hear Jihadi John's real voice. Where possible, Anonymous has restored Jihad John's voice to its normal pitch. We can hardly believe it. The voice in the edited video sounds just like the voice of our driver. Frederic says quietly: "That's exactly how he spoke to you on the first day in Raqqa when he was so furious. And that's exactly how he spoke to me in Mosul when he took my cameras away. I will never forget that. Even though I've tried."

And recently published photos of Jihadi John show an incredible similarity to the man I saw—albeit briefly—without his disguise. And they also match the outline of the masked face that sat diagonally across from and in front of me in the car for so many days. That's not 100 percent proof. And I would never pretend it is. Our "driver" didn't let us photograph him. But I can't suppress our amazing discoveries either.

Everything fit together. The way he appeared to have easy access to the journalist John Cantlie. His irritation when I refused to take part in the propaganda show with Cantlie. His absurd disguise all day and all night. The way he freaked out when I happened to see him one day without his disguise.

FREDERIC READS ME an announcement from the FBI from September 2014 that says Jihadi John belongs to a terror cell called "The Beatles." According to freed hostages, it was his job to guard the hostages and communicate with their families. And that is exactly what our "driver" tried to do when he wanted to arrange and film the exchange of two letters from John Cantlie to his family and to the British prime minister.

He was the "star" of the brutal IS beheading videos that made such a deep impression when they presented the face of the "Islamic

State" to the world. There are probably other executioners besides him, who stood in for him from time to time. Maybe that's why he wanted to be there during my journey through the "Islamic State." To make sure that we didn't distort the image of IS and its blood lust that he had so carefully choreographed.

I tell Frederic about a conversation I had the previous day with an anti-terrorism specialist when I happened to ask him what the striking physical characteristics of Jihadi John were. "A noticeably hooked nose," he'd answered. And no nose could be more noticeable than the hooked nose of our "driver." Even the heavy wrap couldn't hide the bold curve of his nose when he turned his face to us in the car every now and then. People who knew Jihadi John from his youth commented on his magnificent head of dark, curly hair. And when I saw our "driver" without his mask, he, too, had thick hair that fell down the back of his neck.

FREDERIC CALLS MALCOLM and asks him to drop by. Half an hour later, he plays Malcolm the two videos featuring Jihadi John. Without saying a word. Malcolm's eyes open wide. He keeps murmuring: "It can't be." When he's finished looking at the videos, he looks at us completely confused. "That can't be, right?" he says. "That's our driver."

We part wordlessly and somewhat at a loss. At a loss because we're not sure whether I should mention in my book that we probably spent almost every day of our trip in the "Islamic State" with one of the most brutal executioners in the world. We had no doubt IS would deny everything. After all, Jihadi John was one of the most sought-after terrorists in the world.

Freddy snaps his computer shut. The next day, he sends Abu Qatadah the audio Anonymous released with the supposedly true voice of Jihadi John. He asks whether the voice doesn't remind him of our "driver." The terse response comes right away.

"No."

"Are you sure?" Freddy asks.

"Of course!" Abu Qatadah replies.

IX

An Open Letter to the Caliph of the "Islamic State" and His Foreign Fighters

OW POLITE OR distanced should such a letter be? In 1939, one month before war broke out, Mahatma Gandhi wrote a letter to Adolf Hitler "in the name of humanity." The letter began "Dear Friend" and ended "Your sincere friend, M.K. Gandhi." I could not be that amicable. But I also did not want to be impolite. So this is what I wrote.

Dear Caliph Ibrahim Awwad, Abu Bakr al-Baghdadi:

First of all, I thank you for the full compliance with your guarantee of safety during our stay in the "Islamic State." You should invite freelance correspondents from all over the world more often, instead of ordering the execution of journalists.

According to new research by International Physicians for the Prevention of Nuclear War (IPPNW), George W. Bush's war in Iraq, which was illegal, according to international law, killed more than a million innocent people. I can understand every Arab who opposes the West's centuries-old policy of military intervention. I am not blind to the West's iniquity.

You have led a military campaign in Syria and Iraq that has, to some extent, been exceptionally successful and that no one would have thought possible. Although even you will find out how fickle the fortunes of war can be. However, the methods your organization uses in your military actions are, according to the dictates of the Quran, both un-Islamic and counterproductive. You are damaging the whole Muslim world. Above all Islam, in whose name you profess to fight.

Terror has as little to do with Islam as rape has to do with love. Therefore, you and your fighters are not "holy warriors." If such a thing even exists. Perhaps that's not even what you want to be. After all, the expression comes from the time of the Crusades and is "Christian." I have profited greatly from reading the Quran many times. Nowhere in it have I found the spirit of brutality that you and your fighters deliberately incite. Unless one rips out of its historical context the description of the aggressive attacks the people of Mecca made on Muhammad's militarily inferior Medina in the years 623 to 630. Enemies of Islam like to do that.

Incidentally, the myths and historical passages in the Old Testament describe far bloodier wars than the Quran. That is why the Jewish evolutionary psychologist Steven Pinker calls the Old Testament "one long celebration of violence." Nevertheless, it is only ignorant people who consider these descriptions of slaughter to be the essence of the Old Testament. The Old Testament is a book about fairness and brotherly love. Like the Quran.

Unfortunately, the central idea of Islam, its call to fairness, equality, and mercy—a call that was revolutionary for its time—appears to be alien to you. Even though this key message is a common thread that runs through the Quran.

No word appears in the Quran to describe God more frequently than the word "merciful." All but one of the 114 surahs begin with the phrase "In the name of Allah, the Beneficent, the Merciful." Certainly nothing is further removed from mercy than your warfare. You carry out your campaigns to expand the "Islamic State" in the tradition of medieval orgies of power like the hordes of Genghis Khan and Pol Pot. Furthermore, you are quite specifically planning the largest "religious purge" in history, the killing of hundreds of millions of "unbelievers and apostates." I keep asking myself where that is written in Islam.

1. In Islam, there is no compulsion in matters of faith (surah 2, verse 256). You, however, have people murdered in the most bestial fashion just because they are Shias, Alawis, Yazidis, or Sunnis who support democracy. Unless they convert of their own free will to your ruthless ideology. In other words, submit to your supremacy. For centuries, religious tolerance was the most famous virtue of Islamic rulers. Where, dear Caliph, is your tolerance?

2. In Islam, wars of aggression are clearly prohibited (e.g., in surah 22, verse 39). The Prophet never engaged in wars of aggression. He was only ever attacked—by the militarily far-superior forces of the Meccans, who followed a different religion. But you, Mr. Caliph, wantonly attack whole regions, towns, and villages that have not harmed you in any way.

3. In Islam, the killing of civilians, women, children, and old people is forbidden. This is expressed in no uncertain terms in many places in the Quran. But your followers execute innocent people in the most repulsive ways. And they rape women, an abomination the Quran condemns in the strongest terms (surah 24, verse 33). That's supposed to be Islamic?

4. In Islam, the destruction of religious sites is forbidden (surah 22, verse 40). But you call for the destruction and desecration of churches, synagogues, and Shia and even Sunni mosques. That, too, is completely anti-Islamic.

There are many more examples that can be added to this list of your almost exhibitionistic violations against the Quran. Essentially, except for outward appearances, everything you do is anti-Islamic, a program that opposes Islam.

I am a Christian. From the Gospel according to John, my religion is familiar with the existence of the "Anti-Christ." Through your deeds and your existence, I am learning that clearly the "Anti-Muslim" exists as well. Not even the most learned heads of Islam foresaw that this Anti-Muslim would call himself the "Caliph of the Islamic State." They had no idea that someone could mock Islamic history and the Islamic religion with such a complete lack of restraint. You should actually rename the area you have captured the "Anti-Islamic State—AIS."

What you say and do is not only a program that opposes Islam but also the ministry of the Prophet. Muhammad was merciful, but you are merciless. Muhammad was a forward-looking revolutionary. You are a backward-looking reactionary. It is absurd to advance the idea that Muhammad, one of the most dynamic reformers in history, would continue to live by ancient customs and practices 1,400 years after his death. Great revolutionaries take care not to rest on their laurels. You, Abu Bakr al-Baghdadi, may be a remarkable military commander. A reformer, a man of God, of "the Beneficent, the Merciful" you are not.

Many terrorist organizations before IS have violated Islam and misused it to mask un-Islamic deeds. And some misguided rulers and religious scholars have also put their own slant on this great religion. There are similar cases in the history of Christianity. Many devilish deeds have been carried out in the name of Christianity. And you, Mr. Al-Baghdadi, are really preaching not Islam but your private religion, your private sharia.

Your followers point to the fact that George W. Bush killed considerably more people than they have. And he did so in a war that was illegal under international law. That must still be the case, at least for the time being, if your advance is not stopped soon. On numerous occasions, I have demanded that those responsible for the war in Iraq be tried by the International Criminal Court. Bush and Blair included.

But you are different from Bush on four very important points.

1. At least the former U.S. president, perpetrator of serious war crimes, did not publicly boast about or gloat over the torture and humiliation of prisoners in Abu Ghraib, Guantanamo, or Bagram. Neither did he gloat or boast about GIs who committed shameful

murders and rapes that had nothing to do with their combat operations. He never made these shameful deeds the focal point of his campaign. And he did not make them the focal point of the message of Christianity either. That is, if you ignore a few rhetorical gaffes at the beginning of the war when he talked about going on a "crusade" and briefly compared himself to Isaiah.

2. Unlike you, he never deliberately targeted innocent civilians, and he never took pleasure in celebrating and filming their murders. Journalists, aid workers, and people like that.

3. Unlike you, he never planned a religious "purge," with the goal of extinguishing all non-Abrahamic religions. A purge in which many hundreds of millions of people would have to die. You are planning the largest genocide of all time. A campaign that will overshadow everything humanity has suffered so far. You are abusing the name of Islam to achieve your goals! That is blasphemy.

4. At the same time, you have officially reintroduced slavery, an institution people in modern times have taken great pains to eliminate. It once existed in all cultures. But all cultures, ashamed, did away with this debasement of people to commodities, to beings somewhere between people and animals, a long time ago. The Jews, the Christians, the Muslim world. Even though the criminal underground still treats many people as though they were slaves or possessions. Unlike you, Muhammad always looked for ways he could help slaves become citizens with full rights. And so he made Bilal, a black ex-slave, Islam's first prayer caller.

You publicly execute people to provoke their countries into military action. And in these actions, it is predominantly Muslims who will die. You want war. Just as bin Laden did when he used 9/11 to lure the USA into the war in Afghanistan. Is that Islamic? I knew the American journalist James Foley personally from the revolutionary days in Benghazi. He was a likeable, shy colleague. A few days after some friends and I were ambushed by Gaddafi's military, he was captured by these men. Gaddafi is difficult to top when it comes to brutality, but Gaddafi treated James Foley a thousand times better than your brutal fighters did.

I personally got to know some of your foreign fighters. I had in-depth conversations with them for hours. And I address this open letter to them as well.

I call on all foreign jihadists to break away from the "Islamic State" and return to their homelands and face the authorities. You will get fair trials. And, hopefully, sensible programs for reintegration.

I am addressing these foreign fighters. I assume that some of you joined IS because of ignorance, youthful naïveté, conviction, idealism, and—maybe—righteous anger. But if you walk through the world with your eyes open, it must have become clear to you that every twenty-year-old armed with a Kalashnikov or a butcher's knife cannot set himself up as a murderous judge over the rest of the world.

The targeted murder of innocent people and religious genocide can never be justified. You do not have the right to harm the reputation of the great religion of Islam by perversely murdering people and trying to eradicate other religions. No one is more delighted by your crimes than the many enemies of Islam around the world. Doesn't Islam already have enough enemies? One might almost think "IS/AIS" is their creation.

Whoever truly loves Islam should no longer play along with this genocidal game. Abu Bakr al-Baghdadi has abused your ideals. If you are true Muslims, you must put an end to this horrific episode and counter the inhuman anti-Islamism of "IS/AIS." Even if it means putting your lives at risk. Then you would be true heroes of Islam. It takes more courage to correct mistakes than it does to simply continue lemming-like down the wrong, blood-soaked path. You are a danger not to the Western world but to the Muslim world.

In Gaza, during the war in the summer of 2014, I asked a Palestinian who had lost almost everything what he thought of IS. He looked at me in disbelief and asked: "Do we have to take the blame for them as well now?"

My wish for you, dear Caliph Ibrahim, is that the warring parties in Iraq and Syria finally unite and so take away the breeding grounds for your military actions.

May Allah stop you! But I wish true Islam and the 1.6 billion moderate Muslims in this world well. Tolerant Islam has a place not only in Germany but also in cultures around the world.

I end this letter with ten passages from the Quran that, in my opinion, characterize this great book better than anything you have done or said over the last few years. You should at least give them a quick look before history sweeps you aside.

Ten key passages from the Quran that, apparently, you are not familiar with.

1. Do not argue with the People of the Book except only by the best manner... Tell them, "We believe in what is revealed to us and to you. Our Lord and your Lord is one." 29:46.

2. We believe in God and what He has revealed to us... and what was revealed to Moses, Jesus, and the Prophets from their Lord. We make no distinction among them. 2:136. There is no compulsion in religion. 2:256. Do you force people to have faith? 10:99.

3. Had God wanted, He could have made you into one nation, but He wanted to see who are the more pious ones among you. Compete with each other in righteousness. All of you will return to God who will tell you the truth in the matter of your differences. 5:48. Those who have become believers (the Muslims), and the Jews, the Christians and the Sabaeans... will receive their reward from the Lord. 2:62.

4. Believe and act righteously. 25:70. God commands (people) to maintain justice, kindness, and proper relations with their relatives. He forbids them to commit indecency, sin, and rebellion. 16:90.

5. Keep away evil with good. 13:22. Compete with each other in performing good deeds. 2:148. God loves people who do good deeds. 2:195. Be kind to your parents, relatives, orphans, the destitute, your near and distant neighbors... God does not love the proud and boastful ones. 4:36. Whatever you (people) have been given are only the means for enjoyment and beauty of the worldly life. 28:60. For a single good deed, one will be rewarded tenfold. But the recompense for a bad deed will be equal to that of the deed. 6:160.

6. (Among) the servants of the Beneficent God are those who walk gently on the earth and when addressed by the ignorant ones, their only response is, "Peace be with you." 25:63. Be moderate in your walking and your talking. The most unpleasant sound is the braying of donkeys. 31:19.

7. One who acts righteously does so for his own benefit, and one who commits evil does so against his own soul. 45:15.

8. Do not abuse the earth with corruption. 2:60. Make peace among people. 2:224.

9. The recompense for evil will be equivalent to the deed. He who pardons... will receive his reward from God. 42:40. Reconciliation is good. 4:128.

10. And here are the surahs you have sinned against most. The killing of a person... is as great a sin as murdering all of mankind. However, to save a life would be as great a virtue as to save all of mankind. 5:32. Take not a life which God has made sacred. 6:151.

These are words to live by. Instead of your ruthless anti-Islamic ideology.

I thank you once again for your hospitality! And for giving me the opportunity to visit—with relatively few constraints—the country you rule. I would very much like to have visited a real Islamic state. It could easily have taken a stand against Western injustices and pretensions. I heartily regret that, in the end, all I got to know was an anti-Islamic state.

Yours Sincerely,
Jürgen Todenhöfer

X

A Warning to the West

ONCE AGAIN, THE West is waging war in the Middle East. Is it the twentieth, the thirtieth war in this oil-rich area of the world? This time the war is against IS, the self-declared "Islamic State," whose demonstrated brutality has sent shivers around the world. But is the West's ultimate goal really to put a stop to its medieval-style brutality? Or is the West intervening because IS is now interfering with its oil interests in Iraq? At any rate, IS fighters have succeeded in gaining control of a strategic crude oil pipeline from Iraq to Turkey, thus destroying the lifeline of the Iraqi oil industry.

The USA has always been ready to wage war to ensure the trouble-free extraction and delivery of oil. As long as IS fighters were murdering and beheading only in Syria, a long way from the much larger Iraqi oil fields, the USA did not try to stop them. They even indirectly supported them. Through their allied Gulf states. In a July 19, 2015, interview on the al-Jazeera program *Head to Head,* the former head of the DIA, Michael Flynn, openly made some very frightening comments on this subject.

The USA also waved through deliveries of cash and weapons to the other large Syrian terrorist organizations: Jabhat al-Nusra, the

Islamic Front, and Ahrar al-Sham. To a certain extent, they even coordinated with one another through their respective secret service agencies. Because they were fighting Assad. Assad, the ally of Iran, who had become too powerful for the USA as a result of the 2003 war in Iraq and the overthrow of his enemy Saddam Hussein. So what is really going on in the West with these wars?

THE RISE OF the West, which began five hundred years ago, has never been about altruism. Nor has it been about bringing civilization to the rest of the world. It has been all about the steady pursuit of its own economic interests. And the ruthlessness of its armies. It is true that leaders of the Western world usually advance noble motives to ensure support for their choices and their actions. First, they slaughtered people of other cultures in the name of Christianity, then in the name of human rights and democracy. But really it is always about money, power, and glory. To this day. The American academic Samuel Huntington agreed with many historians when he stated: "The West won the world not by the superiority of its ideas or values ... but rather by its superiority in applying organized violence. Westerners often forget this fact; non-Westerners never do." Acts of violence by the West knew no bounds. They often exceeded even the bestial acts of IS terrorists today.

Louis de Baudicour, a French author and colonist, described one of the innumerable barbarous acts carried out by the French in Algeria: "Here, for fun, a soldier cut off a woman's breast; there another picked a child up by its legs and smashed its skull against a wall." The famous French author Victor Hugo told of soldiers who threw children to each other and caught them on the tips of their bayonets. Ears preserved in salt were worth one hundred sous apiece.

Severed heads were worth more, of course. Until the end of the war in Algeria in 1962, beheadings of Algerian freedom fighters were the order of the day. The severed heads were then put on public show—as they are today in the "Islamic State."

It wasn't any better for Iraqis under British rule. In 1920, after their rebellion against the British Crown, Winston Churchill accused them of being "ungrateful." He was prepared to use chemical weapons "with excellent moral effect," as he proudly remarked.

In Libya, tribal leaders were bundled into airplanes and thrown from great heights. Colonial Italian troops kept Libyan girls as sex slaves. Hundreds of thousands of civilians were locked up in concentration camps in the desert, where half of them died miserable deaths.

NOTHING HAS CHANGED about these sadistic atrocities today. We have simply not been paying attention or we have pushed them to the back of our minds. The Muslim world has not forgotten them. According to people high up in the American military, it was more barbaric in Bagram, the U.S. torture prison near Kabul, than in Guantanamo. Taliban prisoners were raped by camp dogs (!) until they confessed to everything. I published the eyewitness testimony of a Western security specialist. No one was outraged. What would have happened if American GIs had been raped by dogs?

Western "campaigners for human rights" were similarly brutal after the 2003 war in Iraq. Manal, a young Iraqi girl, was forced to watch an American GI rape a young Iraqi resistance fighter in the airport jail in Baghdad. She screamed her humiliation out to the world hundreds of time and was dragged before the courts. No one was interested. It was, after all, not an American girl whose life had been shattered.

Recent reports state that prisoners in Guantanamo have been abused by female guards. Sometimes by two women at the same time. After the sexual attacks were publicized in the USA, the guards were simply given a warning. It seems that sexually abusing Arabs is not a crime in Western eyes. The acclaimed German news magazine *Der Spiegel* covered the story extensively. No one was interested in the scandal.

When IS fighters commit similar crimes, Western outrage knows no bounds. Governments sit down together and military staff brainstorm to come up with strategies so that we can put a stop to these shameless attacks on "our values." Crimes carried out by Arabs are clearly in a different category from crimes we carry out ourselves. This is racism in its most repulsive form.

According to the French philosopher Jean-Paul Sartre, the West has always dealt with Arabs as though they were lesser humans on a level with the higher apes. They were the "inhabitants" of Arabia but not the real "owners" of the land. Even the great French politician and journalist Alexis de Tocqueville stated: "If we reason from what passes in the world, we should almost say that the European is to the other races of mankind what man himself is to the lower animals: he makes them subservient to his use, and when he cannot subdue them he destroys them."

IN THE PAST two hundred years, an Arab country has never once invaded a Western country. The aggressors have always been the European superpowers. Millions of Arab civilians have been brutally murdered in these conflicts. Talk of the cruelty of the Muslims turns all the facts upside down. The West has been far more cruel.

And not only for the Muslim world. When Mahatma Gandhi was asked what he thought of Western civilization, supposedly he answered: "I think it would be a good idea." He found the reality of Western dominion as experienced in India "satanic." In 1975, when I was a young member of parliament, I gave the Indian prime minister Indira Gandhi an unsolicited lecture about the importance of human rights in Western politics. She asked in astonishment, "Do you really believe that?"

Former NATO supreme allied commander Wesley Clark reported that shortly after 9/11, the Pentagon gave him a secret list of seven rogue states they wanted to attack in the next five years. Iraq, Libya, Syria, and Iran were all on the list. Bush's warmongers didn't want to miss the unique opportunity presented by the September 11 terrorist attacks. In the words of Clark, they wanted to seize the moment to instigate a number of wars so that they could "destabilize the Middle East, turn it upside down, make it under our control." Honorable justifications would be found.

It is difficult for the Western public to see through such cynical Western political maneuvers. They really believe we are on the side of "good." The bogeyman of Islam, as portrayed by the West for hundreds of years, has made a deep impression. But it is a manipulated image.

It was not the Muslims who invented "the holy war" and butchered more than 4 million Muslims and Jews during the Crusades. It was Christians in Jerusalem who "waded up to their ankles in blood until they came crying tears of joy" to the grave of the Redeemer. It was also not the Muslims who massacred 50 million in the name of colonization in Africa and Asia. It was not the Muslims who instigated the First and Second World Wars, which left 70 million dead. And it was not the Muslims but the Germans who murdered 10 million Slavs and 6 million Jews—fellow citizens, neighbors, and friends—in a cowardly and shameful way. When have our so-called Christian politicians been a credit to Christianity, that wonderful religion of love? When and where have they treated the fellow religions of Judaism and Islam with love and respect?

Continents and countries conquered by Western powers in the last five hundred years have not passively accepted our barbarity. Although the majority of the population usually fell into line, nearly everywhere there were resistance groups. Either peaceful like Gandhi's "civil disobedience" in India. Or armed like the erstwhile FLN (National Liberation Front) in Algeria or the legal Iraqi civilian resistance to the U.S. invasion in 2003, an invasion that was illegal according to international law.

Certainly, as the French writer Jean Cocteau recognized: "The purity of revolution lasts at most two weeks." Legal resistance quickly morphs into murderous terrorism. Not only in the Muslim world. Apart from Christian terrorists such as George Habash, founder of the Popular Front for the Liberation of Palestine, who allowed Jewish settlers to be brutally murdered, there are also Zionist terrorist organizations such as Menachem Begin's Irgun (the National Military Organization in the Land of Israel) or Yitzhak Shamir's Lehi

(Fighters for the Freedom of Israel). The latter self-identify as terrorists. The terrorists Begin and Shamir later became prime ministers of their country. Both were heavily courted and supported by the West.

TERRORISM IS A global phenomenon, not a Muslim phenomenon. According to the Global Terrorism Database, one of the official centers of excellence funded by the U.S. government, there were 239 terrorist attacks in the Western world in 2013. Only 2 were carried out by Muslims. The year before, the number was 6 out of 196. Most of the 239 were carried out by persons unknown, followed by separatists, extremists on the left, extremists on the right, Protestants, and such.

The oft-repeated sentence: "Not every Muslim is a terrorist, but every terrorist is a Muslim" is malignant nonsense, even if the "Islamic" terror attacks have been disproportionately bloody. In Germany, at the time of writing, in 2015, not a single German has been killed by "Islamic" terrorists, but since 1990, twenty-nine Muslims have been murdered by right-wing radicals. Think of the NSU murders (the National Socialist Underground is a far-right German terrorist group uncovered in 2011) or the murders of Mölln (in 1992, right-wing extremists set fire to Turkish-inhabited houses, killing three girls) and Solingen (a politically motivated arson attack against a Turkish family in 1993; five died and fourteen were injured, some severely). Anti-Islamic hatemongers do not let such facts get in their way.

The "Islamic" terrorism of recent years rages first and foremost in the Middle East. Stirred up by the USA's wars on terror in Afghanistan, Iraq, and Libya, which were veritable breeding grounds for terrorism. But this terrorism, as dreadful as it was for its victims in the East and West, didn't really disrupt American global strategies. On the contrary, it delivered important pretexts to continue intervening in the axis of oil and natural gas—the so-called axis of evil—with the consent of American voters. According to former U.S. secretary of state Henry Kissinger, oil was far too valuable a commodity to be left in the hands of the Arabs.

Terrorists are the "villains" U.S. politicians always need to legitimize their military interventions. There is the famous pronouncement of the distraught former general Colin Powell after the collapse of the Soviet Union: "I'm running out of villains!" If there were no terrorists, the USA would invent them. And sometimes they do.

You can read a lot about the aggressive American strategies for oil and gas in official documents. It was around May 1997 when the U.S. government declared that it was obliged to intervene militarily to ensure "unimpeded access to key markets, energy supplies, and strategic resources." Only idiots don't get what it's all about in world politics today: "It's the oil, stupid!" Oil, the black gold on which American prosperity depends. Oil, the Devil's most malicious gift.

TERRORISTS SEE THEIR attacks as a justified answer to the aggressively exploitative policies of the USA, which treats their countries as though they were nothing more than American gas stations. And employs the most brutal methods. Day after day, year after year, young Muslims in Germany and in Iraq see how Muslim men, women, and children in Afghanistan, Pakistan, Iraq, Yemen, Somalia, and Palestine are severely wounded or killed by Western weapons, Western allies, and soldiers from the West. Until some of them, at some point, react. No one comes into this world a terrorist.

Those who bear the brunt of this terrorism—allegedly to liberate the Middle East—are the civilians who live there. Muslims and Christians in equal measure. Just as they bear the brunt of the bombing raids with which those in the West believe they can "combat" this terror. The overwhelming majority of Muslims and Christians stand defenseless and desperate in the middle of this vicious vortex of power.

Terrorists in the Middle East know they are only a minority. They know the overwhelming majority of Muslims would like to find peaceful ways of freeing themselves from their misery. Terrorism in the Middle East is a minority phenomenon. But terrorists see it as their duty to save the Muslim world. A duty they supposedly cannot avoid. Above all, not when the West ridicules and walks roughshod all over their religion and the holiest of Muslims. The West does not understand that ridiculing the Prophet Muhammad inflames and provokes extremists just as much as a bombing raid does. And this doesn't interest the West either. What is important, after all, is to defend our values and not those of the Muslim world.

Most terrorists know that, militarily speaking, they don't stand a chance against the West. They understand that, above all, they are destroying themselves and their own world. Jean-Paul Sartre described this self-destructive despair in 1961, during the fight for the liberation of Algeria: "Suppressed anger circles in on itself and causes devastation in the oppressed. In order to escape it, they butcher each other. Tribes fight other tribes because they cannot engage the real enemy and they can be sure that the colonial powers will stir up their rivalries. The raging torrent of power rips down all barriers. That is how a boomerang works. The powers-that-be retaliate and we understand no better than before that they are using our own power against us."

There has been a struggle in the Muslim world for some time about whether to imitate predominantly Western views in many areas or whether people should orient themselves more closely to Islamic values and traditions. Terrorist organizations seek redemption in a more or less "puritanical" and intolerant Islam. They do this with massive financial support from the rigidly Wahhabi Kingdom of Saudi Arabia. Wahhabis see the Quran as a timeless communication from God that contains clear, immutable instructions for every social, cultural, and political situation. Wahhabis are a financially powerful small minority. Only 2 percent of the 1.6 billion Muslims in the world belong to this strict denomination of Islam. And then only if you count the so-called Salafis among their number. The majority of Muslims today try to reconcile the message of the Quran with the realities of modern life. They represent a clearly more numerous, milder, modern, tolerant Islam.

This religious conflict within Islam is hidden behind the question of how the Islamic world should respond to the aggressive military policies of the West. IS gives the most radical answer. It combines the absolute fight against the Western world with the just-as-relentless fight against all Muslims who do not submit to its brutal, medieval ideology. For IS, the answer to all the questions of our time is the "Islamic State." At the moment just in the Middle East, but in the long term globally as well.

All of this is by way of an explanation and not an apology. Terrorism cannot be justified. And the terrorism practiced by IS absolutely cannot. When civilians are killed, it is always murder. That is not up for discussion. Whoever does not take this paragraph to heart has not understood the significance of the historical trajectory of IS.

IN MY LIFE, I have met many extremists and terrorists. In 1960, as a student, I met fighters with the FLN in Algeria. In 1971, as a judge at terrorist trials, I met members of the RAF (Red Army Faction). In the seventies, as a member of parliament, I met freedom fighters and terrorists in Mozambique, Angola, and Namibia. In the eighties, I met the Afghan mujahideen and their in some respects extremist but at the same time moderate leaders. In 2007, as the manager of a media organization, I met IS fighters for the first time in Iraq. In 2010, I met Taliban leaders in Afghanistan. In 2012, I met al-Qaeda terrorists in Syria, and so on. All the terrorists I met maintained they were fighting a noble war of liberation for their people "who lie in chains." They believed the admonition "Thou shalt not kill" did not apply in their case. They all argued and behaved as though they had been brainwashed. It was as though someone had flipped a switch in their heads. Suddenly, everything was allowed. After all, they were fighting for a good cause. Apart from their ideological delusions, they were mostly fairly normal people. And yet they were out-and-out murderers.

But aren't the people behind wars of aggression judged to be illegal according to international law also terrorists and murderers—and their soldiers as well? Throughout the West, in North America and in Europe, al-Qaeda has killed more than 3,300 people in the last fourteen years. However, according to a recent study by IPPNW, George W. Bush killed more than a million people in the war in Iraq alone. In

Iraq, he did this in a war that was illegal under international law. A war whose justification was constructed overwhelmingly from lies. Isn't that terrorism? Wasn't the British actor Peter Ustinov right when he called wars of aggression the "terrorism of the rich"? For an Iraqi child, it makes no difference if she is blown to bits by a "Muslim" suicide bomber or a "Christian" bomb. War is the terrorism of the rich; terrorism is the war of the poor. To date, I have found no qualitative differences.

Edward Peck, deputy director of the working group for the Reagan White House task force on terrorism, outlined the difficulty in distinguishing between state terrorism and normal terrorism with a mixture of sarcasm and resignation: "We produced about six [definitions], and in each and every case, they were rejected, because careful reading would indicate that our own country had been involved in some of those activities."

Terrorism is never religious. In reality, there is no "Islamic terrorism," just as the terrorism of Northern Ireland's IRA (Irish Republican Army) or of the Norwegian Anders Breivik was never "Christian." We call Muslim terrorism "Islamist." But we would never call Western terror "Christian." We manipulate the public sphere the moment we choose the language we use to characterize our enemies. Whoever uses diabolical methods as a terrorist cannot invoke God. The assertion that terrorism is above all a religious problem is an atheist cover story. The mass murders of the German National Socialists and of the Soviet and Chinese Communists are sad proof that humans can be the most savage creatures of all. With or without religion.

WESTERN WARS AGAINST terrorism have always been disappointments or disasters. Just look at Afghanistan in 2001 or Iraq in 2003. The number of terrorists in the Middle East simply exploded. In bin Laden's time, there were a few hundred international terrorists. Today, there are more than 100,000.

Even the current American coalition conducting bombing raids against the "Islamic State" will not reach their stated goal, which is to deal terrorism a deadly blow. Mostly, they will, above all, kill more civilians than terrorists. They always do. Even today, innumerable Sunni civilians have died because of the "peace bombs" on Mosul, Fallujah, Hawija, al-Alam, Saadiah, or Raqqa. The pictures are gruesome. Arab media are filing detailed reports, but Western media are not. These bombardments fuel the Sunni IS terrorists and bring them new fighters every day. Every child murdered by a Western bomb brings out at least ten new terrorists.

The West has learned nothing from the disasters in domestic policy resulting from its military operations in Afghanistan, Iraq, and Libya. Not even from the simultaneous explosion in terrorism. As a rule, children burn their fingers on a hot stove only once. The West, however, initiates its counterproductive bombing strategy time and time again. Einstein supposedly once said two things are apparently infinite: the universe and human stupidity. And he wasn't completely sure about the universe. The unfathomable depths of human stupidity are no longer a matter for debate. All you have to do is look at the American war on terror.

What it boils down to is that only Arabs can fight Arab terrorists without giving rise to new terrorism. In Iraq, IS was initially defeated when the warring Iraqi Sunnis and Shias buried the hatchet and stood side by side to combat IS. After the U.S. invasion in 2003, the once-powerful Sunni minority was ruthlessly excluded from political life. Members of the former ruling Baath Party were persecuted with particular brutality. Many times, the Sunnis, including the Baathists, offered the Shias reconciliation and peace in exchange for a return to political life on an equal footing. I was there for two of these conversations.

National reconciliation in Iraq would deal a decisive blow to IS. First, Iraqi Sunnis and Shias would no longer fight each other but would fight together against IS. Second, the populations in the important Sunni cities of Mosul, Ramadi, and Fallujah would no longer quietly endure IS. For the Sunnis, IS would no longer be the lesser evil opposing the greater evil of the Shia-dominated government. IS would instead become the main stumbling block to the reintegration of Sunnis into Iraqi society. In 2007, IS in Iraq (which was called

ISI at that time) failed because the Sunni tribes withdrew their support. In return for a lot of American money. It was one of the few U.S. flashes of genius in that stupid war. If one day the USA resolved to deal with the whole Muslim world as generously as they deal with Israel, success against terrorism might even be achievable. But is that what the USA wants?

Once again: IS is a murderous terrorist organization. Its existence can be explained but never justified. However, if Western political leaders were honorable, they would have to admit that politicians such as George W. Bush, Cheney, Rumsfeld, and Blair, at least according to the number of their victims, are even worse terrorists. Wherever they intervene militarily, not just thousands but hundreds of thousands of civilians die painfully. A vast number are humiliated, tortured, and violated. The methods used by the USA in Guantanamo, Abu Ghraib, and Bagram are sadistic and medieval.

Rarely are there photographs or films of death by bombs or missiles. Therefore, the moment a mother and her children die when a U.S. missile hits their house makes no emotional impact on us. We don't see that moment, so it almost always remains anonymous.

IS, however, has deliberately personalized its murders. IS gives us enough time to build an emotional relationship with the victims. To become one with them. One day, we see our friends sitting in the desolation of the desert wearing orange overalls. Next to them stands a faceless knife-wielding monster. He is getting ready to cut the heads off people we have taken into our hearts. Or perhaps he is going to burn them to death. When the monster kills them, he also sadistically kills something in us. And he creates fear. And readiness for war.

THE REACTION OF the West will, as always, be "noble." At least that is what many believe. For the West is ostensibly defending the values of Western civilization. And so it is that many people cheer when they see on the television news the result of the first Western "morally justified missile." What they don't see is its deadly impact. Mostly, they don't see its casualties either. Or whether those who were hit were innocent or guilty.

IS uses repulsive methods of killing on purpose. Methods that are not on the West's list of acceptable ways to kill people. A large part of the Western public reacts to the deaths of civilians by Western bombs, missiles, artillery, and gunfire with a shrug. Just as they do to court-ordered executions by injection or electrocution. These methods of killing are, to some extent, socially acceptable. The long knife IS uses for murder is not on this list. And neither is fire, which IS used with unsurpassable brutality to execute an enemy pilot (Jordanian pilot Lieutenant Muath al-Kasasbeh was caged and burned alive in February 2015). The fact that innumerable victims of our air strikes slowly burn to death just as painfully is of no interest. After all, bombing seems legitimate, and the occasional fiery death is the unavoidable "collateral damage" of a legitimate military operation.

It's kept under wraps that the Western-financed Syrian rebel group the FSA also carried out beheadings and cut countless throats. When this information somehow surfaces, little heed is paid to it. Just as the sword of the Saudi executioner is ignored. Unfortunately, most media outlets do not oppose this manipulation of facts.

IS won't complain. For IS wants the world to know about its limitless brutality. In order to spread fear and dismay among its enemies. Especially where it is outgunned. It wants to provoke the USA. It wants to inflame domestic political discussions to such an extent that the U.S. government gets dragged into mobilizing troops on the ground.

FORMER SECRETARY GENERAL of the Council of the European Union, Javier Solana, and the June 2014 issue of the *American Journal of Public Health,* estimate that 90 percent of those who die in modern wars are civilians. Western wars of aggression, illegal under international law, are therefore also terrorism. State terrorism. Any civilization that does not admit that George W. Bush's Iraq War was pure terrorism is a civilization in name only. I know you are not supposed to say that publicly in the West. But life is too short to keep talking around the truth.

We live in a dishonest world. Full of murderous warmongers and murderous terrorists. Neither group is interested in making our world a better and more humane place to live. Both groups are interested in power, wealth, and fame. And they risk all to get them. The reputation of their religion, which they shamelessly abuse. The lives of their fellow human beings, whose suffering means nothing to them. If there is a hell, one day they will meet each other there again. Because every day, they violate the basic law of human coexistence. The fifth commandment: "Thou shalt not kill."

SOURCES

Abu Qatadah interview in Mosul available online with English subtitles at juergentodenhoefer.de/interview-islamic-state/?lang=en, accessed October 1, 2015.

al-Zawahiri, Ayman to Zarqawi (letter) at www.ctc.usma.edu/posts/zawahiris-letter-to-zarqawi-english-translation-2, accessed October 1, 2015.

Clark, Wesley, "destabilize the Middle East . . ." at www.salon.com/2011/11/26/wes_clark_and_the_neocon_dream, accessed August 8, 2015.

de Baudicour, Louis, *Histoire de la colonisation de l'Algérie* (Paris: Challamel Aine, 1860).

de Tocqueville, Alexis, *Democracy in America* (New York: Vintage, 1945).

Flynn, Michael, *Head to Head* interview with al-Jazeera, July 29, 2015, at www.realclearpolitics.com/video/2015/08/10/former_dia_chief_michael_flynn_says_rise_of_isis_was_willful_decision_of_us_government.html, accessed October 1, 2015.

Huntington, Samuel, White House coordinator of security planning for the National Security Council, in *The Clash of Civilizations and the Remaking of World Order* (New York: Simon and Schuster, 2011).

IPPNW (International Physicians for the Prevention of Nuclear War), *Body Count: Casualty Figures after Ten Years of the "War on Terror,"* first international edition, March 2015. Available at www.ippnw.de, accessed October 1, 2015.

Manal's story is reported in Jürgen Todenhöfer, *Du sollst nicht töten (Thou Shalt Not Kill)* (Gütersloh: Bertelsmann, 2013).

Peck, Edward, on the differences between state terrorism and normal terrorism, at www.democracynow.org/2006/7/28/national_exclusive_ hezbollah_leader_hassan_nasrallah, accessed October 1, 2015.

Pinker, Steven, "one long celebration of violence," in *The Better Angels of Our Nature* (New York: Penguin, 2012).

Quran translation by Muhammad Sarwar at corpus.quran.com, accessed October 1, 2015.

Soufan Group, "The Islamic State" by Richard Barrett, November 2014 at soufangroup.com/the-islamic-state, accessed October 1, 2015.

Todenhöfer, Jürgen, *Du sollst nicht töten (Thou Shalt Not Kill)* (Gütersloh: Bertelsmann, 2013).

——, *Feindbild Islam* (Islam as the Enemy) available in German on YouTube at www.youtube.com/watch?v=Fh7NkooQUIk, accessed October 1, 2015.

INDEX OF PERSONAL NAMES

Numbers in bold refer to the photo section

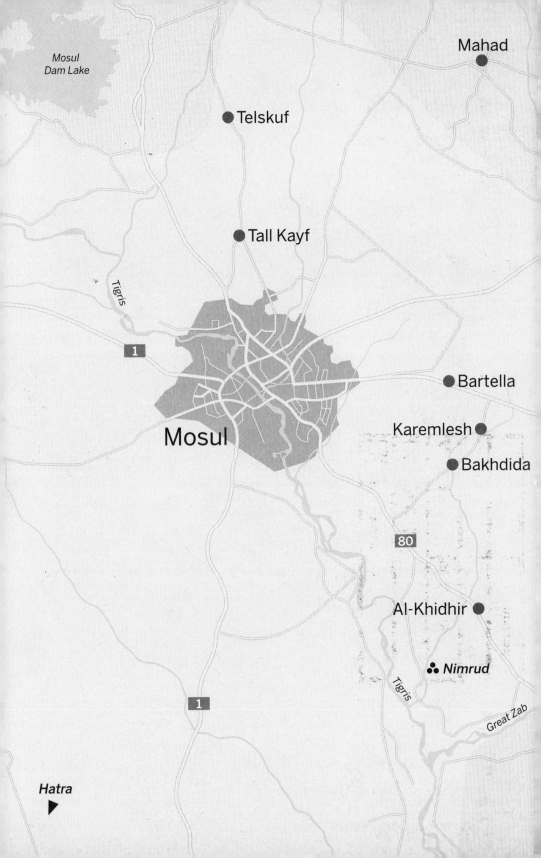